To Frankie

A remarkable couple
with an outstanding
record of public service.

In friendship

Fred

London
September 1997.

A LIFE IN THREE CITIES:

Frankfurt, London and Jerusalem

A LIFE IN THREE CITIES:

Frankfurt, London and Jerusalem

Fred S. Worms

PETER HALBAN
LONDON

FIRST PUBLISHED IN GREAT BRITAIN BY
PETER HALBAN PUBLISHERS LTD
42 South Molton Street
London W1Y 1HB
1996

British Library Cataloguing in Publication Data

A catalogue record for this book is available from the British Library.

ISBN 1 870015 64 6

Typeset by Computape (Pickering) Ltd, North Yorkshire
Printed in Great Britain by
WBC Print, Bridgend

To my grandchildren
who wanted to know

Contents

CONTENTS

CONTENTS

Introduction

THE TROUBLE WITH writing a book of this kind is the capital letter "I" appears too frequently but it can hardly be avoided. The memory of one's early years, although vague, is usually better than of recent events, but how early is early? How much is one appropriating baby and childhood photographs, anecdotes and recollections of family and friends into one's own recalled experience?

To avoid this particular pitfall I have relied on the memoirs of my remarkable aunt, Claire Kevehazi (née Lowenthal), the sister of my late mother, who lived with us in Frankfurt during my early childhood. Fortunately she dictated her memoirs to my daughter, Hilary, who has inherited my interest in the family's antecedents. In later years the *Jewish Chronicle* has faithfully recorded my trials and tribulations as a communal activist, and I am grateful for the editor's permission to reproduce some of the articles and photographs.

I have no delusion *de grandeur* that my life has been an extraordinary one, but my generation has spanned an extraordinary period from the inflation-ridden post-Versailles years in Germany, the advent of Nazism and the Holocaust to the post-War agony of the confrontation of the young Yishuv (the Jewish population of Palestine) with HM Government.

In due course, Jerusalem became our second home and with three daughters and 10 grandchildren there, its attractions are tangible as well as historical.

Looking back over the last 70 years, I can only marvel at my good fortune, and I thank the Lord daily that he has given me Della, my life's companion since I "cradle-snatched" her when she was 19. Her serene beauty, her passionate concern for her family, her intellectual curiosity, her tolerance of my idiosyncracies have enabled me to lead the life of an industrialist, banker, communal worker, sports enthusiast and frustrated academic on the basis of a solid and cultural home background. Her encouragement and critique have been vital factors in the writing of this book.

It will be noticed that the chapters in this book do not flow in strict time sequence. I followed a classic precedent. *Ein mukdam umeuchar batorah*. There is no chronological order in the five books of Moses on which I have spent endless hours over the years.

Since I was involved in so many activities concurrently, it would have been irritating for the reader to flit from subject to subject. Telling the various stories under their chapter headings gives a clearer picture, as long as it is appreciated that at times there were tremendous pressures simultaneously which made for the occasional 18-hour working day. For example, in the 1969–71 period, I was involved in the building and financing of the new Hillel House, in moving the Tudor Factory from Hayes to Wales and in running an active property company, whilst continuing with my many communal activities and spending – what is nowadays known as – quality time with the family.

This book would not have materialised without the infinite patience of Pamela Tollworthy, my secretary for over 20 years, and her word processor. Her good humour and tact, allowing me to change my mind and text *ad infinitum*, her interest in my family and her deep Christian faith have made it a pleasure to work with her for so many years.

My thanks are also due to the editors of the various journals who have allowed me to quote from my work in their publications, to Judge Israel Finestein, who has gone through the manuscript with his usual precision and perceptiveness and who has made a number of invaluable suggestions, to Martin Paisner, for reading the proofs to make sure that I have not been libellous and to Bob Glatter who bullied me to get on with the book.

Peter and Martine Halban, my publishers, have taken great personal interest in the progress and distribution of this book and have introduced Judy Gough whose painstaking final editing has been invaluable.

The decorative symbol used in the text and on the title page is based on the lotus flower motif which is incorporated in the ceiling of the Cochin Synagogue.

Fred S. Worms
London–Jerusalem
June 1996

PART 1

Frankfurt and London

I

Childhood

MY ARRIVAL INTO the world on 21 November 1920 was announced, as was customary at that time, by circulating an embossed card:

FRITZ SIMON
POLDER WORMS UND FRAU
META GEB. LOWENTHAL
ZEIGEN DIE GEBURT EINES SOHNES AN

Frankfurt am Main   21. November 1920   Schwindstrasse 12

Looking at my immaculately maintained childhood records, I see a long series of photographs of Fritz with nannies; Fritz in his swaddling clothes; Fritz in one of those classic curving 1920s' baths; in a velvet suit on mother's lap on the balcony with its elaborate wrought-iron railings; and at the age of 18 months in a peasant smock with a white floppy sun hat which, more than anything else, reflected my status as the lineal descendant of good cattle-dealing farmers. As a three-year-old I am embarrassingly shown in a "Lord Fauntleroy suit" with lace collar surrounded by children's books.

I had a feeling of total security and happiness during the first six years or so before I went to school. I was a proud brother and looked upon my younger sister, Vera as another boy. This was quite justified because, from the age of three onwards, she participated actively in our daily football matches performed with great ceremony and ritual in the long courtyard which connected the front of the house with the back garden. Football became my all-absorbing passion when I was about five years old, and I would spend every spare minute in the courtyard with friends from the same block or the immediate neighbourhood. Outsiders were not admitted.

Whilst nannies came and went, we had one housekeeper – Minna Schmidt – who stayed with us for 15 years i.e. virtually the whole of the time that I lived in Germany. For some unknown reason I called her Nierle. She was the epitome of the devoted servant/housedragon, and the only person who could make me eat spinach. Whenever I misbehaved, which was often, Nierle would say, "This would not have been tolerated at the Von Arnims." Before she came to us, she was one of the many domestics employed by an East Prussian aristocratic family whose exemplary behaviour was a constant source of annoyance to me. (Interestingly enough, in 1994 their family saga appeared on English television. It told the story of their efforts to regain the family castles and vast landholdings which the Russians and then the East German Communists had confiscated.)

My Aunt Claire recorded the early years of my parents' courtship and marriage:

> After having had a lot of admirers, Meta met Polder, who became her husband. His real name was Leopold. It was a great love affair. He was a good-looking, impressive man. I liked him very much. He was 10 years older than Meta, and therefore 20 years older than me. Polder had the gift of charming everybody – Meta, with his kindness and beautiful letters; my mother, by *davening* with a blessed voice; my brothers, with his adventures and experiences, and I – well, I looked up to him admiringly for his "knowledge of everything". He was kind and generous and during the first few years of their marriage became a partner of my brothers. It was a very happy time for Meta and for all of us. The greatest fulfilment of their happiness was when Fred and Vera were born.

After my birth, my Aunt Claire ran through the streets of Hoesbach shouting, "Meta has a boy!" She and her family came to Frankfurt for my circumcision. Her lessons in babysitting started with me. In vain were the efforts of Fraulein Minna and Lieschen, the nanny. I wanted only her when I went to bed and she had to

4

hold my hand and sing "Mandelbaumchen" – a lovely children's song – until I went to sleep.

As a little boy I suffered from middle-ear inflammation and my mother took my sister and me to Nordernei, a fashionable seaside place in the north of Germany. This helped my ears but one of my eyes was affected and my aunt remembered my mother crying all the way home, not because I would have to wear glasses, but because she was afraid the glasses would hurt my eyes when playing football.

When Aunt Claire finished her schooling in Aschaffenburg she came to Frankfurt to live with my mother. She regarded this as her finishing school in place of attending the Jewish Household Training Academy in Aschaffenburg as some of her friends had done. She recalls that my mother arranged everything for her and so Aunt Claire learned shorthand and typing, attended courses at the University for General Knowledge and, what was for her best of all, went to dancing school My mother gave a houseball for Aunt Claire at Schwindstrasse 12 where both my sister and I were born.

Meta and Polder were excellent hosts. There were also the Lodge Balls, the New Year's Eve Balls and one really beautiful one at the Frankfurter Hof (the leading hotel). I remember I was dressed as a page boy with a grey silk suit with a white wig. I can't remember what Meta was wearing but I know it was something very, very beautiful.

My aunt described the bedroom where my sister Vera was born:

The furniture was dark mahogany and there was a dark lilac-coloured carpet, the same colour quilt and silk couch, beautifully embroidered white bedlinen and Meta, in a matching lilac nightgown. The room was filled with white and lilac chrysanthemums and orchids.

Alas, these sylvan years did not last. Polder was an inveterate and, indeed, incurable gambler. Meta had been warned before they married but she was so much in love that she was not prepared to listen. In any event, she thought she could cure him. I could never understand how such an intelligent, charming man could throw his life away for the sake of betting on horses. It became a real illness. He pawned or sold whatever he could lay his hands on and borrowed until he had no friends left. Divorce became inevitable and it became final in 1930 when Fred was nine and Vera was six. Meta said it was the unhappiest day of her life.

My parents' divorce left me bewildered but not shattered. My mother had been crying a lot, money became scarce and while the family had come through the terrible inflation years relatively unscathed, just when other families were recovering financially, we seemed to suffer. To this very day I am puzzled why my father should have been possessed by a gambling *dybbuk* (possessed soul). He was a pillar of the Unterlindau Synagogue, a small place of prayer near our apartment. I remember him as such a gentle courteous man who would never raise his voice in anger.

On one occasion my father went to the Ostbahnhof to pick up his father-in-law. Old Lazarus Lowenthal was a canny farmer/cattle dealer and very careful with his money. They took a taxi, which was a great treat for the old man who was used to his droschke with a couple of horses. "Tell me, Polder, how much did that cost?" he asked when they arrived at our apartment in the West End of Frankfurt.

Embarrassed, my father quoted a ridiculously low price, a fraction of the true cost. "One mark."

"I enjoyed it. For that money let's do it again!"

My father had the manners and foibles of a nineteenth-century aristocrat without the means to support them. My parents' wedding photograph shows him with his pince-nez, white gloves casually dangling from a languid hand and a somewhat detached look in his eyes. He emigrated to France during the Nazi years, survived the War and died in Paris in 1949. I was in close touch with him during those few years after the War and spent the week of his final illness with him. He was buried with a sadly small attendance.

Strangely enough I recall the earlier, happy years much more clearly than the tragic divorce period. There were wonderfully hot summers and cold winters. We used to toboggan down the little hills in the park and, on special excursions, in the Taunus, the mountainous holiday area near Frankfurt. The tennis courts in the Palmengarten, our favourite abode, were regularly frozen over and we went ice skating. My early ambition was to become one of those well-padded ice hockey players who were my heroes. In the summer we swam in the various pools, and in particular the one in the new stadium. My sister and I were also enrolled in a fashionable swimming club known as EFSC – a German acronym for the First Swimming Club of Frankfurt. During the autumn we would walk to Ginnheim – famous for its apple orchards. There we would drink the cider of the season into which we would throw peeled new walnuts.

My first day of school is recorded in a photograph where I am holding a large "fortune's fillhorn" a traditional sweetener for continental schoolchildren and which looked like a giant ice-cream cornet. I had piano and violin lessons – the latter I gave up very quickly for the benefit of the neighbours, but I kept up the piano lessons for a number of years, mostly because I had a crush on Fräulein Ziegler who – looking at photographs – was not very attractive but I remember smelt beautifully.

When I was six years old I joined Bar Kochba, the local Maccabi Sports Club, and I played football for the junior XI. At the same time I joined Habonim – the left-wing Zionist Youth Organisation – which had a very formative influence on my early years. One of my good friends who was not Jewish was Helmut Roeder who lived above us in the same apartment block. His father was head waiter at the Frankfurter Hof and I clearly remember that Helmut's birthday was in June when his mother used to make enormous strawberry cakes covered in whipped cream. I met Helmut again after the War. He was then a night porter at a minor hotel in Frankfurt. He had served on the Russian Front and fate had not been as kind to him as it had to me.

Another friend was Eric Freudenstein who was the son of a wealthy textile merchant. They had a magnificent home with extensive grounds near the Palmengarten. Eric was taken to school in a chauffeur-driven Mercedes and occasionally I was given a lift. When my mother had to work after the divorce and was struggling hard to provide for her family, Eric's father told her, "The only way to run a business is to plough all the profits back into it. One should have an independent income, preferably from property." The advice was pretty useless to my mother then but I have remembered what he said and I have tried to shape my business career along these lines. Eric became a leading food scientist in New York and I am still in touch with him.

At about the age of nine my great love affair with opera began. My friends and I used to get cheap tickets and we sat up in the gods listening to such stars as Franz Volker and Richard Tauber. Occasionally the opera house had operetta performances such as *Das Weisse Roessl* (White Horse Inn). I can sing its principal songs, and the arias in *Zauberflöte* etc. until this very day.

My mother was born a Lowenthal. Her mother's maiden name was Appel. The Appels came from the small village of Schoelkrippen, near Aschaffenburg. My Appel grandparents were farmers and cattle dealers and lived in the same house in which their great-grandfather was born in 1780. I treasure his birth certificate. I remember the house with its Breughel-like atmosphere at the traditional "learning" which took place on the night of Shavuoth (Pentecost). The custom is that the men study the holy scriptures all night long. The reality was that it became a bucolic eating and drinking party. The women brought in tin bathtubs filled with pastries – if the quality of the learning had kept pace with the quantity of food consumed, it would have been a rare intellectual feast.

I was a frequent holiday visitor to my uncles and aunts in the country which was no more than 20 minutes' driving time from Frankfurt. We often went to Aschaffenburg where my mother's oldest brother Adolf lived with his family. They had a large cattle yard with fruit orchards at the rear of their house. Uncle Adolf's son Lothar, who became Laurence on his emigration to England, was brought up by my mother after her escape to London. He was a virtual brother to me. His sister, Helga, escaped to the United States. Their parents were to perish in the Holocaust.

Two incidents from those visits are etched in my mind which illustrate the "humour" of the farmhands, who were working for the family. I was rarely without a football; I dribbled, kicked, headed, scored against a wall and was deeply appreciative of any adult who would play with me. (Interestingly enough, my grandsons in Jerusalem show similar tendencies). One day I played with two of the farmhands in Schoelkrippen. We headed the ball to each other. A nice high one sailed across the farmyard straight on to my forehead. The ball had been rolled in cowpats which smothered my hair, face and shirt. Typical "Max and Moritz" Germanic sense of humour!

In the course of my voracious reading as a child and as a youth, I must have come across most German fairy stories and fables, ranging from Hoffmann's *Struwelpeter* and Wilhelm Busch's Max and Moritz to Christian Morgenstern's sardonic verses of which I was particularly fond. I recently reread some of Wilhelm Busch's "moral tales" and quite frankly, I was appalled. Two naughty boys, Max and Moritz, get up to some devilish tricks in the course of which they deprive a poor widow of her chickens, cause a poor tailor to fall into the river, put gunpowder into the teacher's pipe and bugs into the uncle's bed and, finally, are caught and baked in the oven by the baker whose pretzels they wanted to steal. Max and Moritz manage to escape from this predicament only to be caught by the miller whose sacks of grain they had slashed open. He puts them into the sacks with the remaining grain and pours the contents into the grinding mill. The mixture is then fed to the ducks!

What astonishes me now is that when I first read this as a child this did not strike me in any way as extraordinary. What is disturbing is that Max and Moritz fables continue to be as popular as ever in present-day Germany.

My maternal grandmother's brother-in-law, Samuel Oppenheimer, had a horse and cattle farm in nearby Rohrbach. The daily routine was to take the horses to the pond in the centre of the village where they would drink and splash about. The stable lad offered me a ride back which I accepted with alacrity. What I as a five-year old did not know was that the horses had a habit of galloping home on the familiar road to get back to their lunchtime hay in the stables. I clung, saddleless, to the mane of the unexpectedly virile steed, thundered through the village and ducked my head just in time before we reached the open but very low stable door!

The name Worms had been known in and around Frankfurt for many hundreds of years. I have a copy of *Stammbaum der Frankfurter Juden* published in 1907 which shows that from 1356 there were Jews with the names of Worms in Frankfurt, and throughout the subsequent centuries they were amongst the principal tax payers. One of the reasons why there were so many Jewish families spread around small villages near Frankfurt goes back to the pre-Napoleonic ghetto days. Only the eldest son in each family was allowed to marry and stay in Frankfurt. The others had to leave.

My great-grandfather, Simon Worms, was born in Sulzbach in 1807 and so was my grandfather, Simon, who died in 1909 in Aschaffenburg. He had four sons, one of whom died in infancy, and a daughter: Moses lived in New York where he died in 1941. Heinrich was a victim of the Holocaust and Benno, the only one I knew, was a butcher in Aschaffenburg whom we visited whenever we called on Uncle Adolf and Aunt Sophie Lowenthal. Benno's wife Paula made the most delicious ice-cream in a barrel-like contraption, full of ice-cubes which would be crushed by turning a handle. Their son, Simon emigrated to South Africa in the early 1930s where he was very successful. His daughter Beryl with her husband Heini Wohl, have lived in London for many years and Heini is one of my leading colleagues in the B'nai B'rith Housing Society.

Aunt Johanna, Simon Worms's daughter, sold chocolate wholesale. She was, needless to say, very popular with us. Her daughter Ilse, a charming and good-looking woman, married Dr Max Solomon. For a time they lived in Frankfurt before moving to New York.

In my immediate family I believe that I am the only male Worms left although our family tree (three metres wide) prepared by a distant relative Stephen Warner (formerly Worms), who lives in America, shows very wide ramifications with scores of well-known families in different parts of the world.

My maternal grandparents had moved to Frankfurt from Hoesbach in the early 1920s and my uncles Julius and Benno came with them. They had a large apartment in the Liebigstrasse near our little synagogue. Every Saturday there would be a Kiddush which was quite lavish. There was a regular clientele of guests and apart from the *Schnapps*, a delicacy known as *gaensegrieben* (roasted goose skin) would be served – terribly unhealthy. I loved it but used to break out in little pimples on the back of my neck if I had more than a small portion.

The Samson Raphael Hirsch ultra-Orthodox school chosen by my parents for its excellence, in spite of the considerable distance which I had to travel every day, was very demanding. Hirsch was the founder of the famous "Frankfurt Orthodoxy". He arrived there in 1851 at a time when the community was dominated by Liberal Jews. Indeed, it was against the local by-laws to establish an Orthodox synagogue because it was considered a retrogressive step. Rabbi Hirsch fought, won and introduced a modern type of Orthodoxy which he called *Torah Im Derech Eretz*, that is the study of the Torah combined with secular knowledge. It was a revolutionary concept, since to the hidebound ultra-Orthodox, a university education was anathema.

In addition to keeping up with secular subjects we had at least two to three hours a day on *limudei kodesh* (Torah and Talmud study). Joseph Breuer was a brilliant Torah teacher. He had a sonorous voice and showed the kind of dedication which is so rare these days. He was an educator *par excellence* and my great love for the five books of Moses which I study weekly, is, undoubtedly, due to his inspiration. Breuer's didactic approach interwove Jewish and secular teaching. For example, he illustrated the meaning of onomatopoeia by quoting a sentence from the book of Judges. When Deborah the prophetess was Judge in Israel and waged a successful war, her triumphant victory song recalls the thundering hooves of the horses, *Midaharous Daharous Abirov*. Listening to Dr Breuer's declamation, we sat in frightened awe of the warlike noises.

Our Talmud lessons, on the other hand, were given by a gentleman from Poland who employed the old-fashioned "learning by rote" methodology and totally failed in securing my interest.

By the time I was 13 I had read hundreds of books. Occasionally I was asked by the history teacher to "lecture" to my class. I recall speaking on a translation of Gibbons' *Der Kampf um Rom*. Goethe, Schiller, Heine, Rilke, Franz Werfel, Hans Fallada, Lion Feuchtwanger and Edmond Fleg were amongst my "classics". Karl May and my parents' hidden sex book by Vandervelde were raced through enthusiastically.

My parents did not belong to the Breuer-Austritt (secession) community whose synagogue was in the Friedberger Anlage near the school. When S. R. Hirsch, the progenitor of the Breuer family took his followers out of the established Frankfurt Jewish community to go their own way, another Orthodox rabbi, Marcus Horovitz, took the contrary decision to stay in. His main synagogue was to be at the Borneplatz, adjacent to the former ghetto site. This magnificent building with its rounded dome was immortalised in Max Beckman's painting which hangs at the Staedel Museum in Frankfurt. We prayed at the Unterlindau Synagogue, an affiliate of the Boerneplatz, in the fashionable West End. The choice was not made purely on geographic considerations. The Breuer Agudah anti-Zionist ethos was not ours. They were also too *frum* for my much more relaxed family.

Aunt Claire went to the Leipzig Fair together with my uncles and there fell in love with a Hungarian – Zoltan Kevehazi. Zolly, with his dark hair and moustache, looked like a central European film star. He was a beautiful tango dancer and had a fine voice with which he sang the then popular pop song *Ich bin verliebt in meine eigene Frau* ("I am in love with my own wife"). They were married in Frankfurt in 1930 and moved to Budapest. Miraculously they survived the Nazi and Communist years, went to England in 1956 and then moved with their son Michael and his family to Israel.

1930 was the watershed. Everything turned brittle and fell apart. My parents' divorce went through, Aunt Claire moved to Hungary and the Nazis were becoming more and more aggressive. By 1932 it was made clear to us in the swimming club that it would be better if we were to withdraw before we were thrown out. In 1933 large notices appeared in our beloved Ginnheim pub which clearly proclaimed that our presence was undesirable – *Juden sind hier unerwuenscht.*

2

The Hitler Years: 1933–1937

MY MOTHER JOINED Colibri (the family cigarette lighter business) in Frankfurt and became the manageress for the whole of Germany. My Uncle Benno moved to Zurich in 1932 and Uncle Julius to London in 1935. The senior employee at the Frankfurt firm, Ibelo (an acronym for Julius and Benno Lowenthal) was one Herman Zahn, a non-Jew who took over the company after my mother's emigration. He became a multi-millionaire.

As the treatment of the Jews deteriorated month by month, they withdrew into their own circle, gave their own concerts and had their own *Lehrhaus* (house of study) with eminent teachers such as Martin Buber whose lectures I regularly attended.

After my uncles Julius and Benno had left Germany, my mother's mother, our Oma (later Clock Oma) moved in with us. She had lost her husband, Lazarus Lowenthal in 1923. Oma was born middle-aged and was exceedingly pious in a simple way. She prayed with great devotion three times a day, occasionally annoying "the boys", her sons, when prayer had precedent over their demands. She either wore a hairnet or a sheitel, a wig that Orthodox women wear to hide the beauty of their natural hair from other men. This was not the glamorous concoction which nowadays changes plain women into sex symbols – the very opposite of what they are supposed to be – this was a tightly woven upside-down bird's nest. Typical of her devout practice was the Pesach preparation cleaning period, a veritable nightmare. For three weeks before Passover we had to eat in the corridor. All the rooms that had been thoroughly turned inside out, were out of bounds. However, she did make the best cocoa in the world!

Our football matches had to be played within a Jewish league but at least until I emigrated we were still allowed to travel to other towns. The Second Maccabiah – the Jewish International Games – was held in Palestine in 1935. The German Maccabi team was picked not only on the basis of sporting prowess but also on their professional or agricultural qualifications. Hardly any of the team returned. They stayed in Palestine and became part of the famous German *aliyah*. By that time Robert Weltsch had become the brilliant editor of the *Juedische Rundschau* – a weekly publication of quite outstanding quality. Weltsch coined the famous sentence after the Jews were compelled to wear the yellow band with the word "*Jude*" on it. He said: "Wear it with pride – the yellow patch."

In 1935 I was 14 years old and Hitler had been in power for two years. At Habonim we were taught Zionism and scouting. We walked about in our blue shirts and blue and white scarves until this became too dangerous. Slowly but surely the atmosphere became poisoned. It is now known that the art of Dr Goebbels was to effect changes in such a gradual way that one got used to it. Visitors from abroad would say that the Nazis were not that bad after all.

Two incidents stand out. On Hitler's birthday in April 1935, he addressed the nation. All schools had compulsory assemblies to listen to the broadcast. At the Samson Raphael Hirsch School Jewish teachers and Jewish pupils had to stand and listen to the outpourings of maniacal hatred. Hitler screamed at the top of his voice … "I will rub out the Jews". (He used the word "*ausradieren*".) For some contemporary historians to say that Hitler himself never knew of the final solution is ludicrous. They only have to study his openly declared intentions in his speeches.

A year earlier Hitler had paid a visit to Frankfurt. It was announced that he would speak from the outside balcony of the Opera House. The Opernplatz in Frankfurt is a big square, rather like a miniature St Peter's in Rome. SA and SS Stormtroopers made sure that "half Frankfurt" turned up and the square was packed tight. I could not resist the temptation of going. I did not tell anybody and had my mother known she would have been frantic with worry. Why should a boy of 13 go into the middle of a fanatical, screaming, hysterical mob who were after his blood, raising their arms in unison and shouting "*Heil Hitler*" and "*Juden raus*"? Yet such is the folly of youth that I was amongst them. I pretended to be squashed so near to the man in front that I was unable to lift my arm. Fortunately nobody took any notice of me. I remember Hitler appearing on the balcony and screaming with a demented but at the same time compelling voice his tirade against the allies, the Freemasons, the Jews, the Bolsheviks and, indeed, against almost anybody who was not a pure Aryan.

It struck me at the time that very few of the Nazi leaders lived up to their ideal picture of an Aryan. Hitler himself with his Slavic face, jet black hair and moustache; Goering with a piggy face and enormous stomach; Streicher completely bald, bandy-legged and fat; Rosenberg and Milch (both reputed to be of Jewish descent) – they were all very far from the slim blond Aryan whose ubiquitous pictures symbolised the New Germany.

Fortunately at that time the insidious fear which crept into the bones of every German Jew who stayed on beyond 1938 was only latent. We had a foretaste of what was to come. The Hitler Youth would march with a rousing band and a cheering public, singing their mantras. "*Wenn's Judenblut vom messer spritzt dann gehts nochmal so gut*" ("When Jewish blood spurts from the knives we'll feel twice as good.")

Surprisingly in 1935 we, the youngsters, still laughed and had a good time, although Jewish schools were prohibited from going on their traditional outings. After 1933 it was not possible for Habonim to have their summer camps in Germany so they were moved to Switzerland. Our Swiss *chaverim* (friends) rented a large meadow from a farmer in Flims and there we were, sleeping under canvas, near the source of the River Rhein which was so cold, even in summer, that one could not stay in it for more than thirty seconds. Preparing the camp was a privilege reserved for the "old timers" who had done it before. The first thing to be erected was a large wooden watch tower on which the blue and white Zionist flag (which became the Israeli colours) would be hoisted daily at an early morning ceremony. This was reminiscent of the water towers which were the hallmark of the Israeli kibbutzim which they would put up as soon as they took possession of their land.

The camps were the highlight of the year and my mother, in spite of the worries and financial pressures following her divorce, made it possible for me to go in 1933, 1934 and 1935. 1935 was a special year. Hitler had introduced the strictest exchange control regulations. No holiday money was to be taken abroad, with the exception of Italy where one could take the equivalent of three hundred marks, not in cash, but in traveller's cheques endorsed for Italy only. This was, at that time, quite a lot of money. So what was going to happen to our summer camp? The leaders of Habonim, who were in their early twenties, summoned me: "Look, you have been to two summer camps before so you know what it is all about. We have got a very special task for you, because we are unable to get away early. We want you to take the traveller's cheques for all of us to Italy and then to bring back the money to Switzerland."

I felt very proud of this special responsibility. After all, I had already been a *Madrich* (youth leader) for two years and had led youngsters of the ages of eight to 10 to minor weekend camps in different parts of Germany when it was still possible. I chose as my Sancho Panza a young chap called Rosenfelder. I cannot remember his first name but I can still see his curly hair over his boyish face.

We collected the traveller's cheques for over 100 youngsters and off we went. The thought of carrying such large cash equivalents did not bother me in the least. After all I was already 14! Today, I think, I would be more apprehensive. We travelled by train to the Swiss frontier because we were no longer allowed to hitchhike in Germany. In Switzerland we "tramped" as we had always done, and in no time at all we were at the foot of the St Gotthard. We had already worked out that the best way to get the money back into Switzerland was to go to a little Italian town called Cannobio, which was only an hour's distance from Lugano. We had great difficulty in getting a lift. There we were, standing at the foot of the mountain on a blisteringly hot day in the month of July. We carried the typical German rucksacks and we were virtually indistinguishable from members of the Hitler Youth travelling out of uniform.

Car after car passed by. Although we cursed them we could not really blame them. Driving up the St Gotthard was a challenge for any car without the extra weight of two youngsters and their enormous rucksacks. Then – lo and behold – an open-topped Mercedes with German number plates drew to a halt. A big man with shaven bullet-shaped head and enormous stomach covered by belted trousers with a swastika as a buckle got out. His only passenger was a woman who could have played the leading part in a Wagner opera. She too was enormous and her blonde hair was pulled into a big bun at the back of her head.

"Where are you fellows from?" he barked.

"Frankfurt," I replied.

"*Heil Hitler*. Jump in."

We got into the car with mixed feelings. The fat Nazi didn't stop talking. He told us it was the happiest day of his life. He was the newly-appointed Ambassador of Germany to Egypt and *en route* to Cairo they would have a holiday in Switzerland. That very morning, he told us, he had had the personal privilege of shaking hands with the Führer.

Did I not know the Gauleiter of Hesse (local Nazi Chief) who lived in Frankfurt, he asked? I replied I did not, which was the truth.

Our host told us that he was delighted to help two young Germans and he could not do enough for us. "On the other side of the St Gotthard at Airolo is a marvellous little restaurant. We have been going there for years, haven't we birdie?" (he used the German "*Voegelchen*") he said, as he turned to his wife.

My friend and I looked at each other, firstly because we thought "birdie" was rather big and secondly I – but not my friend – was strictly kosher.

"They make the finest pork cutlets in the country" he went on.

"Thank you very much indeed," I said, "but just before you came we had the most enormous sandwich lunch. We cannot eat another thing."

"Nonsense," he said. "You come inside and I will buy you a piece of cake and a cup of coffee."

When we got to Airolo he ordered a whole apple cake and much to his amazement we finished the lot in five minutes flat.

"Well," he said. "I wish I was as young again. Young people can always eat. What appetites you have got. Pity you didn't taste those lovely little cutlets."

He had intended to go to Locarno but when he heard we wanted to go to Lugano he drove us there.

"Right, now here is my address in Egypt and here is the address of the Gauleiter in Frankfurt. I want you to go to him specially and tell him you travelled with me and give him my very best regards. *Heil Hitler*."

We all shook hands and parted.

By that time it was evening and it was too late to cross into Italy. In any case there was no point because the banks would be closed. We did not have enough Swiss money to stay at a youth hostel never mind a hotel, so we slept in an unfinished house. In the morning we went to a kiosk, had breakfast of rolls and coffee and then walked to the frontier.

"I am sorry," said the customs officer, "but your friend cannot enter Italy."

"Why not?" I asked.

"He has only a child's passport and our regulations are that children can only enter with their parents.'

"Oh well, never mind," I said to Rosenfelder. "You wait here. I won't be long."

He looked very apprehensive. After all, he was only thirteen and he had only a few francs in his pocket.

"Don't move away from here," I said. "I will be back in a couple of hours."

The walk seemed interminable and I got hotter and hotter. Some workmen were digging up the road, their bicycles lying in the adjacent field. I pointed to one of the bicycles and shouted *"Cannobio returno!"* in my best Italian, and added, *"trente minutos."* They nodded vigorously and clapped me on the back as I pedalled off to Cannobio. Unfortunately at the bank I had to wait one and a half hours. They made all kinds of enquiries. After all, a young chap in shorts with so many different pre-signed traveller's cheques did not turn up every day, and I had great difficulty in getting the money. When they finally handed it over to me the manager said, "Now don't forget. It is illegal to take the money out of Italy."

Well – nobody had told me that before! What the hell was I going to do now? I had been in the bank for well over two hours and as I cycled back I could see the labourers walking towards me, obviously looking for the original bicycle thief! I tried to explain. *"Banco attende, attende."* I was lucky to get away without a beating!

When I got to the frontier I waited until the Italian customs officials were busy examining a number of cars. I showed my passport which they stamped, and walked into Switzerland. The Swiss, of course, could not care less. They will take and change anyone's money. I felt elated. I had saved the summer camp single-handedly in spite of the exchange control difficulties. But my friend Rosenfelder was in tears.

"What's the matter? Why are you crying?"

He sobbed. "The police came this morning after you left and took me to the police station. They wanted to send me straight back to Germany. They said as soon as you come back from Italy you are to come to the station. They have kept my passport." I realised immediately what had happened. The Swiss love all kinds of tourists – except penniless ones. The only thing which is unforgivable is to arrive in Switzerland without money and to sleep rough. Tramps are illegal.

"Don't worry," I said to my friend. "Just watch what's going to happen now."

We walked into the police station with typical German arrogance. Now, the Swiss themselves can be very dour when they turn off their tourist charm. The station sergeant said, "Just a minute young man, just a minute. Don't you barge in here like this."

"How dare you take my friend's passport away!" I shouted. "I will report this back in Germany."

The sergeant didn't know what I was talking about until an officer came from an adjacent room and commanded: "Come in here and sit down." He then proceeded to read the riot act. "Do you realise that sleeping in an unattended house is against the law and I could have you put in jail and sent back to Germany immediately?"

"But that's ridiculous!" I shouted. "We are tourists. We are going to camp in Flims, the same camp which our organisation has organised there for the last three summers."

"How are you going to pay for it?"

"How are we going to pay for it? With money, of course!" I replied angrily.

"What money?" asked the officer with a smirk on his face.

That was the moment I had been waiting for. Before calling at the police station I had gone to the bank and changed the Italian money into lots and lots of small notes of 20 and 50 Swiss francs. I spread out the loot. It was a joy to behold the man's face. It literally fell by inches.

"Well, well," he said. "Um ... I am very sorry, there seems to have been a misunderstanding. But why were you sleeping in an empty house?"

I thought quickly. "Because it was too late to get into a youth hostel and we did not fancy a hotel."

"Don't do it again," he warned. "Now take your money and go off and enjoy yourselves." That was my last summer camp in Switzerland.

Before going back to Frankfurt I thought we would call on Uncle Benno who was on holiday somewhere in the Swiss mountains together with his wife, Dorly, and some other members of her Guggenheim family.

A young doctor gave us a lift. He explained that he would have to call on a patient in a small village. We soon fell asleep in the car. Some two hours later we were woken up. "Time to get out boys. I am turning left to that little place up there."

We sat ourselves down in a meadow full of buttercups, daisies and cows to enjoy our sandwich lunch.

"Where's your satchel?" asked Rosenfelder.

Where indeed! My precious belted passport and money carrier was travelling up the steeply winding mountainside in the doctor's car.

"No use losing our heads," I said. "That village is obviously the end of a cul-de-sac. Let's walk up. Either we'll catch him coming down or we'll visit the few houses in the village till we find him."

We ate our sandwiches and then started climbing up the hairpin bends. After an hour's toil we recognised the doctor's car coming towards us. We signalled excitedly but with a stern face and a negative waving of a hand he drove straight past us.

"Take my rucksack!" I shouted at Rosenfelder. "I'll cut him off at the bottom of the hill."

In my youthful optimism I reckoned that by running straight down the mountainside I would get to the main road faster than the car which had to negotiate all those hairpin bends. I hopped, skipped and jumped, fell and rolled over the steep meadows. In full flight I negotiated a barbed wire fence, reached the main road and sat down exhausted. My leg was bleeding profusely but there was no sign of the car. I had missed him.

Just as Rosenfelder came down, swearing under his two rucksacks, the doctor's car returned.

"When I saw you lunatic falling down the mountainside I wondered what you were trying to achieve. Then I looked round – sorry – here's your satchel." He bandaged my leg and thereafter we had no difficulty in getting lifts.

3

From Samson Raphael Hirsch to St Paul's

I CAME TO England in April 1937 when I was 16 years and four months old. Strictly speaking, I was brought over by Ferdinand Metzger, who was an old friend of the family. He came to England to prepare for his own immigration which followed a year later. The third member of our party was my young cousin, Jack (Hans) Lowenthal. He was a difficult child who had frequent tantrums, particularly when he was with his mother. He was sent to Frankfurt to spend some time under the firm hand of my mother and became the first of several cousins who followed in his footsteps.

I lodged at Sichel's Boarding House in Greencroft Gardens. The Sichels were members of the famous German wine family. They were refugees themselves and every paying guest originated from Germany. They charged two pounds for weekly *demi-pension.*

Within a week of my arrival I was a pupil at St Paul's School in Hammersmith. The High Master (it was St Paul's privilege to give this title to the Head of the school) John Bell, was a particularly compassionate man. He allowed a number of refugee boys to enter St Paul's without the usual entrance formalities but relied on the reports of the headmaster of their German school.

The culture shock was tremendous. Just two weeks before leaving Frankfurt I was still a pupil at the Samson Raphael Hirsch School in the eastern part of the town, opposite the Zoological Gardens. It was in the East End that the poorer immigrant Jews from Poland and Russia were concentrated. We lived in the West End and had practically no contact with the black-coated "foreign" Jews on the other side of town. The old-established members of the community who had been in the country for hundreds of years looked down on their fraternity from Eastern Europe, who in their eyes conformed so closely to the anti-Semitic caricatures.

If German Jews who, after the formation of the State of Israel were to be known as "Yekkes" (allegedly because they wore jackets even on the hottest summer days) had delusions of grandeur, this applied even more to the Frankfurt Jews. They considered themselves the élite and regrettably suffered from a superiority complex. I wished that I could say that my own family was different but in fact we were no exception. I have already mentioned that they never subscribed to the Frankfurt type of Orthodoxy, as typified by the Breuer stream. The Breuers dominated the Samson Raphael Hirsch School. They were direct descendants of Rabbi Hirsch and looked upon themselves as the guardians of his particular tradition. I was in continuous rebellion against the Agudah Orthodoxy which the school imposed on all its pupils. Throughout my life I have found myself unable to fit comfortably into any narrowly defined religious camp. Rabbi Soloveitchik, a leading American talmudist, said that the best type of religion is that which arises from internal friction. On that basis I am a deeply religious man. Contemporaneously with my attendance at the Hirsch School, I was an active member – and later a leader – of Habonim. At school I was known as the "abicores" (Greek for the non-conformist) and in Habonim I was labelled a religious fanatic. This suited me well. Tolerant Orthodoxy has been my style ever since.

Thus I found myself transplanted from this relatively protected environment to one of England's oldest church schools. Dean Collet founded St Paul's in 1509 for the education of Christian gentlemen. It was also a famous army school and one of its best known graduates was Field Marshal Montgomery. Among many distinguished "old boys" who became friends later were Sir Isaiah Berlin and Marcus Sieff (Lord Sieff of Brimpton).

The school uniform in 1937 was still black suit, white stiff collar and black tie with school cap in winter and straw hat in summer. In the sixth form one was entitled to wear a bowler hat and carry an umbrella. The night before my first day at school was dedicated to practising putting on the stiff collar. These, mercifully, have gone out of fashion today, but I defy any young man to put on a stiff collar with the elusive stud for the first time in less than an hour. Well – it took me two hours! I lost three collar studs and finally, in desperation, left the collar on and sat up in bed the whole night. I wanted to be sure that I was not going to be late on my first day.

I travelled on a No 28 bus to Hammersmith. My English was that of a foreign school boy – no better, no worse. My accent was atrocious. The prefectorial system, whereby boys could punish other boys and the captain of the school could apply a beating, was completely unknown in Germany. Within a few days I was in trouble. One of the prefects had seen me on the bus without my school cap. I was given a detention. This was an interesting new experience. After class the captain of the school, together with two prefects swinging walking sticks, walked in. I, an arrogant young German, who had no idea of the mores of public school, immediately complained about the injustice of the detention. The captain of the school, who was the nearest thing to God, gave me a withering look and said: "Worms, you are lucky not to be beaten," and gave me 200 lines!

A few days later one of the prefects came into Mr Stubbs' class (Stubbs was a very fine history master with a habit of turning up late) and threw some of my books on the floor. "Pick them up!" he yelled at me. Whilst by that time I had some inkling of the power of the prefects and their right to commit minor injustices amongst new boys, I also had a temper which, though slow to rise, was fairly fierce. I said to him "You pick them up." He threw down another book. Ten seconds later he had a black eye. By the time Mr Stubbs entered the classroom we were on the floor, both bleeding, our shirts torn. He saw instantly what had happened and said quietly, "I think you chaps had better go and wash and then come back here." We went out, cleaned up and rejoined the class as though nothing had happened. That was the end of the first and last persecution to which I was subjected at school.

One of my contemporaries was young Hanfstaengel. His father, Puzzi Hanfstaengel, was Hitler's clown and companion. He was a Munich publisher who made a fortune out of the Nazis, fell out with Hitler and had to flee. His son entered St Paul's at the same time as I did. He was an enormous chap – six foot tall, with Falstaffian girth, short hair, and with an unremitting nostalgia for the "good old days in the Hitler Youth." He really could not understand why he had to leave his beloved Germany and join that "dreadful" English school. Amongst the large teaching staff at St Paul's were two masters who symbolised the polarised outlook of our educators. One was Eynon-Smith, who sympathised with the German and immediately took Hanfstaengel under his protection. The other was a Mr Parker, a pencil-slim, typical Englishman with jet black hair and most elegant manners. He showed a marked sympathy towards the few Jewish boys.

One of these was a young superman called Cohen. He was an American, well over six feet tall, beautifully built, an outstanding sportsman and brilliant scholar. Eynon-Smith realised that the only way he could make Hanfstaengel more popular amongst the boys was to get him involved in sport. Whilst Cohen already had his school colours in rugby, rowing and boxing, Hanfstaengel was far too clumsy and too heavy for these sports. Eynon-Smith decided that he should become a shot-putter. When Parker heard of this little stratagem he arranged for Cohen to take up that sport as well. Strangely enough my name was also entered and I went into serious training. I got nowhere. Hanfstaengel, who had practised hard and assiduously, broke the school record for five minutes until Cohen's turn came to break Hanfstaengel's record!

Cohen stayed in England, joined the Eagle squadron (the American sector of the RAF) and was killed in action five years later. Hanfstaengel and his father emigrated to the United States where his father was interned.

Mr Parker took me in hand to improve my accent. "Worms, have you practised speaking in front of a mirror?"

"Yes, sirrr," I replied.

"Worms, will you please stop rolling your r's!"

I could never understand why the class greeted what I considered a relatively harmless sentence with such amusement. Mr Parker was tireless in his efforts, and if from time to time I get away with mimicking the then fashionable BBC accent, it is entirely due to his persistence.

He was also responsible for making me take up boxing. He said "If you must fight, Worms, you might as well do it properly." For many decades St Paul's had been the best boxing school in the country. We had an old army sergeant who had taught generations of boys. When I put on boxing gloves for the first time he said "Hit me!" and I rather gingerly put out a dainty fist. He said, "No! Hit me as hard as you can!" I let fly but could not make contact with his body at all. Every time I aimed for his face his glove intervened like lightning. I became annoyed. I aimed for his body; I aimed for his ears. It was just impossible. He was ducking and weaving, always out of reach of my frustrated fists. He took me in hand and I boxed for the school's second team as a welter-weight. After one of my fights against another school my face was swollen for a week! By that time I was a sixth former, proudly wearing my bowler hat and carrying my umbrella.

One of my friends, the secretary of the school Boxing Club, Howard Stone, was a lanky, thin fellow with an enormous reach. He was knocked out one day, fell on the back of his head and spent the rest of his life in an institution.

I joined the Officers' Training Corps within a few weeks of entering the school. We were taught shooting and were initiated into the barrack drill and "bullshit" of the British Army. My boots glistened like mirrors; my putties and my uniform were immaculate. Alas, my power to obey commands was determined by the speed of my linguistic limitations. English was a foreign language to me with which I had encounters of varying success. Whatever somebody said to me went via the German synapses in my brain which would then send out the equivalent of "message received and understood". I was therefore unable to react instantly and became the bane of the lives of my sergeants. When they shouted "ATTENTION!" 300 boys would click their heels and stand erect like one man. A split second later there would be a separate click produced by Worms. Matters were not helped by the "Left turn by the right quick march!" which sounded to me like a number of incoherent animal noises, and the best I could do was to follow the examples of my fellow recruits on either side. That again involved a time factor. Thus I was never promoted.

Although St Paul's was considered, with some justice, to be one of the best academic schools in the country with one of the highest percentages of places and scholarships at Oxford and Cambridge, I found the standard considerably inferior to that of a good German school. I had come to England without any knowledge of physics or chemistry. The High Master advised me that these were essential subjects unless I was going to specialise in the classics. I devoted the summer holidays to studying physics and chemistry and in two months caught up with a three-year curriculum. I was due to sit for the Oxford and Cambridge School Certificate, which is the equivalent of what was later known as "Matric", in December of that year. For the compulsory Shakespeare play we were given *Twelfth Night*. Shakespeare was about as familiar to me at the time as the Talmud was to my classmates. I felt that I had no alternative but to learn *Twelfth Night* by heart and now, some 60 years later, I can still recite many passages.

Continental language training was far superior to that of an English public school. The prevalent attitude was that it was so much simpler for the foreigners to learn English. My French was actually much better than my English. When the day of my French oral exam came I entered a classroom and there sat three elderly gentlemen, one of whom in painfully accented French enquired whether I had ever visited France. In fairly fluent contemporary French I gave them an impression of the several holidays which I had spent in France until I realised that two of them could not follow me. Perhaps it was my accent. Since that time, things have changed and French teachers are frequently natives of France so this would not happen now. When it came to the publication of the results the Sur-Master (assistant High Master), Mr Cooke, called me over and said "Worms, I have a note from your French examiners which says 'Worms' knowledge of French is good. However, there was no need to show off quite as much as he did.'" Damn it. I still had not learned the English habit of underplaying one's abilities. It was only many years later that I appreciated the old dictum – If you are too fluent start stammering!

St Paul's School was remarkably tolerant in those days. I had no difficulty in having all the Jewish holidays off as well as the Friday afternoons in winter when *Shabbat* came early. It was, nevertheless, with some horror that I discovered that the Practical Physics Examination was due to take place on Friday afternoon at two o'clock. December was the time of the year when I had to leave the school at one o'clock in order to be back in Hampstead in time for the commencement of *Shabbat*. The High Master was most sympathetic. "No trouble at all, Worms. We'll write to Oxford and see whether you can take the examination in the morning."

A week later he called me and said: "I've arranged that for you. However, I cannot spare any examiner so I have to leave you alone. I want your undertaking not to take any books inside the examination room, and I want your promise not to talk to the boys who will be sitting the same examination in the afternoon."

On the appointed day I entered the laboratory where a master was waiting for me. He gave me the question and said, "I will be back in one and a half hour's time," closed the door and left me. The question was to find the latent heat of ice which had to be determined by means of several lumps of ice, a thermometer, jars of water and very delicate scales. I knew the latent heat of ice was 80 but when I had finished weighing and temperature reading the figure came out vastly differently. I adjusted the weight of the ice cube so that the result showed 78.5 which I thought was near enough, and this was one of the subjects in which I got top marks. To my amazement not a single boy asked me what the question was. I left the school entirely unmolested – something which would have been quite unheard of under similar circumstances in Germany.

One of the highlights of the following very hot summer was the visit of General Montgomery, as he then was, to inspect our Officers Training Corps. After the usual marching up and down the school barrack square, we were told to sit down on the tarmacadam surface. Montgomery then climbed up on a platform and gave us a pep talk. The temperature was in the eighties and our uniforms were extremely uncomfortable. At the end of his speech he ordered us, in his clipped accent, "You may get up." Half the boys were stuck on the melted tar!

When I was due to leave school I went and saw the High Master. "Sir, what shall I do?"

By that time the small allowance which my mother had sent monthly to England had been stopped by the Nazis. I had no particular preference for a profession. He deliberated and said, "You had better become an accountant."

"But Sir," I replied, "my weakest subject is maths. Didn't one of my teachers say I would never learn it?"

"My dear fellow," he retorted, "accountancy has nothing to do with mathematics."

I thought at the time he was joking, but of course it was a very profound statement, as borne out by subsequent experience.

4

Articled Clerk

WHEN I LEFT school at the beginning of 1939 I moved in with my
Uncle Benno and his wife Ly, who had a house at 11 Milton Close,
Hampstead Garden Suburb. At that time the Suburb was country-
side; Winnington Road was unpaved; The Bishops Avenue consisted
of relatively few houses, each one of which formed an estate by
itself, and Lyttelton Road, which now forms part of the A1 bore
little traffic and did not divide the Suburb.

Milton Close is a turning off Holne Chase. The plot of No 38
(with an unfinished house) shared our garden fence. We also had an
unrestricted view of No 36 where Anton Wallbrook, the famous film
star and his male companions were disporting themselves. Little did
I realise that some 11 years later when No 38 was completed that
my future wife and her family would live there and that our
engagement party would take place in their garden.

Even more astonishing was that Buya Lehmann and his wife
Ruth, would acquire No 36 and spend the whole of their married
life there. Buya was my best man. His son Colin is one of the senior
partners of Blick Rothenberg, Chartered Accountants, and a communal activist. Buya and Ruth died tragically young. They would
have enjoyed seeing their three children, Freddy, Colin and Nicole
and their cheerful grandchildren as they developed over the years.

Apart from Benno and Ly there was Trudi, who was the nanny of
their little daughter Marlys. Benno and Ly had already begun to
drift apart. He was well into his affair with Trudi, whom he later
married, and Ly left London with Marlys for New York when the
War broke out.

My volatile Uncle recommended me to his accountants, a firm of liquidators and bankruptcy specialists. I was then a relatively innocent 18 year old, devoid of any business experience, gullible and naive. The firm, which shall be nameless, was straight out of a Jeffrey Archer novel. Clients' books were "cooked". The office boy, who was about 26, had a motor car – an unheard of luxury in those days. Part of his finances was raised by acting as a part-time Commissioner for Oaths. Every day 50 or 60 documents relating to bankruptcies and liquidations had to be sworn before a Commissioner. Our young friend had an arrangement with a doddery old solicitor who would come in two or three times a week to sign 10 certificates, for which he would be paid two shillings and six pence each. The office boy would then forge the signature for the remaining 50 documents and put the money in his pocket. The petty cash strictly agreed with the number of certificates sworn and everybody lived happily ever after. Special old army-colonel types who lunched on gin and tonic, kept a regular liaison with the Registrars and Examiners at Carey Street where bankruptcy courts were situated, and ensured that an unceasing flow of liquidation work would be directed at our firm.

After six months of these extraordinary goings-on I saw the senior partner and said, "Sir, I would like to leave."

"But my dear boy, you are partnership material. In another four and a half years you will be qualified and then – the sky's the limit!"

"Thank you, sir. I appreciate what you say but I don't want to make my living as a liquidator."

He released me with regret. I then went to one of the oldest and best-known Jewish City firms – Jeffreys, Alfred, Henry and Marks. The senior partner was a Mr Herbert Marks – an establishment figure, upper-class, avant-garde, a socialist, collector of paintings, leading tax expert and a Russian-speaking snob of the first order. He, too, had been educated at St Paul's and therefore looked at my school reports with some interest. I told him that not only was I unable to pay a premium for my Articles, but that I needed a small salary to live on. He was most co-operative and agreed to pay two pounds ten shillings a week. That was a large sum of money in those days and one on which I could live fairly comfortably, particularly since I augmented my income by giving German and French lessons.

"There is another matter, sir."

"Yes, Worms."

He thought the interview was finished and his head came up reluctantly from the document he was inspecting.

"I am Orthodox, and I do not work on Jewish holidays or Saturdays."

"My dear boy, this is the City of London, not the East End. It is out of the question."

"Well, I am sorry to have wasted your time, but I cannot start."

He removed his glasses and looked at me with amazement.

"Do you mean to say that after the concessions I have made to let you come here as the first articled clerk who does not pay a premium, and who receives a not inconsiderable salary, you would turn down this opportunity because of your old-fashioned religious ideas?"

"I'm afraid so."

"Well, in that case I will take you on."

He explained to me later, when we had established some sort of rapport (he was a most powerful personality and every member of the staff from the manager downwards was terrified of him) that my predecessor had been the son of a *Dayan* (a rabbinical judge) who took off all the Jewish holidays, only to march with the Communist Party. Whilst Herbert Marks, MC, FCA, had no objection to him marching with the Communist Party he did not see why it had to be done in the firm's time.

During my Articles I spent considerable time auditing the books of the United Synagogue, and it was my duty to go through the Honorary Officers' Minute Book. I had the vicarious pleasure of reading the extraordinary correspondence between Chief Rabbi Hertz and Sir Robert Waley-Cohen, the President of the United Synagogue whose son, Sir Bernard Waley-Cohen, later became a director of one of my companies. The two men admired and disliked each other. Chief Rabbi Hertz felt that he was the head of the community whereas Sir Robert looked upon him as a very senior employee who had a certain amount of freedom in religious matters but that was all. Sir Robert, who had built up Shell and Unilever and was one of England's most important industrialists, considered the United Synagogue as another one of his companies. He could never reconcile himself to the limitations which the Council of the United Synagogue tried to impose on him. His tremendous application and outstanding leadership was diminished by his inability to carry those who worked with him along willingly rather than by bullying them into compliance. Similarly, Sir Isaac Wolfson, who was one of his successors as President of the United Synagogue, tried to run the United like his Great Univeral Stores and had little time for committees.

No one thought it strange that Herbert Marks, the militant atheist, should have had a virtual monopoly of the audits of all major Jewish religious organisations, including the Spanish and Portuguese Synagogues, the Federation of Synagogues (whose accounts were frequently qualified), the Beth Din etc. It was a tradition and a privilege which his firm had enjoyed for many decades.

5

My Mother's Lucky Escape

IN ADDITION TO her responsibility for her mother and my sister Vera, my mother travelled throughout Germany as manageress of the family lighter business. She exhibited at the annual Leipzig Fair. She conducted dangerous litigation against a Nazi firm which she won, and when, in 1938–9, the British Home Office agreed to admit refugee children provided a UK family would guarantee their maintenance, my mother became one of the prime movers in getting them out of Germany. She was indefatigable and fearless, travelling with "her children" to England on a number of occasions, and she succeeded in getting scores of youngsters to safety.

On 10 November 1938, the day after the infamous *Kristallnacht* when synagogues were burned down, Jewish shops were smashed and most Jewish males were arrested, she rescued my cousin, Laurie Lowenthal. He lived with his parents, Adolf and Sophie, in nearby Aschaffenburg. When the Nazis went on the rampage Laurie was beaten up. His Uncle Ludwig was shot in the stomach and left for dead.

It so happened that that morning my mother had neither seen a newspaper nor listened to the radio. She was therefore oblivious to the horror of the previous night when the telephone rang. "Meta, can you come over to us right away?" It was Sophie's tearful voice.

Such was the ingrained fear of Jews left in Germany, that the worst was always expected and there was voice telepathy which needed no elaboration. Without asking any questions my mother said, "I'll be with you within two hours." She caught the next train and thinking that Laurie would be safer in Frankfurt, brought him back with her. When a member of the SS knocked at her door to make a routine search for male residents, my mother hid Laurie in the wardrobe. She explained to the SS that ever since I had left for England there were only women in the apartment.

But where was Vera? After my mother had left for Aschaffenburg, my sister had received another SOS phone call from a close friend who had pleaded with her to travel to Düsseldorf to warn her husband not to come home and to hide until further notice. My intrepid 14-year-old sister did precisely that. It is not surprising that I am proud of the courage of the women in my immediate family.

Towards the end of December 1938, on a Friday morning, an SS man in uniform called on my mother. "We know that you are frequently travelling to England. We have reason to believe that you are smuggling money out. I am giving you this private warning. You will be arrested on Monday. I can arrange to have your record card destroyed if you pay me 800 marks." My mother told him she did not have that sort of money in the house and asked him to come back on Monday. She left Germany that night, although it was the Sabbath.

That following Monday the SS man returned. Vera told him my mother had gone abroad. The next day two more SS men turned up. "Have you seen this man before?" they asked, showing Vera a photograph.

"Yes," she replied. "He called here yesterday."

"Did he ask for money?"

"Yes."

"You had better come with us to identify him – he is an impostor."

So poor, noble, brave Vera had to go with them to confirm the identity of the man who undoubtedly saved my mother's life, since she would have never left in time.

Before leaving Germany my mother had arranged for Vera and Laurie to travel to England on one of the children's transports. My grandmother was unable to obtain a permit for England and she therefore joined my Uncle Herman and his young family in Strasbourg in the Alsace. Uncle Ludwig recovered sufficiently to emigrate to America.

At that time England had a very strict immigration quota. The only way for a single woman to get into the country was on the basis of domestic service. The Home Office made sure that this was not just a pro forma regulation but that the condition of entry was strictly adhered to. My mother thus found herself in the extraordinary position of serving as a maid in other people's households after having had never less than two domestic staff at her disposal until her divorce. This traumatic period, fortunately, did not last too long and by 1940 we were installed in a small apartment at Ashford Court, Cricklewood, north-west London.

6

Interned

THE OUTBREAK OF the Second World War in September 1939 was followed by the so-called phoney war before the Nazis swept through Belgium and Holland, by-passed the Maginot Line and occupied a major part of France. England's attitude towards the refugees was ambivalent and hopelessly muddled. To the man in the street a German was a German. The fact that a German Jew had more cause to hate Hitler and his gangsters than anybody else was not immediately obvious. The country was ill-prepared for war and there was general paranoia. Ashford Court contained quite a number of German Jewish refugee families. Spy mania was rampant. There were regular complaints from the ARP (Air Raid Precaution) volunteers at the nearby Smiths Industries factory that coded signals were being sent from the roof of Ashford Court to high flying enemy aircraft. Whilst this may appear laughable today, it was a tragedy at the time. Little did I imagine in those traumatic days that my next contact with Smiths Industries some 33 years later would be a more rewarding one.

Henry Mond, the second Lord Melchett, who converted back to Judaism (Jewish father, non-Jewish mother, non-Jewish wife), and was circumcised as an adult, became an enthusiastic Maccabiah supporter. He attended both the first and second Maccabiot in Palestine in 1932 and 1935 when he led the British contingent on a white horse. He ultimately became President of the Maccabi World Union (see Chapter 34).

It is most ironic, therefore, that he should have been responsible for the internment of one of his presidential successors. In 1940 he

37

wrote to Churchill stressing the diabolical strategy behind Hitler's anti-Semitic policy. ". . . the influx of sixty to seventy thousand refugees to a country like England could easily be accommpanied by two to three thousand agents. The introduction of two to three thousand agents by themselves would be an impossible task." He suggested that the best way to combat such a well-thought-out and ingenious policy was to intern all refugees, enemy aliens and ex-Germans naturalised since the War. When in doubt "In".

Thus it was that I was His Majesty's guest for a few weeks in 1940 until the absurdity of interning Hitler's greatest enemies was recognised and I was released.

I was lucky. In June and July over 4,000 internees including prisoners of war, were deported to Canada. Seven hundred drowned on the way when the *Andorra Star* was torpedoed by a German U-boat. Those sent to Australia on the *Dunera* suffered terrible hardship and tough internment conditions.

By that time I had been in the country for four years. I had been to public school and commenced my Articles and begun to feel truly at home in England. I was animated by an all-pervading hatred of Germany and her torturers. I had detailed knowledge of the atro-cities of the concentration camps from which members of the family and friends were released as shadows of their former selves before being allowed to emigrate. To be interned in England, therefore, came as a totally unexpected shock. Somehow I had an instinctive faith in the fairness of the English and I was sure that it would not last long. When a policeman called for me, my suitcase was already packed.

Much has been written about the various internment camps. My own recollections are those of a very badly run holiday camp. In the first place we were sent to Lingfield racecourse where we slept in provisional accommodation under grandstands. After a few days we were sent to Sutton Coldfield. That was a blow to the solar plexus. We arrived on a barren site with a few draughty army tents. I was young and fit and used to sleeping under canvas, but there were many older men who suffered badly under those conditions.

Already there was mounting pressure in Parliament against the injustice of interning Jews and Nazis together and Churchill himself began to look into the matter. Within a week we were transferred to Yorkshire to more comfortable quarters. We soon organised football matches against the guards and enjoyed a period of intense cultural activities. There were many university professors who lectured on every conceivable subject. Amongst my dormitory companions were Simon Bischheim (Eric Beecham's father), Albert Lieven, the famous German actor, Willy Frischauer, a writer from Vienna who later became one of England's leading journalists and Issy Geiger who practised on his fiddle all day long. After the War he played regularly with his orchestra at the BBC and at Lyons' Corner Houses.

Whilst I may be able to write light-heartedly of this extraordinary experience in retrospect, it must be borne in mind that the married men were absolutely frantic with worry about their wives and children whom they had left behind, in many cases without money or adequate knowledge of English.

One of the reasons for early release was emigration to another country. Without consulting me my mother went to the American Embassy and got a visa for the United States. How this was to be taken advantage of during the War with the lack of shipping and the menace of U-boats we shall never know.

One day the Camp Commander called me in and said, "Look, Worms, I want you to go back to Lingfield because that is the Release Centre, but I am afraid I cannot spare you an escort. Just give me your word that you will go there."

It was less than two years since I had had a not dissimilar conversation with the High Master of St Paul's. I asked permission to telephone my mother so that she could meet me at Euston Station where I had to change trains. This was given. At Euston there was my mother in tears accompanied by my sister and Ilse Ledermann, a close family friend. They did not see me at first for the simple reason that they expected me to be tucked between two large military policemen. It was only when I assured my mother that I would probably be released within a couple of days that she stopped insisting that I should come home and go to Lingfield the following day.

Back at Lingfield, which was surrounded by barbed wire, I

walked up to the guard with my suitcase and said, "May I come in please?"

The young soldier snarled at me. "Go away – this is Government property. Stop clowning."

I was enjoying myself. I said, "No, seriously, I do want to come in. I have a letter of introduction."

The soldier looked at me as though I was crazy, released the safety catch, rattled the bolt of his rifle and pointed it at me. Just then his sergeant came out.

"Hello, hello, hello! What's going on here then?"

"Would you kindly convey to Major Layton that Mr Worms is waiting outside and would like to pay his compliments to him."

Thus I was readmitted to Lingfield, into the care of Major Layton who later on became a good friend, my co-director at the Bank Leumi UK PLC and the senior partner of my stockbrokers. He considered the whole episode a marvellous joke and introduced me to his fellow officers as the young man who travelled by himself to be reinterned. I was sent home the following day.

Julian Layton was a remarkable man. Of German Jewish stock he, together with Professor Norman Bentwich, Leonard Montefiore, Sir Robert Waley-Cohen and Ernest and Oscar Joseph was the principal activist in rescue operations conducted by the Central British Fund's Jewish Refugee Committee. He risked his life by travelling often into Nazi Germany and saved many from concentration camps. Over 3,000 men found refuge in the Kitchener Camp in Kent which he helped to set up.

Within one week of my return home I volunteered to join the RAF for flying duties. I wanted nothing as much as to throw bombs on Germany. I passed my physical but was referred to a Harley Street consultant whose name was Morcelli Shaw, for a special eye test. Mr Shaw, after two sessions, gave me the shattering news that I had been living all these years with the use of one eye only. Ever since the age of four when I had inflammation of the middle ear, my left eye had been badly affected. He said that not only had I no chance of getting into the airforce but that it was extremely unlikely that any of the fighting units would have me.

I did not fancy cleaning lavatories in the Pioneer Corps and repeated this to Herbert Marks, to whom I was articled. He was delighted that my services would continue to be available to him. He obtained special permission from the Home Office for me to travel and visit Government weapons factories as reporting accountant, which was apparently necessary to keep the war machine going.

Ever since I have been running around with the knowledge that I have the use of one eye only. Over the years I have learned to compensate to some extent for this deficiency. As I got older, I had to admit to myself, albeit reluctantly, that a one-eyed tennis player lacks the breadth of vision of a two-eyed one, but I never use it as an excuse for my many unforced errors.

When I qualified Herbert Marks offered me a partnership, but I decided that accountancy was not for me. Rather than reacting to clients' business ventures by auditing their books, *post factum*, as, mistakenly, I then saw it, I wanted to shape my own destiny.

7

Bachelor Years: 1946–1950

THE POST-WAR YEARS were a tremendously exciting period. It was wonderful to get back to normal living in so far as we knew what that meant. Those of us who were teenagers at the beginning of the War suddenly found ourselves as adults confronting a way of life that was altogether unfamiliar.

It could hardly be claimed that the late 1940s were a particularly easy time. The euphoria of victory quickly vanished. There were not enough jobs for all the returning soldiers; Churchill, the engineer of the survival, was thrown out by the electorate and Messrs Attlee and Bevin were running the country. Petrol rationing was not abolished until 1950. It was a dark period for the Jews in Palestine and the relationship with Great Britain, the mandatory power, reached its nadir.

Refugees who had miraculously survived the death camps and who were longing to reach the Promised Land, arrived in their thousands in worn out ships, only to be turned back at the very shores of Haifa and Tel Aviv, and were sent to new concentration camps in Cyprus.

Ernest Bevin, the strong man from the unions, had become a very powerful Foreign Secretary. Spurred on by the Arabists in the Foreign Office it was only "over his dead body" that more Jews would get into Palestine. He accused them of "jumping the queue", an insult to the very people who were outcasts of Europe and desperate to leave German soil. It has been said that the State of Israel should erect a statue to him in grateful memory for his stubborn opposition without which the declaration of independence might have come much later.

It was his very ruthlessness that incensed the *Yishuv* and spawned Menachem Begin's underground organisation, the Irgun. When the King David Hotel in Jerusalem was blown up and two British sergeants were hanged in retaliation for the execution of some of Begin's men, Chaim Weizmann and his followers were in despair. His beloved England, the Bible-loving nation, had turned against him and his peaceful methods. He was out-manoeuvred by the militants and he deplored the bitter irony that the State of Israel was to be created by the gun rather than by universal acclaim.

It was not a time when it was easy to be a Jew in England. It was in 1946 that my aunt Claire Kevehazi brought her son Michael to London. They had miraculously survived the onslaught of the Nazis, the hardship of the Budapest ghetto and the Russian "deliverance" which made the beautiful town of Budapest whilst under their sphere of influence into another drab spiritless Iron Curtain city. Michael was then a tall, thin, underfed boy with enormous black eyes blinking into the light of newly-won freedom and fresh air of London with considerable apprehension.

On the first Sunday after his arrival the London cousins went for a walk on Hampstead Heath; Laurie and Jack Lowenthal, Michael and myself. We were showing Michael the spectacular beauty of Kenwood which forms part of the Heath when suddenly we heard cries for help. We ran towards a gang of bullies beating up a young Jewish boy whilst his girl friend stood by, crying. We were incensed. I said to the leader, "Okay, that's enough, leave him alone."

He said, "Do you want to make something of it?"

I would have loved to have said "No" but there was that part of my temper which is very rarely roused but becomes difficult to control when it raises its ugly head as mentioned earlier.

I replied, "Leave him alone or fight me."

They formed a circle around us and, with fear in my heart and the boxing experience of St Paul's, I knocked him out in less than two minutes. The horde then descended upon us. When we got back to Beaufort Park with bloody noses and torn shirts, but triumphant in spirit, Aunt Claire was wondering whether it would not be safer to take Michael back to Budapest with her! She did not. He stayed in

London to commence a remarkable success story.

Michael followed in my footsteps and became a chartered accountant. In June 1952 he married Gene Preger. This was the last wedding that Clock Oma, my grandmother, was able to attend. Because Michael's parents were not allowed to leave Budapest, the occasion had a melancholic undertone. My mother wrote to Claire and Zolly describing the wedding in great detail. Michael worked his way up to a partnership in Blick Rothenberg and Noble, who were my auditors, got involved in Maccabi and, at the height of his professional career in England, gave up a house in Finchley with two cars and decided to emigrate to Israel. This was a courageous step motivated entirely by idealistic considerations.

He took his parents, who had settled in London in 1956, and his four children to start a hazardous new career in Tel Aviv. I well remember my long chats with Fritz Metzger who was then the senior and dominant partner in Kesselman and Kesselman, to ensure that Michael would be given every opportunity for early promotion. I also recall that Michael said to me, "Do you think our Maccabi colleagues in Israel will let me come in? I hear Israelis freeze out new *Olim* from senior positions."

This was perfectly true because quite a number of my acquaintances who were capable professionals who had tried to settle in Israel, came back to England after receiving the cold shoulder from their Israeli colleagues. In due course Michael became senior partner in Kesselman and Kesselman and Chairman of the Maccabi World Union.

The immediate post-War period was an historic one at Maccabi Compayne Gardens. We had an outstanding youth club and even today, nearly 50 years on, I am frequently stopped by people in different parts of the world: "Aren't you Freddie Worms? Don't you remember me from Maccabi?" (Freddie is my pre-1960 Maccabi trademark). Pierre Gildesgame was Chairman; Fred Oberlander was Sports Director: I was Cultural Director continuously fighting the other Fred for the use of the large hall. The Executive included such names as Jack Salmon, Jack and Bryna Richman, Ken Gradon, Ivor Taylor, Asher Rebak, Con Abrahams, Sidney Simons, Cyril

Blausten and Sidney Farleigh to mention just a few of those evocative names.

Selig Brodetsky, the prominent Zionist leader and President of the Board of Deputies, was also the President of the Maccabi World Union. One of the finest mathematicians in the country, he was a professor at Leeds University, but spent most of his time on communal affairs.

In 1946 we held the first European Maccabi Conference. It was a reunion of Maccabi survivors from the concentration camps with whom we could only communicate in Yiddish. Amongst the "Yekkes" this had been a despised language but after my first exposure to it, I became very fond of it and am able – with the inclusion of too many German words – to communicate in it.

My sister Vera married Ken Gradon on 9 October 1947. They had met on the running track of Maccabi, whose athletic section at the time was training at Parliament Hill fields. They were both good track athletes. Kurt Gradenwitz metamorphosed into Kenneth Gradon when he joined the British Army where he served throughout the War, and took part in the invasion of France. He came from a well-known Berlin medical family.

He was, and still is, a member of the Munk Shul in Golders Green, named after the charismatic Rabbi Eli Munk who founded this congregation of truly Orthodox Jews mostly hailing from Germany, after the War.

My cousin Laurie Lowenthal married Cecily Stern of the eponymous Hotel family three months later on 17 December 1947. After the ceremony Laurie felt ill and had to lie down. It thus fell to my lot to receive the guests standing next to Cecily until such time as Laurie was able to return. Everybody who shook my hand and congratulated me said "Please God by you" and gave me a significant look. Others were more forthcoming. "Isn't it about time you stood there in your own right?"

I went to Switzerland on my first skiing holiday. Skiing had always been one of my dreams. As a boy I had tried it with inadequate equipment in the Taunus mountain range near Frankfurt, and I was eagerly looking forward to the day when I could take it up seriously.

Food was still strictly rationed in England in 1946. We had the "five shilling maximum price" meals in restaurants. When I walked through the Bahnhofstrasse in Zurich I thought I was in paradise. Fruits and food which I had not seen for years were available in abundance. I lunched at the Café Huguenin, which is now the Café Krantzler, and I asked for trout. I expected to see a little dead fish which – with a bit of luck – would have some horseradish with it. There came a vast oval platter on which two trout were swimming in butter sauce, surrounded by little mountains of peas, mushrooms, new potatoes, artichokes and asparagus. My eyes filled with tears and I felt quite guilty at destroying this work of art. Ahh . . . the land of milk and money!

I went to St Moritz, the mecca of fashionable skiing. The annual holiday allowance available to residents of the UK was £35. The pound in those days was a pound and this sum was enough to stay in a small hotel and live carefully for some ten days. I joined a ski class but, with my usual impatience, found the slow progress somewhat boring. Occasionally I would zoom off on my own with minimal technique and maximum cheek. My preferred way of travelling was "*schuss*" – straight down.

On one occasion, when I was inadvertently racing toward a particularly steep incline, the teacher shouted "*Bremsen*! [Stop!]"

"What a fool he is," I thought to myself. "If I could brake would I be racing down like this, out of control?"

One of my fellow pupils was the Hon Billy – a charming, chinless aristocrat. He said, "Tonight we are going to have a party."

"Thank you very much," I replied.

"Come along to the Carlton Hotel at nine o'clock."

"But," I queried, "the Carlton is closed."

"I know," he said, "but they are opening it for me."

I looked at him with different eyes. I had never met anyone to whom money was no object. Where was he getting the Swiss francs from? He hired a band, we had a marvellous party and at six in the morning we adjourned to the Palace Hotel for breakfast. Some of the other English chaps and myself then went over to him.

"We would like to make our contribution, even if it means cutting short our holiday."

He roared with laughter and gave us all a pitying glance.

"Don't you worry," he said. "All this will be paid for in England."

This was my first encounter of a special law for the very rich!

Harry (Buya) Lehmann and I spent our summer holidays together in typical carefree bachelor fashion. Discretion is the better part of valour and a veil shall be drawn over our indiscretions.

We motored through France to vacations in Biarritz, St Jean de Luz, St Sebastian in Spain and Rapallo in Italy. Did not Ecclesiastes tell us that in life there is a time for rejoicing? We grasped the opportunities after the Hitler and war years eagerly and gratefully.

8

Marriage

MY BACHELOR YEARS continued. I had a wide social circle and was extremely busy building up my company, Tudor Accessories. I was an active sportsman and even in those days was involved in a number of communal organisations. Skiing in winter, and summer holidays by the Mediterranean had become a fixed pattern. But then the unexpected happened.

In 1950 Norrice Lea synagogue was a small one-storey hall. The men sat in front and the women at the rear. I caught myself looking backwards more and more frequently. The attraction was a young girl who was somehow different. I could not take my eyes off her. I met her formally at a party given by Buya Lehmann. Della Rosenberg and her family, lived next door to the Lehmanns. She was a tall, 19-year-old with black hair, large trusting eyes, and a face of luminescent beauty and with such obvious shining integrity that I thought to myself "there goes the mother of my children".

I took her out in the company of Laurie and Cecily Lowenthal. After the third meeting I knew that I had truly fallen in love.

Della's parents hailed from Eastern Europe; her father Myer, or Mick as he was generally known, was born near Kiev and had arrived in this country as a baby whilst her mother, Esther Ehrlichman, had come with her family from Bendzyn in Poland after having spent some time in Antwerp. Mick was a prosperous textile merchant.

Della was educated during the war years at Amersham and later at the Henrietta Barnet School and was then sent for a short spell to Switzerland to a finishing school. When I met her she worked for her father as a commercial traveller after having studied economics, and – luxury of luxury in those days – had her own car, a Hillman Minx.

Seven weeks after I had first set eyes on her I proposed to her on a fine day in late May. I cannot remember the exact words but I know that half an hour later she nearly lost me for ever. We were on a beach in East Wittering on the south coast of England. There was a warning notice to the effect that the currents were treacherous but I saw it only later. I swam out a fair distance, probably to show off, and soon realised that I could not get back because the tide was going out, and so was I. Fortunately the bay was crescent shaped and I allowed myself to drift sideways rather than engage in a futile battle with the sea. All this took a considerable time. Della had lost sight of me and ran up and down the beach enquiring with increasing concern whether anybody had seen a balding football-shaped head bobbing about on the water, or words to that effect.

I reached the shore a long way from where I had set out. I was exhausted and walked back a considerable distance to a greatly relieved Della. We were both somewhat embarrassed and I was too tired to say no when she suggested we should go for a run!

I was anxious to obtain Mick and Esther's permission to get engaged as soon as possible. I talked quietly to Mick who was delighted. Not so Della's mother. She was not at all certain that she wanted her beautiful young daughter to get married to a Yekke (who needs a mixed marriage?), a man 10 years older with thinning hair and a reputation of having been around. She skilfully avoided a showdown, but kept her options open by inviting me to lunches and suppers. Here I had my first culture shock. We sat down to large plates of mixed salad garnished with nuts, raisins, seaweed, cucumber and other kinds of green herbs as described in the creation process in Genesis. "Where is the steak?" I asked.

This was my introduction to healthy living and over the years we have swung more and more to the Rosenberg diet and perhaps this is why Della has retained the skin of a young girl and I ski as irresponsibly as ever.

Every time I visited Della's parents I tried to sit down quietly to talk with Esther but she jumped about, fetching this or that, making tea, asking Della to play the piano for me – in fact, she went to great lengths not to stay in the same room with me for more than five minutes unless others were present.

Mick said to me, "I am sorry Fred, but you will have to get Esther's permission," so one afternoon I arrived when I knew both Mick and Esther were at home. "Mrs Rosenberg," I said, "I want you to come for a ride with me."

"Why?" she asked, in apparent innocence. "You'll see," I replied.

Mick asked whether he could come along too.

I replied hesitatingly, "Well, provided you don't talk," a considerable sacrifice for him.

So Mick sat in the back and with Esther next to me we went for an aimless yet purposeful drive. In the meantime Della went to her regular class where she was studying the Margaret Morris system of Greek dancing. She told her fellow pupils, "I think I am getting engaged this evening!"

She was perfectly right. I must have been persuasive because by the time we returned to Holne Chase Esther had said "Yes", perhaps a small price to pay to get out of my car. Mick, who unusually for him, had not opened his mouth said that he had not enjoyed himself so much for years!

My mother-in-law became one of my biggest fans. I could do nothing wrong in her eyes. Our only differences arose when she smuggled garlic into her cooking which, whilst it may have fooled my palate, led my stomach to rebel later.

Della and I were married by *Dayan* Dr Lew in the Norrice Lea Synagogue on 6 February 1951. Following the ceremony Della walked over to Clock Oma who was sitting next to the *Chuppah* in her wheelchair. Della bent down to receive her blessing and there was a hush in the synagogue giving that poignant moment special significance.

The party took place at the Porchester Hall in Bayswater. Because of the very large number of family and friends on both sides, I had suggested (which was my mistake) that we should invite another younger crowd to come for the dessert only. Benny Guggenheim has blamed me ever since because he was not allowed to finish his main course in comfort as the waiter whisked his plate away to clear the table for the second house. Anyhow, a great time was had by our guests who danced long after Della and I had disappeared.

Ours must be the only wedding photographs taken by a professional that turned out to be total failures. My father-in-law employed a traveller who said to him: "My son-in-law is a budding photographer. Please allow him to take the wedding photographs – it will be one of his first assignments." Sir Sidney Samuelson, as he became later, the doyen of the British Film Industry, succeeded in getting every picture out of focus. When I met him 35 years later he said "Please offer Della my apologies. I think today I could do a better job!"

Johnnie Morton, our faithful driver at Tudor, took us the following morning from Grosvenor House to the airport on our way to a skiing honeymoon in Arosa. We stayed over in Zurich where Benny and Lydia Guggenheim entertained us for a special meal when seven blessings were recited. Lydia had asked me during our wedding dinner what I wanted for supper the following night at her house in Zurich. "Steak," I replied without a moment's hesitation, not realising the culinary complications for what turned out to be quite a party. To this very day Della and I have wondered how Lydia managed to serve 30 people with rare, medium or well-done steaks to their specific requirements. The Guggenheims have remained close friends and Maccabi colleagues for over 40 years.

I see the early years of our marriage through a golden glow. Eric and Jean Beecham, whose wedding took place a week after ours, joined us for a holiday in Scotland and the Lake District. Then Della and I travelled to Paris, to Spain and to Tangiers. I remember saying to Della as we walked along the deserted coast at Marbella that I would not be surprised if this were to become a popular place one of these days, and if one had any money to spare one should buy some land there. I did not have any money to spare but my forecast was right.

On 8 March 1952 we celebrated Della's 21st birthday by holding a fancy dress party.

Della travelled everywhere with me and we attended the different motor shows in Europe where Tudor exhibited. After the Kevehazi wedding in June 1952, Della and I went off to Devon later that summer where one of our suppliers, a Mr Ayers, owned a sand yacht. This is a specially adapted boat with wheels and nautical sails. We learned to race along the hard sands of Devon, often falling off but thoroughly enjoying ourselves. Little did we realise that Della was in the early stage of pregnancy but her experience seems to have done no harm to Nadia. (This pales into insignificance when compared with the exploits of the late Alison Hargreaves who conquered Mount Everest without carrying oxygen and who was six months pregnant when she ascended the north wall of the Eiger in 1988.)

Nadia was born in 1953 and Della and I came to the conclusion that what we needed was our own house with a garden. I went to the various estate agents in Market Place, Hampstead Garden Suburb, to register our interest. Properties in those days were a rare commodity. "For sale" boards were unheard of. What we wanted was a modest house suitable for a young married couple at the bottom of the ladder. One of the estate agents was McCraith and Brooks. They had a reputation for being somewhat anti-Semitic and for never introducing a property to a Jewish family. I took no notice of that and went and saw Mr McCraith.

One day he telephoned me, "I have something for you. It is a plot of land in The Bishops Avenue." I said "You must be joking, Millionaire's Row – one of London's most expensive streets. What would I be doing there? I am afraid you have the wrong number."

"I suggest you go and have a look anyhow," he replied.

At that time The Bishops Avenue was really in a class of its own with enormous homes, many of them standing in acres of ground. This was before the post-War redevelopments and despoilation when some of the larger properties were broken up into estates of vulgar houses.

Della and I inspected the site which was on the corner of The Bishops and Bancroft Avenues. It formed part of one very large garden. The owner had felt that it was too expensive to maintain. He wanted to dispose of the corner site.

I went back to Mr McCraith and said "How much?" He said, "£1,500." Now £1,500 in 1953 was a lot of money, but nevertheless it struck me as an extraordinary bargain. I drove back to the house of the owner, a Mr George, put my visiting card through the letter-box with the word "£1,500 – sold" written on the back. Esther, my mother-in-law, remonstrated with me: "Why didn't you bargain?"

I said, "When I see something that is already a bargain, I don't risk losing it."

Ernst Pollak, a Czech architect, who had never designed a house before but who had built our factory at Hayes, pleaded with me to give him the job. At that time there were building restrictions. 1,500 sq. ft. was the maximum that could be put up at any one time. He created a modern house of distinction with a partial glass front elevation. He introduced us to large, rectangular, unencumbered double-glazed Swedish windows with venetian blinds between the sheets of glass. It was altogether a departure from the pseudo-Georgian houses that were the norm for The Bishops Avenue. He lined the walls of the living rooms with rare wooden veneers similar to the recently built Festival Hall. Thus we had a virtual maintenance free lounge and dining room which needed little attention throughout the nearly 40 years we lived there.

We had some difficulty in getting planning permission. The conservative Barnet Council was not then used to new ideas, but over the years Esher House became a classic. In due course, the loft became another elegant floor; we had the first and one of the largest open air swimming pools in the Garden Suburb and under the supervision of Della and the brilliant gardening expertise of Stanley Peglar, we had a show garden once it came to its glorious maturity.

Vera and Stanley Peglar provided the infrastructure of Esher House for over twenty years. We bought an apartment for them in East Finchley and Mr Peglar, as we invariably called him, was our gardener/chauffeur whilst Vera, a brilliant cook and baker, ran the household under Della's supervision. These were ideal arrangements which left Della free to pursue her interests as a very active magistrate (Justice of the Peace) for a period of 25 years, which apart from sitting in court, usually taking the chair, involved continuous refresher courses. There were also her many charitable activities in Emunah, the Art Museums of Israel, and B'nai B'rith in addition to her eternal quest for improving her Hebrew and her fitness through Greek dancing which led to yoga and aqua-aerobics. The Peglars became friends and took a passionate interest in the affairs of the wider family. When they retired we bought them a cottage in the country and with my trusted Vauxhall, which they took as an additional farewell present, had a number of contented years before Vera Peglar passed away in 1994.

Hilary was born at Esher House in 1956 and Caroline in 1958. We settled down to a routine, taking the children to Switzerland in winter and to Frinton, on the Essex coast, to Canford Cliffs near Bournemouth or to Paignton in Devon in summer but, most of all, we enjoyed the facilities of Esher House.

The children expected, as a matter of course, their nightly bedside stories. For years I ran a regular series for them, dealing with a variety of characters who virtually became honorary members of our family. Even nowadays the younger grandchildren in Jerusalem often greet me with a sing-song voice, "Mossy story, please!"

One summer we hired a dormobile and spent two glorious weeks in Scotland, climbing the hills and swimming in the lakes. None of our daughters had reason to complain that there was sex discrimination. There were the same requirements from the female of the species as there would have been from boys. Nadia, Hilary and Caroline were expected to climb mountains, ski fast, swim stylishly and follow their father's outdoor challenges. One day we climbed up a waterfall, clinging to slippery stones and overhanging branches. The girls were aged between five and 10. Della, who was apprehensively watching us from the adjacent path, was accosted by some tourists. "Who is that lunatic with those little girls?"

Della replied with a mixture of pride and embarrassment "I am afraid that's my husband toughening up my daughters ..."

The annual apple harvest and the building of the *Sukkah* in our garden was another cause for the young cousins in the family to come together to help and get under our feet!

Esher House was not only the family's but also a communal focal point. Anniversary celebrations, charitable functions, dinner parties often in large marquees, and a home from home for overseas colleagues were the order of the day.

Our regular Swiss mothers'-helps and *au pairs* provided logistic support. One, a charming country bumpkin asked when seeing a bidet for the first time in her life, whether this was provided to "wash the baby in". Vera Peglar explained that to the contrary, it was to wash the baby out!

After we had built the pool we were almost always praying for bad weather during weekends. We never realised that we had so many friends. People happened to have their costumes with them when they dropped in on a sunny Saturday or Sunday afternoon. Della and I found ourselves as permanent caterers until we came to the reluctant decision to put up a metaphorical board "By appointment only".

Della taught me at a fairly early stage that she was quite capable of asserting herself, forcefully, if necessary. One fine summer's day we were all ready to go out. I was wearing a smart grey suit. However, we had a difference of opinion and before I knew where I was I was floundering in the pool.

"You pushed me in," I gasped, "fully dressed!"

"That's right," Della replied. "Let this be a lesson to you."

The children were delighted and applauded. They thought their mother was wonderful and so did I.

In 1959 we had one of the most memorable Maccabi European Sports Championships at Copenhagen. Pierre and Maniusia Gildesgame, Lionel and Cissie Schalit, Lord and Lady Nathan – all came along. It was one of those sylvan summers. We took Nadia aged six, and Hilary aged three, and an *au pair* and rented a property with a boathouse outside Copenhagen. It was the perfect combination. Swimming and sailing with the children, sports and meetings with Maccabi colleagues and long sociable evenings.

A typical English summer included tennis at Wimbledon and opera at Glyndebourne. We made it a practice to spend a few days in Sussex and to go to Glyndebourne for two or three evenings in succession where we entertained family and friends which, in the early days, included (Viscount) Edwin Samuel and his wife Hadassah, who divided their time between London and Jerusalem, and more recently that remarkable musician, the Lord Chief Justice, Peter Taylor and his wife, Irene who, alas, passed away in 1995.

One year Mick decided to come along at the last minute. "Dad, I've only got four tickets. It's sold out!"

"You'll manage, Fred, I'm coming."

Nan Merriman was singing that evening. I had met her in Milan, courtesy of Count Lurani.

"Darling," she welcomed me in her dressing room, "No, I can't help you with a ticket. Why don't you see John?"

Sir John Christie was generosity personified.

"Of course, my dear boy, you must give your ticket to your father-in-law."

I sat between him and Pilar Lorenga in the private box. Mick was not in the least surprised. Other guests at Glyndebourne were Hannah and Moshe Raviv who came back to London in October 1993 to represent Israel once again, this time as the official ambassadorial couple. They have won the hearts of the community and the trust of the Foreign Office. They were and remain very good personal friends.

Della has a younger brother, Arthur, who not only became my brother-in-law but over the years also one of my best friends. Mick influenced Arthur, really against his wishes, to enter the textile industry. He said, "I am just an ordinary wholesaler but if you become a production expert, one day you will be opening your own mills and you will be in a different league." Arthur studied textile engineering, worked for Monsanto, and rapidly climbed the ladder of promotion. He combined expertise in this field with a special gift of human relations. It was no wonder, therefore, that Monsanto asked him to open up factories for them in Ireland and Israel.

After Arthur had married Bernice Woolfson from Glasgow, he wished to settle down. Staying at Monsanto would have meant uprooting himself every few years and working in a different part of the world. He and Bernice wanted to bring up a nice Jewish family, difficult if you are in perpetual motion. There was also the consideration that the textile industry was in decline and the manufacture shifted gradually from Europe to the Far East. At the age of 37 Arthur took the enormously courageous decision of changing careers. He became a chartered accountant, joined Hacker Young,

Stuart Young's firm, and quickly became a partner. He also became a Fellow, and later Chairman, of the Council of the Textile Institute and in later years specialised in working on assignments for the Fraud Squad as a fully fledged DTI Inspector. He also became the Vice Chairman of the Institute of Arbitrators and, with Bernice, had the satisfaction of watching the successful careers and marriages of their two daughters, Dorit and Leora and their son, Daniel.

Arthur is one of my regular tennis partners, Bernice and Della are very close and we see a lot of each other.

Occasionally, Della and I travelled to the south of France or the Italian Riviera. We knew the children were in good hands because Mick and Esther would move into Esher House. One summer in Italy we found the noise from the motor-bikes of the young Italians who expressed their machismo by revving up their engines whilst talking to their girl friends quite exasperating. We drove to Switzerland and checked into a quiet hotel on Lake Geneva. Della wanted to go back to the casino in Evian. She had been there with her father but was too young to be admitted. Alas we did not take our passports and once again she was refused admission because she looked too young. We did manage to get in eventually on condition Della didn't play! With chips in my left pocket I placed my own bets; from the right pocket I placed Della's bets. Della won and I lost.

Esher House truly lived up to its name. Where does the word Esher come from? Does it have some connection with the little town in Surrey? No, it is a play on the Hebrew word "Esher" which has two interpretations and we have often been asked which of the two we had in mind. In Hebrew there are two ways of spelling Esher. If you use an *aleph* the word Esher means happy; if you spell it with an *ayin* the word means rich. We prefered the former but were not averse to either offering.

We sold the house in 1994, much to the regret of our daughters and grandchildren, who looked upon it as their stately home with the beloved garden, fruit trees and swimming pool that was always available for their holidays.

"What on earth are they doing to your house?" has become the standard greeting of my Suburb friends. What indeed? The purchasers, who said they wanted the house because they had fallen in love with it, utterly demolished it. They had in fact paid us for the site value. In its place stands a pretentious edifice with pseudo-Greek columns, ready to be marketed to a Middle-Eastern potentate.

In 1992 we moved into Highpoint, a large "Bauhaus" apartment block in Highgate put up in 1935 by Sigmund Gestetner, some 15 minutes walking distance from Esher House.

It is often referred to in architectural circles as Lubetkin's masterpiece and it is now a Grade II star listed building. Whilst it is agreeable to live in an architectural showpiece, it has disadvantages. What would be a routine renewal job in a normal block of flats, necessitates the involvement of English Heritage and the local planners, often a protracted and tedious process.

John Allan, formerly Lubetkin's junior partner, looked after the redesign of the layout of the duplex penthouse which we acquired. It was his mission to follow in the footsteps of the Master, insisting on 1930s' replacements where more modern fixtures and fittings would have been preferable. We have a 250 degree view of London from our balcony, ranging from the Canary Wharf in Docklands to the City, West End, Surrey Downs, Hampstead Heath, Harrow and St Albans.

Birds whom we used to be familiar with by looking at their undersides now look us straight in the eye. The sunsets and the seasonal changes of the trees are a daily tonic. We have three acres of gardens, two tennis courts and a heated outdoor pool. And yet ... one cannot help yearning from time to time for the golden days of Esher House, its laughter-filled garden with its apple trees and floribunda ... but as *Kohelet* says: "There is a time for everything in life."

9

Three Daughters

OUR THREE DAUGHTERS have completely different personalities; they do not look alike, they lead different lifestyles, yet they have a similar educational background. Coincidentally they have chosen careers where human relations are paramount.

All three girls went to Norrice Lea Synagogue's Kerem House Kindergarten started by the redoubtable Stanley Frankfurt, where Mrs Bornstein-Cohen was the *sympathique* Headmistress. Next, they went to Henrietta Barnet Junior School (unlike Della, who went to Henrietta Barnet Senior School) and finally, on to North London Collegiate School. They were active in B'nai Akivah and became *Madrichot*.

To assert their independence all three left the family home at the age of 18 to go to Israel. For Della and me these were mixed pleasures. On the one hand, we were proud of our girls who preferred the challenges, trials and tribulations of the young State to the home comforts of Esher House. On the other hand, we would have loved to have shared in their tertiary education from closer quarters.

Nadia entered Machon Gold, a religious girls seminary before reading Jewish Philosophy at the Hebrew University. Soon she was to meet her future husband, Alan Hoffmann, who was born in South Africa but had made *aliyah* in 1967, joined the Israeli Army and over the years became one of the country's leading educationalists. In due course he was to become the Head of the Samuel Melton Centre of the Hebrew University for Jewish Education in the Diaspora and later the Chief of Staff of Mort Mandel's Institute which, together with Seymour Fox and other top academics, endeavours to reshape and revitalise Jewish Education in the United States and Israel.

Nadia and Alan spent two years at Cambridge, Massachusetts, where she studied for her second degree at Harvard i.e. an MA in Education. Later, she, Alan and their children spent a year at the University of Michigan at Ann Arbor and then she read for her third degree in clinical psychology at the Tel Aviv University. Today, Nadia is practising in her field, counselling on campus, hospitals etc. Her four children, Ayelet, born in 1979, Noam, born in 1982, Matan, born in 1985 and Tal, born in 1991, having spent some part of their lives in the United States are completely bilingual.

Hilary went on *hachsharah* (preparatory training for *aliyah*) at Kibbutz Lavi. This particular Kibbutz up in the Galilee not far from Tiberias has always been very close to our hearts. We have many friends there and in particular the Obermans have always been looked upon by our daughters as role models. It is, by the way, a matter of some concern to us that these wonderful people with their knitted *kippot* have moved so far to the political right but that is another story. Hilary then also read Jewish Philosophy at the Hebrew University where she met her husband, Jeremy Milgrom. Later, whilst Jeremy was qualifying for the Rabbinate at the Jewish Theological Seminary in New York, Hilary got her Masters at Columbia University in Social Work. They have three children Kineret born in 1982, Maor born in 1985 and Ma'ayan born in 1987. It is said that one in three marriages ends in divorce and unfortunately our family falls into line with these statistics. Hilary and Jeremy live near each other and have joint custody of the children. Hilary runs her family therapy practice with some partners and part of the time works at the Womens' Counselling Centre where Nadia has now joined her.

Hilary fondly recalls her childhood memories and the fun they had when Della organised charade games and free dance improvisation, which Hilary now often incorporates in her work. She uses psychodrama in her groups of women who suffered child abuse and has led drama groups for children, based on folklore of their countries of origin, thus helping the children to appreciate the diversity of Israel's immigrant population.

Caroline, our youngest, also went on *hachsharah* to Kibbutz Lavi but she was determined not to follow in her sisters' footsteps and to carve out her own path. Instead of going to university straight away she became a tour guide and qualified in three languages. She was particularly popular with German pilgrims. and she could have had a lucrative and interesting career in this field but she found it too corrupt. She said there was no way in which bus drivers could be weaned from the habit of taking tourists to favoured restaurants or souvenir shops where the kick-back system was well-ingrained.

She then studied at the Rubin Academy of Music and acquired her diploma and BA in Music and Movement. She became a teacher and deliberately selected one of the under-privileged schools in Jerusalem's East Talpiot. Large classes of up to 40 contained many immigrant children to whom the concept of classical music was totally alien. Caroline always said that one of her great ambitions was to wean them from pop culture to enjoy some of the classics. She invited us on a few occasions to attend some of her classes. To me it was a complete eye-opener. How she kept 40 unruly children totally disciplined was amazing. She brought along her collection of primitive African instruments to demonstrate the development of music-making through the centuries. The greatest punishment to any of her children was to be sent outside. Caroline married Nitzan, a graphic designer, who has worked for most of the leading Jewish organisations. They have three children – Sigal born 1988 and twins Roi and Barak born 1993. Caroline is at present commuting between Jerusalem and Netanya where she is reading for her Masters Degree in Therapy through Remedial Movement.

With 10 grand-children ranging in ages from three to 16 at the time of writing this in 1996, Jerusalem's attraction is irresistible.

One's children are a mixed pleasure. After all, one had the responsibility and worries of bringing them up, nursing them through illnesses, educating them and seeing them go their own way, whereas the grandchildren are there for one's pure delight. You are pleased when they come, and enjoy building up a rapport with each one individually, and also relieved when they go. The ultimate responsibility lies with their parents. In fact, one of the first lessons grandparents have to learn is not to interfere with the upbringing of the grandchildren. I hope we have learned our lesson. I believe that when one talks about the future world that this is largely tied up with the happiness of one's grandchildren who should feel the souls of their grandparents benevolently hovering over them.

10

North London Collegiate School

DAME KITTY ANDERSON became a legend in her own lifetime. She was an outstanding educator with a national reputation. When Nadia entered NLCS, Dame Kitty was in her last year as Headmistress. There was a great party where Dame Kitty unpacked her farewell present. This was a suitcase within a suitcase within a suitcase with a handbag inside the smallest one which held a cheque. That cheque enabled her to circumnavigate the world after her retirement.

The journey was prepared in her usual meticulous way and she boasted that she did not have to sleep one single night in a hotel. Wherever she went, even to obscure places, she found an Old North Londoner with whom to spend the night. Part of her journey took her to Israel where she was the guest of my cousin Ruth Fluss, an Old North Londoner, who lives with her husband Barry in Haifa.

I became a Governor of the School after my three daughters had left and after Madeleine McLauchlan had become the Head Teacher. During her period of office the school facilites were substantially expanded whilst maintaining the country house atmosphere with its many acres of green belt land at Canons Drive, Edgware.

Since the school was amongst the top two or three girls' schools in London, there was an enormous demand for places and only a fraction of the girls succeeded in getting in. Admission was strictly on merit although siblings of former pupils received a modicum of preference. As the Indians established themselves in London, both culturally and financially, a growing number of Indian girls became pupils.

Next in line as Headmistress was Joan Clanchy, a tall imposing Scottish woman who exuded authority and vitality. I invited her to our home and I asked her whether she was aware of the fact that a substantial percentage of the girls at the school were Jewish. She said that she did know but she doubted whether she had met more than half a dozen Jews in her life, so that this new assignment would be an interesting challenge for her.

Joan Clanchy became a friend, and I suggested that it would be for the benefit of the school and an interesting experience for her as a practising Christian if she were to visit Israel, and she accepted my invitation with alacrity. We advertised in *The Jerusalem Post* that there would be a reunion of former pupils of NLCS at Mishkenot in Yemin Moshe, Jerusalem to greet the new Headmistress.

At the urging of Professor Alice Shalvi, the Headmistress of the Pelech School, the top private girls' school in Jerusalem, I had joined their Board of Governors as well. Alice was an eminent Professor of English at the Hebrew University and became famous as an activist, fighting for equal rights for women both in the religious and social fields. She is a speaker of international renown who frequently travels at the invitation of a variety of overseas organisations. I asked Alice to take care of Joan Clanchy during her stay in Jerusalem. The two became firm friends and have been in close touch ever since.

Della took charge of the reunion. I had to fly back to London on urgent business but in any case, this was an "All Women" affair. It was sensationally successful. Ladies of all ages converged on Yemin Moshe. They came from kibbutzim, laboratories, universities or as housewives and mothers. They fell around each other's necks – many meeting for the first time since leaving England, not knowing of each other's existence in Israel.

Joan Clanchy said it was one of the most moving experiences of her life. She travelled up and down the country and, to her delight, met some girls who were currently at the school. She began to understand why most modern Jews feel an affinity to the Holy Land. She even forgave me for the considerable difficulties which she had with the Israeli airport security who thought that she was an Irish terrorist and submitted her to the most searching and embarrassing cross-examination. Had she only brought along my letter of invitation that difficulty would have been avoided. North London Collegiate School is all the better for the experiences of their Headmistress in the Holy Land.

11

My Almost Favourite Synagogue

I HAVE BEEN going to Norrice Lea synagogue in Hampstead Garden Suburb since 1938. This is where I see many of my oldest friends; this is where we walk to on a *Shabbat*, half an hour each way; this is where I first set eyes on Della, and this is where the rabbis for over 50 years have become close to us. Let me deal with just three of them.

Dayan Dr Lew was a gentle man, a quiet intellectual, tiny in physical stature but large in compassion and tolerance. Della and I were happy that he performed our marriage ceremony and participated in many family celebrations.

Isaac Bernstein, the fiery Irish orator, was a powerful speaker, a great teacher, happiest with his books preparing for his famous *shiurim* (study group), which attracted large crowds. He saw problems in black and white. There were no religious compromises for him.

For many years, the seat allocated to me has been the one nearest to the rabbi, with all of whom I have had the privilege of instant communications, sometimes of a talmudic nature, more often than not with an intimate wisecrack.

Isaac Bernstein, shortly after his arrival, gave his first Kol Nidre address. He told the community in clear, unequivocal terms that unless they changed their ways, prayed daily, stopped eating in non-Jewish restaurants etc. he would not be able to be their minister. When he had finished, there was a hushed silence for the wrong reason. The majority were appalled. After the service the view of the many I talked to was that this was not our man. I could not sleep that night of the fast. The following morning in synagogue I said, "Rabbi, I know it is Yom Kippur, but could you come outside for a few minutes." In those early days we were still on formal terms.

I told him that he had delivered his resignation speech the previous evening, that he had completely misjudged the composition of our membership and that there was absolutely no chance of his words being heeded by 95 per cent of the community. He listened in silence, uttered the two words "thank you" and returned to his seat. He addressed the congregation again in the afternoon. He said, "I have, metaphorically, speaking, torn up the sermon which I have so carefully prepared. It appears that last night I was completely misunderstood. That was my fault. All I am asking for is improvement by *madregot*, by steps. Those who come to shul three times a year, let them come on the joyous holidays. Those who come *Shabbat* morning only, why not try and savour the atmosphere of Friday evening etc. etc."

We became close friends. He taught Hilary and Caroline privately. When Hilary married Jeremy Milgrom he officiated at the ceremony in Jerusalem. I was able to help him and his family leaving London for New York and returning to London later on. In New York we spent *Shabbatot* with him and his patient wife Ruth. It was a great tragedy when in 1995 he died at the age of 53.

Rabbi Edward (Eddie) Jackson, the present incumbent, has retained his youthful looks, except for his white hair which he did not have 40 years ago when I first met him. He is a man with charisma. He would not claim that he was the greatest talmudist or that his sermons should be published in book form, but he can claim that he is probably the best community rabbi in the United Synagogue. He has the charm, the energy and the tact to keep a fissiparous community united. His synagogue is always full. There are usually three services going on simultaneously. Not only is the community a powerhouse of daily activities for all age groups but, uniquely, it is getting younger.

One likes to be missed when one is not there and nowhere do I feel this sense of comradeship more than when I return to Hampstead Garden Suburb Shul after one of our frequent trips abroad.

I have had to change my aversion to *chazanut* (cantoral art) in synagogue. Avromi Freilich, the gifted young cantor recently given tenure in Norrice Lea, prays with dedication, sings melodiously and finishes at twelve o'clock just to show it can be done, without troubling the Almighty to go into overtime. Avromi lives up to the family tradition set by his great-uncle Reverend Meyer Freilich.

I am allergic to long services. At twelve o'clock I leave. That is fine because the service usually finishes just then. Maybe I played a small part in this discipline. On special occasions I stay longer. Then my neighbours throw me significant glances, tap their watches and make it clear that they expect nothing less from me than to live up to my reputation. In Judaism tradition is everything.

When the Synagogue celebrated its 60th anniversary in 1994, Bernard Taub and Alfred Kleiman called on me. Bernard was the senior warden and Alfred was and continues to be the Editor of the Synagogue's half yearly journal, a local publication of exceptionally high standard (although I have a regular column in it). They invited Della and me to host the function at the Dorchester, in view of our long and close relationship with the Synagogue. We accepted with great pleasure, not least because our youth group would derive considerable financial support from what turned out to be a great family party. At Norrice Lea we are at home.

12

Skiing

Skiing has been one of the great passions of my life. Swinging down a *piste* on new snow under blue skies and alpine sunshine is the epitome of happiness.

One of my great regrets over the years has been that I have never had the opportunity of skiing long enough in one season. Essentially we lowlanders are glorified "Sunday-skiers." If we are lucky we get 10 to 20 days on the slopes in any one year and that is on the assumption that there are no blizzards or injuries whilst on holiday. We are obviously at a disadvantage *vis-à-vis* the Swiss, Italians, Austrians, Norwegians or all the other nationalities that are blessed with snowy mountains and whose children learn to ski as soon as they can walk.

Still, I must be grateful for what I have enjoyed over the last 50 years. If I add up the various holidays I find to my surprise that I have spent more than one year on a variety of laminated pieces of wood and plastic, otherwise known as skis.

Taking Della on a skiing honeymoon was perhaps a little unfair. I was a reasonably experienced skier; she was a total novice. Little did she realise that her fate was to ski winter after winter until God called a halt. Her ambition was to become a competent skier, which she achieved with aplomb. The highlight of her skiing career was in 1985 when Evi Guggenheim (Benny and Lydia's daughter), our daughter Nadia and her husband Alan – all dashing skiers, Della and I had a glorious day on the slopes. Evi exclaimed, "Isn't it marvellous when five skiers of the same standard can have such a wonderful time together!"

Our daughters have been skiing from early childhood. For years we took an apartment, Chalet Helena, in Zermatt. Those were blissful holidays. I would get up early in the morning, go to the baker, fetch aromatic rolls, set the breakfast table, get the children up, put on their ski boots (which before the modern clips came in was quite an operation) and get them all off to ski school. On one particular occasion Hilary said impatiently, "Get a move on, Dad, we are late!" The harassed father replied, "Where is it written that I have to do all this for you? You are big girls now. Look after yourselves." And for three days I went on strike. There was chaos. I do not remember whether in the end the girls got on with it themselves or whether I relented because nobody was keener than I that they should not miss their ski lessons. We skied in Adelboden, Wengen, Grindelwald, Davos, Arosa, St Moritz, Verbier, Val d'Isere, Tignes, Klosters, Celerina, Sas Fe, Crans Montana, Flims and Lenzerheide.

Nadia, Hilary and Caroline are accomplished skiers. Nadia has had more practice because she has had the opportunity during the last 10 years to go skiing on a number of occasions whereas the two younger girls have been too busy with their families and professional commitments. They ski with the effortless elegance which can only be acquired if you start in childhood. Alan, Nadia's husband, had never been on skis when he married Nadia. He is a man of the utmost determination, and a capacity for analysing physical movements for the different sports. Today he is one of the best and certainly the fastest skier in the family. We have had the enormous pleasure of skiing with them and their three eldest children in Lenzerheide.

My grandson, Noam, then aged 10, fearless as ever, came down a red run with me. I deliberately set a fairly fast pace. He followed me as though his life depended upon it. At the bottom of the hill he said "Fred, that was wonderful. You ski like an Olympic champion ..." "Thank you, Noam," I said. He completed his sentence "... all speed and no style!" So young and already so much chuzpah!

One of my regular companions over many years has been my brother-in-law, Ken Gradon. 1957 was one of the coldest winters on record. We stayed in Klosters. Ken and I, undeterred by the minus

20 degree temperature, were out on the slopes. As usual I skied ahead but where was Ken? After some minutes I began to worry and started the exhausting climb back. The feared accident, which normally happens to other people, had struck. Ken had had a bad fall and broken his shin. The problem was how to prevent him from freezing to death before the rescue sledge arrived. Other skiers stopped to offer their help but all we required were their anoraks to keep Ken warm. We jumped about, flapping our arms, until the "blood wagon" arrived from the Parsenn Hut. A blood wagon is an elongated sledge with long handles, rather like a farmer's cart, but instead of a horse pulling it, there is an experienced skiing paramedic between the shafts who slaloms the victim down to the valley. This is fine in deep snow but very painful when going down on a hard *piste*. These human St Bernard dogs race down the slopes (they know every inch of the terrain) to get the injured party into hospital as quickly as possible. I had great difficulties, unencumbered as I was, to keep up with the sledge and its handler.

We travelled back to London with Ken on a stretcher the following day. The London specialist told us that the fracture was even more serious than was first thought. The fibula, the tibia and the ankle were broken. Six platinum/steel pins were needed to hold the shattered parts together. These pins are there for life but this has not stopped Ken from continuing to ski in his own inimitable style ever since.

An early highlight was our Arletsch-Glacier tour in 1955. We hired a private teacher for one week in Grindelwald. Herr Burgener's task was to toughen us up to a fitness standard necessary for this challenge. On day five we took the first cable car to the Jungfrau Joch. We breakfasted up there at 7 a.m. and then started our painful climb. For a long ascent animal skins are fitted under skis to stop them sliding downhill. My skins did not fit particularly well and I had to stop frequently to adjust them. Burgener shouted at me to get a move on. We climbed steadily for over four hours, passing the Concordia Hut and crossing the glacier in glorious sunshine. The intensity of the light and the reflected heat from the sun were quite overwhelming. We were then in our early thirties and reasonably fit but at the time I thought that I had never been so physically extended.

We stopped for lunch at the Loetschenluecke, a mountain pass where we sat and watched a couple who seemingly flew up the mountain. Their ascent appeared to be so effortless that we could only marvel in astonishment.

"That's Molitor and his wife," said Burgener.

No wonder, I thought; he was only one of the greatest champions and a Swiss skiing legend!

Burgener produced a thermos flask containing hot tea from his capacious rucksack. If he had charged us £100 a cup I would gladly have paid. It was probably the most welcome drink I had ever had.

We skied down to Goppenstein, a remote, poor, little village. The "street" was so narrow that we could touch the simple wooden houses on either side. Burgener took us into a primitive café/pub. By then we were totally dehydrated. I had some 10 glasses of sparkling water and beer and four cups of coffee, but the expected call of nature after such an intake of liquid was conspicuous by its absence. We then embarked on a circuitous train journey that brought us back to Interlaken and Grindelwald.

Amongst other skiing friends were Count Giovanni (Johnny) Lurani and his partner Franco Cortese. They happened to be Tudor's representatives in Italy and through the business connections we developed a great personal friendship. Johnny Lurani was the scion of an old Italian family. He had a 19-room apartment in Milan with 15 servants. On one particular occasion I could not stay with him because two of his servants were ill and that was a major catastrophe because it upset the well-drilled routine of the household! He had a villa in Celerina and a palace outside Milan where, he explained to me, he lives officially for tax reasons.

The Italian men have a style all of their own. Beautifully dressed, fastidious with their food and their motor cars, they confirm my long-held theory that Milan in particular is a town entirely dedicated to upper-class men. On one occasion I was their guest at the 24-hour race at Le Mans. From Le Mans we were driving to Italy and throughout most of the journey Johnny and Franco performed the *Marriage of Figaro* for me. Both were former Grand Prix racing drivers.

One summer Franco invited me to be his guest at his apartment in Cervinia. He waited for me at Milan airport. With our skis on top of his Alpha Romeo GTA he set off in the worst possible weather conditions. There was a cloudburst the like of which I had never seen and with which the windscreen wipers, even at double speed, were unable to cope. We travelled along the Milano–Turino Autostrada, a marvellous highway under good weather conditions but rather dangerous when wet. He raced through enormous puddles with a deafening roar as though a motor torpedo boat had struck a rock.

As a concession to the weather, Franco slowed down from his customary speed of 180 kms to 130 kms It was quite an experience to have a real professional at the wheel, particularly when he shot round the hairpin bends at St Vincent at the end of the Aosta Valley. He fairly slalomed into the corners during our 1,500 metre ascent to Cervinia whilst I braked hard on the floor of the passenger seat, reinforced by my heart in my shoes and a prayer on my lips.

The following morning we rode up to the Plateau Rosa (Testa Grigia) at 3,500 metres. It is reached by a series of cable cars via Plan Maison. The plateau is basically an enormous glacier which runs from the foot of the Breithorn down to the Theodul Pass which connects with the Zermatt skiing facilities. One lift goes up to 4,000 metres from where it is possible to ski some six kms on a variety of runs. During the summer, skiing usually stops at 2 o'clock when the snow turns into slush.

During another year I enjoyed some summer's skiing with Ken Gradon on the same glacier but this time we stayed on the Swiss side at Zermatt. We had seen the village in different evolutionary stages. When we first went there in the 1960s the only way to get over to the Italian side was to climb on skins, hard labour indeed! Some five years later we were given a ride on tractors, known as snow-cats. Today, the connection is easily made by a series of ski lifts which take one effortlessly from one side to the other.

We played tennis in the afternoons since skiing had to finish at lunchtime. The court we played on belonged to the Zermatter Hof, a hotel in the middle of the village. We soon had a partisan crowd of locals watching us. "Play on his backhand!" was the shouted advice to Ken, and very good advice it was too!

Ken and I also did some summer skiing in Tignes and Val d'Isere.

Alan Cohen and I have also been skiing in Klosters, the royal family's favourite place, and to which he is also particularly attached.

Della's skiing career ended in 1995 with a bang and a whimper. A Swiss boy of 12, out of control, crashed into her whilst she was in a refresher class with a ski teacher, causing her to fall forward and break her pelvis. This was particularly unfortunate because the previous day she and I skied together, although weather conditions were unfavourable and most people stayed in the hotel. I had the enormous pleasure of seeing her fly down the mountains with effortless elegance. After three months' long and painful recovery she was back to her normal activities and her yoga exercises but she says she will never go on skis again.

In March 1996 I skied with Hilary and her three children in Lenzerheide and Nadia and Alan and their four children in St Moritz. Della was there, of course, lending moral support but this time in après-ski boots.

13

Parasailing

IF IN YOUR old age you get into a bit of a rut as far as new experiences in the field of sport are concerned, why not take up parasailing? It's a fascinating sport which I started at the age of 66 whilst on holiday in the Greek Islands. You stand on a jetty and a local tough guy puts a harness and a lifebelt on to you. Two men hold up the enormous parachute which is tied to your harness. A long rope which curls in a pretty pattern (to take up the several hundred feet that are required to make you soar into the sky) connects you with a powerful motor boat. The boat starts off slowly then accelerates; the snakelike rope straightens and suddenly there is a jerk, the line is taut, you step forward and soar into the air.

There is no particular technique required except that during take-off it is essential that you hold on to the harness of the parachute with both hands. Somebody who took off before me let go with one hand and promptly finished up in the water! Once in the air your hands are free and there is no reason why you should not wave and sing, which is precisely what I did. Della was sitting in the boat dividing her time between taking photographs and saying silent prayers for me.

Up in the sky it is amazingly chilly. One has the freedom and exhilaration of a gliding bird. A relaxed inspection of the country-side is called for. "Ah, that is what we find on the other side of the bay. Another hotel!"

People wave and you reply with a royal salute. The boat races across the bay where mountains loom up. Occasionally in para-sailing one boat steals another's wind, and this is what happens. The mountains reduce the available wind and you rapidly descend to water level. Your feet get wet and you have to pull up your knees or be dragged into the water and that would hurt. Of course, the driver of my boat is very experienced and makes allowances for this. He turns round and as we draw away from the mountains and gain new impetus I soar once again heavenwards.

Landing is not difficult. The boat slows down and stops in a pre-determined position to bring you down as near to the jetty as possible. You then descend slowly into the water and undo the buckle which releases the harness and the parachute, otherwise you get dragged underwater. You then have the option of being picked up by boat or of swimming back. I chose the latter and felt strangely triumphant. As the assistant on the raft took the harness off me, he recited in his strong Greek accent in one breath ... "Alergictopenicillin." He then asked whether that was my name, because that's what is written on the little medallion which was attached to the gold chain round my neck. There was not enough time for explanations – so I said "Yes"!

This first experience of parasailing was at Elounda Beach on the island of Crete. My second attempt was at Faliraki on the eastern beach of the island of Rhodes. There they have refined parasailing into a science. Under their system you don't even get your feet wet. You take off from a raft, and although the take-off technique is similar to the one in Crete, the landing is very much simpler. The boat drives slowly past the raft. The umbilical cord which connects you with the boat is therefore rather low. The assistant who stands on the raft then hooks into the line and brings you in like a fish. Hopefully you land on your feet. Next time I'll try it with a bowler hat and a city suit, perhaps at Eilat where I have practised since.

What are the dangers? I thought there were none at all, but I am told that in the unlikely event of falling out of the harness and crashing into the sea, it is like falling on concrete, or where perhaps an unskilled boat driver allows the parachutist to come down on rocks. That could be somewhat painful! Apart from this, there could be a tumble into the sea either on take-off or an unfortunate landing, but these are minor hazards which are part of the fun!

My last attempt was made in January 1996 in Mahé, the capital island of the Seychelles, which has been described as the nearest thing to paradise. I was strapped up and connected to the parachute. This was going to be a comfortable sandy beach landing, so I did not bother to change into a bathing costume. To be on the safe side I gave my wallet, pen and spectacles to Della. She said: "You are as *meshugge* [mad] as ever."

"Okay, when the engine starts and the rope tightens, take three steps forward and you'll take off," was the attendant's command

"Understood."

I gave a thumbs-up signal. The engine started, the rope tightened, I took three steps but no lift-off. The rope kept pulling me so I kept running, which is preferable to being dragged. I sat down with a splash in the water, the rope slackened, I stood up and walked back to the beach. The engine had lost its power, they could not restart it and I reported back to my commanding officer, DW, feeling very wet and dishevelled that the mission was not accomplished due to *force majeure*.

14

Back to Frankfurt

IT IS A TRAUMATIC experience to revisit the town of one's birth after an interval of over 50 years. I had been back once or twice for hurried motor show visits but these were not suitable occasions to rediscover my childhood environment, and it was only in December 1987 that I had this long overdue opportunity.

Frankfurt went through some dramatic changes both during and after the War. Its centre was virtually flattened. The Altstadt was completely wiped out. The once so elegant stretch of the Kaiserstrasse between the Hauptbahnhof and the Frankfurter Hof (still Frankfurt's best hotel) became a no-go area. It was overrun by brothels, drug addicts, drunken soldiers and the remnants of human wartime debris which found this a tolerant locale. Strangely enough, the police did very little about this, probably because of their acute awareness of having over-reacted under the Nazis.

It was at that time that the better-off families chose to move out of Frankfurt into the surrounding Taunus area, to idyllic small places such as Kronberg, Koenigstein and Bad Homburg where the Frankfurt accent is heard more frequently than in the town itself. For me, the virtual absence of this familiar "dialect" with which I had grown up was most strange. Another phenomenon which made me almost paranoid, was the difficulty in finding an adult who was actually born in Frankfurt. The older generation – the Frankfurters – have disappeared. One would expect non-local hotel employees but officials, taxi drivers, shop assistants – all seemed to have come from somewhere else. It is – as a genuine old Frankfurter said to me – a town of "*Zugelaufeners*".

Since the mid-1970s Frankfurt has become an attractive town once again. Its profile, when seen from the Staedel Museum at Schaumainquai, that is the other side of the Main, is quite startling. In the foreground are the old houses which front the river, many of them rebuilt in the original style, whilst the backdrop is provided by skyscrapers, some of extraordinary beauty including Helmut Jahn's post-modern Messe Turm, Kohn-Pederson Fox's DG Bank Building and the latest 60-floor tower for the Commerzbank by Sir Norman Foster, reminiscent of the modern architecture of Chicago by the lakefront.

The Kaiserstrasse has been cleaned up and has become a pedestrian precinct. The demise of the famous tramways which crisscrossed Frankfurt has had some beneficial effects. Both the Hauptwache and the Old Opernplatz have become car-free pedestrian precincts. So has the famous shopping street, Die Zeil. I did not realise the advantages of clean air shopping until I strolled through these large squares and wide streets without a motor car in sight. However, many famous old stores: Kaufhaus Wronker, Kaufhaus Hansa, Leonhard Tietz, Bamberger & Herz have all gone to be replaced by Kaufhof, the ubiquitous C & A, and other names totally unfamiliar.

The original Opernhaus, where I saw virtually every single production from the age of 12 to 15, has been restored to its former glory. The legend – *Dem Wahren Schoenen Guten* – is again chiselled into its masonry over its famous balcony. There it was that Hitler addressed a crowd of some 20,000 in 1935. Amongst them was a rather nervous schoolboy who pretended to be too squashed to raise his hand in the Hitler salute. I had been warned not to go there but found the challenge irresistible.

One of the last impressions that I took away from Frankfurt in 1937 was my visit to the officially sponsored exhibition on the theme of *Entartete Kunst*, or degenerate Art.

Dictatorships, whether fascist or communist, require conformity. Heroic workers wielding a hammer, strong lithe women realistically portrayed, preferably in a warm optimistic glow were "in". Innovation, abstraction, avant garde and, of course, communist or Jewish artists, regardless of the quality or theme of their work were *"verboten"*. The banished artists included Emil Nolde, Oskar Kokoschka, Paul Klee, Ernst Barlach, Max Beckmann, Hans Grundig, Otto Dix and Felix Nussbaum amongst many other non-Germans such as Chagall and Picasso who wrote: "Painting is not done to decorate apartments. It is an instrument of war for attack and defence against the enemy."

Hitler and Stalin were not prepared to allow any artistic controversy. Banishment or death for those who did not toe the party line was their solution.

History has had its revenge. Museums all over the world, including Moscow and Berlin are proud to feature the "degenerate" artists, whilst the heroic worker paintings have been relegated to the dustbin or the basements as curiosity items of a degenerate past.

Frankfurt has become the banking capital of Europe and has overtaken Zurich in financial importance. It has 460 different banks, all of which need accommodation. It is thus that the lovely tree-lined Bockenheimer Landstrasse has had its character completely changed. Gone are the patrician villas, the small elegant office blocks, the desirable apartments with 15-foot-high rooms to make way for marble and steel palaces of the banks and insurance companies. The house in which I was born in the Schwindstrasse, the house in which my grandmother lived in the Liebigstrasse, the Synagogue in which we prayed – the Unterlindau – have all been demolished to give way to ultra-modern offices. I felt like Alice-in-Wonderland looking through a distorted mirror where familiar objects gave a different reflection.

I was desperately trying to find something that had not changed on which I could anchor my memories and finally found it in the Café Laumer. There it was, in the middle of the Bockenheimer Landstrasse, totally unchanged with its curved high bay terrace windows, its gilt chairs, its vast selection of cakes and its aroma of freshly ground coffee and chocolate. The owners told me that they had acquired the café in 1955, that the building itself was listed and that they felt like custodians of an ancient heritage.

The Palmengarten was even more attractive than I remembered. Its basic layout remains the same but there are now steeply raked glass palm houses which, quite apart from the Kew Gardens-like flora which they accommodate, are architectual features in themselves.

Of course, there is the well-known phenomenon that everything in childhood seemed bigger. Frankfurt, on re-examination, is a much smaller town that I thought it was. It is possible to walk through the town from Bockenheim via the Opernplatz and Hauptwache to the Zoo in under an hour.

The search for Jewish landmarks is, alas, a most depressing undertaking. The Boerneplatz Synagogue and the famous Breuer Schul on the Friedberger Anlage have disappeared. In 1990 the garden and cemetery department of Frankfurt's Municipality published and illustrated a booklet called *Die Synagogue an der Friedberger Anlage*. The short history of this architectural monument is faithfully recorded. It does not shy away from the vicious thoroughness, tantamount to sadism with which the authorities dealt with the community after *Kristallnacht* in November 1938.

The Synagogue was built in 1907 following an architectural competition. Of the seven judges, four were leading non-Jewish architects and the other three were members of the Breuer Shul. At the opening ceremony regional and municipal representatives vied with each other to identify themselves with the magnificent building with seats for 1,600 worshippers. Rabbi Dr Salamon Breuer (1850–1926) pronounced the blessing of the House. Incidentally, the chosen architects, Urgensen and Bachmann, were non-Jews. None of the 129 submissions from all over Germany came from Jews.

I remember the building well, with its double arched gates leading to the forecourt, its twin towers on either side of the triangular elevation and the impressive two entrance doors, one for men and one for ladies. Many of Germany's leading technical building journals reviewed the project and were unanimous in declaring it an architectural gem.

Thirty-one years later, less than one generation, Nazi hoodlums set the gem on fire. There was only limited damage, so on the following day (10 November 1938) the locals were entertained by four further attempts to complete the operation by rolling in barrels of petrol. The Torah Ark, which was built like a banking vault, was cut open with acetylene torches and the ritual silver was stolen.

On the 3 April 1939 the Jewish community was forced to enter into an official sale of all its real estate including synagogues and cemeteries. The 3,138 square metres of the Breuer Shul was valued at 62,700 Reichsmark. An acre of freehold land in town was, of course, worth many times that ludicrous figure. The final insult came when the community was asked to pay for the removal of the debris, since the purchaser (the Municipality) wanted a cleared site. Whatever money changed hands was soon requisitioned before those Jews who were unable to emigrate were sent to their death. The site was then used for a large air-protection bunker which, after the War, became a warehouse.

The memorial in front of the bunker, redesigned in 1990, an inclined slab between trees, is, to my mind, a disappointing epitaph of the great period of the Israelitische Religions Gesellschaft (IRG) and the Breuer tradition.

My old school, in which I spent the first 10 years of my academic life from the age of six to 16, the Samson Raphael Hirsch School, opposite the Zoo, has now been replaced by another secondary school – the Von Gagern Gymnasium.

The only famous Jewish building that has remained virtually unscathed is the Liberal Synagogue in the Freiherr von Steinstrasse over which Rabbis Seligmann and Salzberger had presided for so many years. It too, was used by the Nazis as a warehouse. It is now the only synagogue in Frankfurt but it has turned Orthodox, and the Polish-Ashkenazi *Minhag* applies. There is also a small minyan in the Baumweg where they try to maintain the *Minhag* Frankfurt, but I understand they have a struggle.

The interior of the Freiherr von Steinstrasse Synagogue has been redecorated in what I can only describe as Marie Laurencin style watercolours – pale blue, pale pink, gold and silver. Its vast glass dome and the huge chandelier give it an air of unreality and transience. The accoustics are appalling and the chazan has to work very hard to make himself heard. On the *Shabbat* when I visited the synagogue, the Torah was read by an old gentleman. He made no effort to be audible and the community settled down happily to their private conversations. I was told that on a normal *Shabbat* one

Above My parents' wedding, Frankfurt 1920. Standing left to right: Herman Lowenthal, my mother, my father, Adolf Lowenthal; seated: Julius Lowenthal, Claire Kevehazi (née Lowenthal), Adolf's wife Sophie and Benno Lowenthal. *Below left* Clock Oma, Fanny Lowenthal (née Appel); *below right* "Fritz" Simon Worms, two months old.

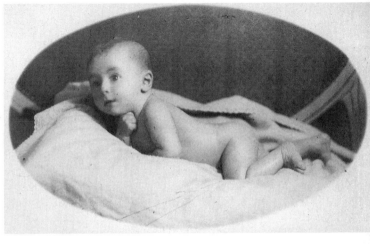

Above left "Fritz", 18 months old; *above right* "Fritz" and sister, Vera, 1925; *below* as Habonim leader, aged 14, 1935.

Above left Officers' Training Corps, St Paul's 1938; *above right* on a hiking holiday, Switzerland 1947; *below* Della and Fred's engagement, 1950.

Above left Fancy dress party – Della's 21st birthday, 1952; *above right* the Lido, Venice 1957; *below left* Celerina, St Moritz 1963; *below right* Della, 1968.

Esher House.

Above left With Lord Snowdon at Maccabi Association, London 1962; *above right* opening of Gordon Court, Edgware 1965 – first sheltered housing project of B'nai B'rith, with Sir Keith (later Lord) Joseph; *bottom left* Leo Baeck B'nai B'rith Lodge 25th anniversary Dinner, Guildhall 1966. Left to right: Philip Klutznick, Della and Maurice Weinstein; *bottom right* Mutti with Lord Jakobovits and Fred.

Above Opening of B'nai B'rith Hillel House, London 1971. Left to right: Ambassador Comay, Emeritus Chief Rabbi Brodie, The Haham Dr Gaon, Chief Rabbi Jakobovits, Mrs Joan Comay, Avraham Harman, President of the Hebrew University, and Fred Worms; *below left* Lord Sieff, recipient of B'nai B'rith Gold Medal for Humanitarian Services 1982. Left to right: Werner Lash, Henry Lewis, Lord Sieff, Fred Worms and Sir Monty Finniston. *Below right* Lord (Barney) Janner, Fred Worms and Pierre Gildesgame.

Above left Hillel Luncheon 1970. Left to right: David Stern, James (later Lord) Callaghan, Fred Worms, Jack Morrison and Hayim Pinner; *above right* "Lookalikes" – with Roy (later Lord) Jenkins 1970; *bottom left* Sir Edward Heath at a Hillel lecture; *bottom right* Board of Deputies reception. Left to right: Della, Fred, Willy Nagel, Lionel Kopelowitz and Lady Thatcher.

could expect between 50 and 100 but on this particular day they had two or three times that number because of a Bar Mitzvah.

In pursuance of my quest I enquired of the Warden whether there was anybody in the community who was born in Frankfurt and he referred me to a Herr Wolff, a benign gentleman in his seventies. He was a mine of information. He told me, for example, that the three men sitting in the row behind us were the owners respectively of the Hilton, Plaza and the Carlton hotels on the Tel Aviv seafront. They conversed in Yiddish.

During the last five years the community has had four different rabbis. It was only when the young Bar-Mitzvah boy himself spoke from the pulpit that the irony of the tragedy of the situation became apparent. Here was this boy of 13 who, in his perfect, unaccented German, represented the new generation that could well start the cycle of the rebirth of German Jewry all over again.

Hats for men were out. Yarmulkes were in but no one except me wore a knitted *kippah*, in spite of, or possibly because of the fact that a number of congregants were former Israelis.

Before the War there were 30,000 Jews in Frankfurt. Now there are no more than 5,000. Mr Wolff thought that those who were strictly kosher would number less than 100. Some two years ago the new community centre in the Savignystrasse, not far from the Bahnhof, was opened. The money came from restitution funds. The complex itself is most attractive. It is built in light coloured stone and one vast tablet soaring to a height of four floors shows a zigzag crack to commemorate the tragedy of the *Shoah*. The centre contains a kosher restaurant, meeting hall and a primary school.

In looking at the older Germans and thinking the inevitable ... "What did you do during the War?" ... one must be careful not to generalise. There are some remarkable exceptions. One of these was Walter Hesselbach, the eminent banker, architect of the phenomenal growth of the Bank für Gemeinwirtschaft, and one of the leading City Fathers. Both Hesselbach and his parents were trained at a Jewish bank and at the age of 18 he became a member of Poale Zion. Two of his three daughters are married to Israelis; he himself had a distinguished record as an anti-Nazi. He was, amongst other things, the Chairman of the Friends of the Hebrew University in

Germany, which raises some $8,000,000 per annum. In 1987 he hosted a dinner in the Kaiserhalle of the Roemer, the old Frankfurt Guildhall. He told us:

> The recent efforts to remove the years of Nazi rule to an isolated place in history and to narrow down further the circle of guilty persons, must be thwarted. And all the more so because of the outstanding performances with which German Jews have enriched our culture and the welfare of the nation.
>
> The atrocities committed by the Nazis are a warning. Again and again they give rise to deep shock. We must not relax our efforts in repeatedly drawing attention to the causes of anti-Semitism and guarding against its revival. We have had to do this frequently in the recent past.

I have quoted Hesselbach verbatim to show that the spark of Goethe and Heine's Germany has not been entirely extinguished but what does the silent majority think?

15

Should One Take One's Grandchildren to Frankfurt?

IN MY CASE YES.

My children and grandchildren had never been to Frankfurt. To my delight they seemed to be extraordinarily interested in the family history. They wanted to know where my parents and grandparents came from and they wanted me as a guide, so we decided to take them to my birthplace and the surrounding villages where the extended family had lived.

In the summer of 1993 we returned with Nadia and her three younger children (Ayelet, the oldest, was in camp in America) and Hilary and her three children. Caroline could not come but kept reminding me that we still owed her such a memory trip. This debt was discharged in November 1995.

I had come to the conclusion that it would not be a good idea to stay in the confines of the town. With six restless children it would have been a difficult task. We therefore followed the example of the wealthier citizens of Frankfurt, many of whom had moved to Bad Homburg. I found a small place with 12 bedrooms in the middle of the forest. The fact that the facilities were rather primitive did not disturb us. We were concerned that the children could run about freely and enjoy themselves without adult supervision when we were not sightseeing.

It is not always easy to have a mixture of three generations at the same time but throughout the whole of that period there was never a cross word; miraculously all six grandchildren were in a good mood! This only goes to show that as long as you keep intelligent children constructively occupied, they are easy to handle. It was fascinating to watch the closeness of cousinhood and the protective attitude Maor, then aged eight, took towards Tal aged nearly three. When they were chasing pigeons on the traffic-free square adjacent to the Romer in the old part of Frankfurt, he held her carefully by the hand to make sure she would not be lost in the throng of sightseers.

I hired a minibus with a driver for three days. Not a cheap exercise but one which, in the event, proved immensely worthwhile. I asked the young driver when we finally said goodbye to him, whether he had ever driven such a large family before, to which he replied, "*Ja vielmals aber nie so sympatisch.*"

Like all major towns, Frankfurt is divided into a number of clearly defined areas. The so-called West End is the most exclusive one. It was so before the War and is still so today. One of the Rothschild palaces is nearby and my own home in the Schwind-strasse is within five minutes walking distance from the Palmen-garten where I spent a great deal of my childhood with the various nannies that Vera and I had over the years.

My mother used to tell us that when I was a little boy, my favourite pastime was to stand in front of the band enclosure in the Palmengarten and conduct the band. I might start a split second late but after that I had them under perfect control. To relive this particular experience we took a number of photographs where the six grandchildren were lined up pretending to be different instruments, and I stood there conducting at the very same spot where I had stood 70 years earlier.

Our faithful minibus took us to the various locations which were associated with my childhood. Alas, most of them had been demolished either by the Nazis who burned the synagogues, or by the RAF. The old town, which was completely destroyed, has been rebuilt stone by stone so that at first glance it looks exactly as it did before the War. In reality the patina of old age is missing. The Jewish Museum in Frankfurt alone justified our visit. It is located in yet another Rothschild palace alongside the River Main at the very street where my father used to have his business, at the Untermain-quai. Its curator is one Georg Heuberger. He assumed his job in 1986 and he and I have been in correspondence ever since. Georg was born in Hungary, brought to Germany as a child, studied at universities in Israel and the United States, is completely trilingual and speaks German without an accent. His wife, Rachel, is an Israeli girl who is an historian. She has written an excellent history of Frankfurt Jews.

Georg awaited our arrival with keen anticipation and took the day off to guide us personally through the museum. I ought to add that it is an official town museum, its employees are paid by the State and it enjoys exactly the same rights and privileges as the famous Staedtel and other museums in Frankfurt unlike our London Jewish Museum which is always short of funds.

For the children the most interesting exhibit was a model of the ghetto. Built in 1462 for 100 families, it was inhabited by over 3,500 by the time it was dissolved by Napoleon at the beginning of the nineteenth century. Living conditions were by then absolutely appalling. The detailed descriptions gave my sensitive eight year old grandson, Matan, nightmares. That same evening, thinking about the ghetto and the Holocaust, he quietly took his bedding and crept into his mother's room.

There is an extension of the Jewish Museum where the old Boerneplatz synagogue used to be. The synagogue was totally destroyed by the Nazis. It stood next to the oldest Jewish cemetery which came into use in 1270. When, in 1987, builders began to erect an office block in this very area, they naturally commenced with excavations. Much to everyone's surprise they uncovered a ghetto street and two *mikvaot*. The developers were keen to cover up the find in order to get on with their work. However, the citizens of Frankfurt, possibly driven by a bad conscience, rallied to the protection of this historic site. They lay down in the street, they demonstrated and they displayed posters which are commemorated in the museum, screaming that this was a "rape of history" and that this old relic of the Jewish association with Frankfurt going back over 800 years must be preserved. Naturally, the few Jews in Frankfurt joined in these efforts and they were successful. Today the whole area is beautifully preserved and the office block is simply built over the museum. The curator was delighted when our Israeli grandchildren read the Hebrew signs so effortlessly.

We spent a wistful day in Aschaffenburg and Hoesbach. Aschaffenburg is the small country town in which Laurie Lowenthal was born and where his father, my uncle, and other members of the family conducted a prosperous cattle-dealing business. They lived opposite a park in a small apartment house which still stands. I looked with nostalgia at the balcony where I had enjoyed so many excellent meals and where they had their *Sukkah*. The house is adjacent to a yard in which cows and horses were tethered. At the other end was a large stable. All this is preserved except that instead of animals it has now become a second-hand car lot. Ma'ayan, alert as ever, trying desperately to get a perspective to suit her six years said "Oh, I can see there used to be animals here; there is a horseshoe nailed to the wall!"

I recalled with horror the Nazi days when the rights of the Jews were diminished day by day, when my stately bourgeois uncle and aunt were forced to sweep the streets before being sent to their death in the infamous cattle trucks. Laurie Lowenthal, who had been back to Aschaffenburg together with my late cousin, Simon Worms from South Africa, told me that the town is trying to make amends. Our Uncle Ludwig, who was callously shot by the Nazis whilst in bed, was according to official Nazi records, resisting arrest. But a memorial now shows what really happened. I still find it difficult to understand how the children of the people who perpetrated these acts can lead normal lives, and this is one of the reasons why I feel so uncomfortable when I am in Germany.

We then motored to Hoesbach, the birthplace of my mother and her siblings. I remembered it as a pretty village, charming, with little gardens and small orchards. Today, it has gone the way of most villages; the gardens have been asphalted over; the houses are larger and what was a truly rural abode has become urbanised. Aunt Claire had given us some addresses and photographs on the off-chance that some of the old people might still be alive. We found our Brunnenstrasse. We also had a photograph of the family house which, alas, we could not trace.

I approached two old men sitting on a bench and told them that my mother and grandparents, the Lowenthal family, had lived in Hoesbach. It was an emotional experience. "Certainly," they said,

"We remember them well. Adolf, Meta and Claire" ... and they indulged in reminiscences such as the annual gifts of matzot to the non-Jewish neighbours at Passover time. In the meantime the children, bored with my conversation in German, roamed around and found the family house with the help of Claire's picture. We rang the bell and introduced ourselves; the people were friendly and welcoming. Was this genuine *bonhomie*? We shall never know.

We then searched for Claire's old friends. We found them in a little supermarket across the road. We walked in and asked whether the old lady was still alive. The young woman behind the counter called out *"Mutter, komm doch mal runter."* An old lady with a clean scrubbed face and shiny, alert eyes came downstairs. I showed her Claire's photographs. She said "Yes, that's me, that's Claire, that's Meta, that's my brother" and a flow of reminiscences of those "good old days" when they lived side by side became almost unstoppable. Each grandchild was handed a bar of chocolate and they invited us for tea but we declined. Remembering the past – yes; forgetting it in convivial get-togethers – no!

Frankfurt's population has changed: there are thousands of immigrants and Turks and various nationalities from the Balkans are doing the menial jobs. Frankfurt is probably richer than ever. It has, however, lost its touch of class, possibly because it no longer has the highly sophisticated and educated Jews who played such a large part in making it what it was.

Nadia and Hilary were impressed by the lifestyle of our family in pre-War Germany, a far cry from the simple boarding house accommodation where I first lived in London or the Ashford Court flat in the "refugee block" in Cricklewood!

In November 1995 I redeemed my promise to Caroline. In my dual capacity as a native Frankfurter and as Honorary President of World Maccabi, I was invited to be the guest speaker at the 30th Anniversary celebrations of post-War Maccabi in Germany.

Ken and Vera Gradon, Bob and Shirley Glatter, Caroline and Nitzan, as well as our oldest granddaughter, Ayelet Hoffmann, came along. Both Ken and Bob hold high office in the Maccabi hierarchy and travelled in a quasi-official capacity. This was another milestone in the history of Maccabi and the normalisation of the return of the

Jews into post-Holocaust Germany, but the events were marred by Yitzhak Rabin's assassination five days earlier.

16

The Rothschilds of Frankfurt

ONCE AGAIN, IN February 1994, Della and I returned to Frankfurt, this time as the guests of (Lord) Jacob Rothschild, an old friend, whose family assembled *en masse* to celebrate the 250th anniversary of the birth of Mayer Amschel Rothschild, the progenitor of the banking dynasty.

The resilience of the Rothschild family is one of the most remarkable phenomena of modern Jewish history. No less than 75 of them, mainly from London, Paris, Geneva and New York, converged on Mayer Amschel's home town.

It is doubtful whether the clan had ever assembled before in such strength. From London we had Lord and Lady (Jacob) Rothschild and their son, Nathaniel (Nat); Edmund (Eddie) de Rothschild, his daughter, Charlotte and son Lionel; Miriam Rothschild's son, Dr Charles Lane, and daughter Charlotte; Amschel, Jacob's half-brother, together with spouses and children. Paris was there in full strength led by Barons Guy and Elie, together with their sons, daughters and grandchildren, whilst Baron Edmond de Rothschild, the grandson of the Baron of the same name who created the Rothschild family's involvement in the land of Israel on such a magnificent scale, led the Geneva contingent.

Where today are the other great German Jewish banking houses which dominated the City of London at the turn of the century? Where are the successors of the great American Jewish banks that played such a prominent part in the development of the North American continent? They have survived, some as bankers but hardly any as Jews.

What struck me most forcibly during the series of two day events was the emphasis which both Lord Rothschild and Guy de Rothschild the heads of the English and French houses respectively laid on their Jewish identity. It would be interesting to determine how many of the 75 who participated were halachically Jewish, but who would query a Rothschild who wishes to identify with us?

The anniversary meant a great deal to Frankfurt which has much to atone for. The Mayor, Andreas von Schoeler, made it very clear how much the town was indebted to the Jews. Since they had first come in the year 1150 they were expelled no less than four times; in 1241, 1349, and 1614 when the ghetto, which was created in 1462, was looted by a mob led by the notorious Fettmilch. He was executed before the Jews were invited back in 1616 when the Frankfurt Purim was initiated on 20 Adar. The last and most lethal expulsion took place under the Nazis which, by 1942, had made the town *judenrein*.

Jacob, in the historic speech which he made in the Romer, the old Town Hall of Frankfurt, referred to his ancestor in the following terms:

> He lived for most of his working life in the Judengasse, that long, narrow street whose inmates were locked up every night and who were confined to the ghetto on Sundays and public holidays. As Goethe wrote, "The filth, the dirt, the multitudes, the accents of a strange language altogether made an unpleasant impression, even if one only looked through the gates from outside." Goethe was not prejudiced but was simply describing what he saw.
>
> My aunt Miriam once wrote that Mayer Amschel had a vision of a network of European countries collaborating and improving their communal lot. He had a vision of the emancipation of the Jews with his five sons as the successful promoters, the emblem of European and personal prosperity. The founder of the Rothschild EEC and his sons, based their highly successful enterprises on some well-defined virtues. If we were to cast a critical eye over his family assembled here today he could not but be touched by there being no less than 75 gathered here

spanning four generations aged from one to 80. His son, N. M. Rothschild, who went to London, once wrote to his four brothers, "After dinner I usually have nothing to do. I do not read books, I do not play cards, I do not go to the theatre, my only pleasure is my business and in this way I read Amschel's, Solomon's, Jacob's and Carl's letters."

Fortunately no one in the present generations would expect similar dedication ... concluded Lord Rothschild,

and indeed, the family, over the last 200 years spent as much energy on philanthropy and the arts as on business.

There are records of Mayer Amschel's grandparents' graves in the old Jewish cemetery which served the community from 1240 until 1812. Mayer Amschel was one of the last to have been buried there. It was the first location which our party visited. This old Jewish cemetery presents a sorry sight. Where once there was a dense forest of tombstones, all with Hebrew lettering, there is now a green lawn. The tombstones were removed by the Nazis and used for building purposes. Miraculously some survived and they are huddled like an evocative Jacob Kramer painting in one corner of the cemetery. Amongst them is Mayer Amschel's. He is referred to as Moshe Meir Roit Schild, son of Anseln. When I, tongue-in-cheek, invited Amschel to change the spelling of his name he declined saying he had got used to it. It appears that in the transliteration from Hebrew to German the n became an m. The i in Roit reflected the Yiddish-German pronunciation.

Arthur Fried, the Chief Executive of Yad Hanadiv – the Rothschild Foundation in Israel – led the Kaddish at the old cemetery. Jacob and Amschel from London, Guy and Elie from Paris, and Edmond from Geneva stood behind him in silent prayer. It was a moving occasion, not only because of the tragic desolation of the cemetery but also because it was immediately adjacent to the ghetto excavations. It was at this very spot that the Judengasse started and where the old Boerneplatz Synagogue once stood.

We visited the "new cemetery" in the Rat-Beil-Strasse in which Mayer Amschel's wife, Gutele, was buried in 1849 and later his son, Amschel Mayer von Rothschild (by that time the family had entered the ranks of the aristocracy). Gone were the days of the plain, Hebrew-lettered tombstones such as the one which stood over Mayer Amschel's grave. By now, the rich Jews had assimilated to the custom of elaborate catafalques over family tombs.

In this cemetery are also buried many of the Jews who made Frankfurt famous including Samson Raphael Hirsch, Dr Paul Ehrlich, the Nobel Prize winner, Leopold Sonnemann, the founder of the *Frankfurter Allgemeine Zeitung* and Leopold Casella, the founder of the small chemical firm which ultimately became IG Farben. My grandfather, Lazarus Lowenthal, was one of the last to have been buried there in 1923.

Rabbi S. R. Hirsch's influence ultimately extended far beyond the confines of Frankfurt. When, in the middle of the ninetenth century, Reform Judaism was recognised by the local authority as the only legitimate form of the Jewish religion, a number of Orthodox Jews were affronted. Their leader was Wilhelm Karl von Rothschild (1828–1901), a grandson of Mayer Amschel. He invited Rabbi Dr Samson Raphael Hirsch to become the spiritual leader of a newly formed Orthodox Community which was officially recognised in 1850. By 1876 Hirsch and his followers seceded from the registered Frankfurt Jewish community and the IRG became the Austritt's *Gemeinde*.

Hirsch's slogan was *"Torah im Derech Eretz"* – the study and meticulous observance of the Torah combined with modern university teaching. Talmud and chemistry, Rashi and Goethe, Rambam and physics represented the confluence of his two worlds. He created the eponymous great Jewish secondary school which I was privileged to attend for 10 years.

The signing of the town's Book of Honour by 21 male members of the Rothschild Family in the old Romer was a ceremony which symbolised, in a way, the return of the Rothschilds to Frankfurt. Sir Evelyn and his French cousins established a new branch in 1989 after a pause of 88 years. The last of the Frankfurt Rothschilds was the aforementioned Baron Willi.

What distinguished this historic weekend was the simplicity of the celebrations. Those who expected a Grand Ball with the participation of the international aristocracy, in one of the Rothschild palaces, were to be disappointed. Whilst we lunched at a couple of former Rothschild residences, the principal commemoration venues were the two cemeteries and the Jewish Museum. The most famous, the Staedel Museum, was specially opened (Monday is official closing day) to show us the many paintings acquired with the help of the Rothschilds, including its most famous picture – "Goethe in Italy" by Tischbein. Many of the pre-War treasures were seized by the Nazis and only a handful have been recovered for the Jewish Museum. There is, however, a detailed history of the local Jews which makes it very clear that anti-Semitism has been endemic for centuries.

I was particularly disturbed by a series of posters printed in 1916 accusing the Jews of dodging the army – this at a time of national peril when it was thought that the Jewish population had been wholly integrated and had assimilated into the German way of life. The Jewish authorities demonstrated that by 1916 12,000 Jewish soldiers had been killed on active service (a far higher percentage than that of the general population) but the anti-Semites were not to be confused by facts.

Our party was under continuous discreet police protection. The thought had occurred to the organisers that 250 years of the family's survival could be brought to a sudden end by one strategically placed bomb.

The celebrations came to a climax with a musical soirée in the course of which Chancellor Kohl emphasised the historic contributions of the Rothschilds to Frankfurt and, indeed, the economies of so many European countries. I asked Helmuth Kohl to sign the Frankfurt Hagadah which I had acquired. Both he and Chaim Herzog had written a foreword to the facsimile. Chaim had signed it already. Now I have a collector's piece.

Charlotte de Rothschild (Eddie's daughter), a fine soprano, entertained the guests with quotations from Mathilde de Rothschild's musical diary which was started by her mother, Charlotte. Mathilde, who was born in Vienna in 1832, and lived in Frankfurt at Haus Gruneberg next to the Palmengarten, was a strictly Orthodox woman who would not even eat with the Kaiser. She was a prolific composer of songs.

During the nineteenth century, the family mixed with Felix Mendelssohn, Mayerbeer, Rossini, Chopin and Liszt – some of whom acted as teachers. Musical pieces from these composers, lyrically sung by Charlotte under the generic heading of "Family connections" were a demonstration of the family's manifold cultural interests.

A new era has begun. For the fifth time Jews have resettled in Frankfurt; the Rothschilds have also returned. Will history repeat itself? Ten years earlier I would have been inclined to say "no". The 30,000 Jews thinly spread through Germany's larger towns were looked upon as transients. Today, with the Russian influx, the number has doubled to 60,000. Synagogues and Jewish schools are being built and Ignaz Bubis, the head of the Central Jewish Organisation, has no doubt that they have come to stay.

PART 2

Business

"Without substance there is no learning"
(freely translated from the *Ethics of the Fathers*)

17

The Tudor Story: 1946–1960

IT WAS 1948. Dagenham was one of the largest car plants in Europe. Built by the Ford Motor Company in 1928 it had been added to ever since. The factory had unique facilities with its own river wharves and access to ferry ships. To break in as a supplier was a major challenge and considered by the banks to be a collateral for expansion finance.

The offices of the Chief Buyer, Mr Davis, were utilitarian. He was a bald gentleman with spectacles, rubicund face and a twinkle in his eye. Thank God, I thought! He is human! Sitting behind him were four assistants, scribbling away busily but obviously with their ears pricked. "What can I do for you, young man?" he asked. "Sit down." At subsequent visits he would offer me tea and biscuits but this was a preliminary skirmish.

"I have something which I think may interest you."

"What is it?"

"It's a new type of mirror for commercial vehicles. An exterior rear view mirror where the glass is held by a rubber ring."

"Have you got a sample with you?"

He looked at it. "Young man – what's your name? Worms? Will you take some well-meant advice from someone who has been in the motor industry for over 35 years. Leave it alone. We have our regular suppliers with whom we have worked for decades, and who supported us throughout the War when we were making bits and pieces for the Government. Lucas, Smiths Industries, Triplex, Wilmot Breeden. What can you offer us that they haven't got? Just one ordinary mirror?"

This was a most discouraging start. What was I, a chartered accountant, doing here in Dagenham trying to flog car mirrors to an unwilling buyer at the Ford Motor Company? Somebody less stubborn might have given up. One of the young assistants came forward. "Could I have a look at that sample, Sir?" Davis handed it to him.

"You know," he said, "it's got something. Every time we break a glass at the moment, the mirror has to be replaced. Here, all you do is take the glass out and slip a new one in. Our main dealers would like that." And that's how we got into the motor industry. This initial contact led to our first contract with Ford. The young assistant's name was Bert Walling. He was to become a dear personal friend. A spectacular career led him to become Director of Purchasing of the Ford Motor Company and later of British Leyland. What had led up to this encounter?

After qualifying as a chartered accountant, when the War was over I joined my Uncle Benno's business on a strictly temporary basis. Both my uncles in London – Benno and Julius – carried on with what they knew best, that is selling cigarette lighters and smokers' requisites. There was a desperate shortage of all consumer products at that time. There were no imports and luxury goods were not then manufactured in England. Benlow, as Benno Lowenthal's company was eponymously called, also dealt in lighter flints which it bought in bulk and repackaged for the retailer. Benno was forever inventing new cigarette lighters which were made up for him by a mechanic whom he employed on a full-time basis. The climax in the chequered career of Benlow was reached when some Hungarians who had come to England as refugees, built a very attractive factory in South Wales and made a special lighter for him which became known as the Benlow Golmet lighter. This was made of fluted anodised aluminium and its wheel, which was turned by hand, was of a similar design to that of Dunhill, who were restarting their world-famous lines at more or less the same time.

The fact that I had decided not to become a professional accountant but to go into manufacturing was based on misplaced idealism. I wanted to play a more positive role in the national economy but that did not mean that I wanted to stay in the lighter business for the rest of my life. Nor could I see myself working with or under my uncles. Benno acted spontaneously and to my intense annoyance, suffered from eternal optimism which led to him making extravagant sales forecasts. My accountancy training had taught me to look at the downside.

One day I was filling up my car with petrol and chatting to Fred, the manager of the Castle Garage at Child's Hill, in north-west London. He said, "Why don't you make this? It's what everybody wants."

"What is it?" I asked.

"Its a wing mirror . . ."

In 1946 we acquired a company known as the Tudor Trading Co Ltd which made ghastly bathroom fittings. I had two thirds of the Tudor shares and my cousin, Laurie Lowenthal, one third. I became Chairman and Laurie and my mother became directors. Why my mother? She had run the Colibri German business in Frankfurt right through the Hitler years. She was an experienced businesswoman, she had an extraordinary amount of common sense and – most importantly – I wanted her to have the feeling that she was living from her own income rather than on what I would provide for her.

I had frequent arguments with Julius and Benno. They considered me a naive nephew with too much chuzpah. Julius, in exasperation, said to me one day, "You'll never make a businessman." They looked upon me as an equal, however, when it came to providing for the family. Their mother, Clock Oma, who was staying with my mother, was maintained by equal one third contributions from Julius, Benno and myself.

"Why me?" I asked, when the proposal was first mooted. "I look after my mother. You look after yours."

"No, you have to pay your mother's share." I decided there and then that I would never argue when it came to family finances. Pay up – even when it is inequitable. God will take note and repay you. I did and he did.

After the death of his first wife, Julius married Herta in 1947. He became a different man, happy and expansive. He was active in the JPA (Joint Palestine Appeal) and later in the Joint Israel Appeal and generous to his many ultra-Orthodox nephews and nieces (my Uncle Herman's children) in B'nai Brak. Julius died in 1970 and is buried near Haifa, adjacent to the forest planted in his memory. Herta became a splendid addition to the family. She is a great hostess and particularly close to Ernest and Jack (Julius's sons) and their off-springs. She has homes in St John's Wood and Haifa, adjacent to her daughter Ruth Fluss and her husband Barry.

In 1948 Benlow acquired the lease of an enormous four-storey building in Hayes, Middlesex from Walls Meat Products. It looked like an old textile mill. Some of the floors were sublet by Benlow Properties, a company which I set up and which in the end proved to be more profitable than the Benlow Lighter business itself. In 1947 a small part of the premises had been taken by Tudor where I employed some five people busily manufacturing car parts.

The Ford contract was the first major breakthrough. We had to go through laboratory tests; certain suggestions were made on how to improve our product and when the first delivery was paid for I felt we were well on our way. Little did I realise that a major disaster was looming round the corner. What we failed to anticipate, and not even the famous Ford laboratory with all its sophisticated tests had discovered, was a latent fault in a component which would cause us a virtually negative turnover in the second year of our motor accessory business.

Within some six months of the mirrors being fitted to the Ford trucks the mirror glasses turned blind. They lost their reflection. What had happened? The rubber rings contained sulphur. When the sulphur migrated from the rubber it ate up the silvering at the rear of the mirror which became plain glass. When Mr Davis asked to see me after intimating the extent of the disaster, I felt that the end of my business career had come. He was surprisingly understanding.

"I will give you a simple alternative. I am not going to influence you. It is entirely up to you. Either replace every single mirror that we have in stock free of charge and you take complete responsibility for any returns that may be coming in over the next two or three years, or we say goodbye."

Since the Ford contract was the major part of our business at that time the decision was not quite as obvious as it would appear with hindsight, today. There was the alternative of looking upon this as a second warning and getting out of what appeared to be a business full of latent dangers, pitfalls and snares. We replaced the mirrors; we made a substantial loss in 1948, the second year; we survived and we cemented a bond with the Ford Motor Company that was to stand us in good stead until the very day we sold a flourishing Tudor in October 1973.

The 1950s were a truly exciting period for the motor industry. We were dealing with a varied range of car manufacturers including:

Armstrong Siddeley	MG
Aston Martin	Morgan
Austin	Morris
Bentley	Rolls Royce
Daimler	Rover
Hillman	Singer
Humber	Standard
Jaguar	Sunbeam
Jowett	Talbot
Lagonda	Triumph Herald
Lee Francis	Vauxhall
Lotus	Wolseley

There was little foreign competition. Car production was thoroughly inefficient. Not only did we have to supply components and accessories of different shapes and sizes to many car manufacturers, but these manufacturers often produced a range of motor cars where none of the components were inter-changeable. Lucas and Smiths dominated the accessory field. They had an informal non-aggression pact whereby their respective spheres of activities were clearly delineated. In quoting for certain accessories which cut across the field of either of these two companies we had enormous difficulties. Both Lucas and Smiths would present a package quotation for a whole range of components and accessories which would go into a particular motor car, a range with which we could not possibly compete. To take out an interior mirror or a windscreen washer would bring about a very small reduction in the comprehensive price quoted by either of these giants. Yet, we prevailed.

Germany and Japan were licking their wounds and started rebuilding their economies with brand new equipment. The Americans were busy looking after their own booming home market. It was no wonder, therefore, that in the annals of the history of the UK motor industry the 1950s and 1960s were its golden years.

In 1946 total output was slightly in excess of 200,000 vehicles which climbed to nearly one million by 1959. Exports flourished. Overseas markets were crying out for British motor cars. They were memorable years with outsize personalities; Leonard Lord of Austin; Lord Nuffield of Morris; men who had previously worked together but who detested each other, and the merger which ultimately took place initially proved to be disastrous as antipathy outweighed synergy.

I remember visiting both camps. Instead of standardising their cars to enjoy the advantages of economy of scale, both organisations carried on entirely independently and multiplied non-compatible models. This proved to be a great opportunity for the Ford Motor Company, which was undoubtedly the most efficient and best organised car manufacturer in the United Kingdom. They employed American production techniques, had sophisticated costing systems and laboratories and controlled their distribution network with an iron hand. The British Motor Corporation, the merged Austin/ Morris companies, which had over 40 per cent of the market after the War, began its steady decline. Terry Becket, later Sir Terrence Becket of the Confederation of British Industry, was a manager of the Product Staff at Fords when I first met him. He was a brilliant operator and one of the principal architects of the dominance of Fords in the British motor industry. He refused to copy the "Mini" because he concluded that it would never be profitable.

Our range of products included petrol locking caps, mud flaps and a considerable variety of mirrors. We were famous for our windscreen washers. Needless to say, we also had our failures. One of these was the "Oil Check". It was a very simple device. Basically it was a tube with a small hole at the bottom and a plastic bulb on top. The bulb was transparent and marked with horizontal lines. This oil check served as a dipstick. All one had to do was to squeeze the bulb, the oil would come up and one could tell from the level of the gauged horizontal lines whether the sump was full or not. It seemed to us to be such a simple idea that it was bound to be a winner.

We spent a considerable amount of money on marketing. We had Points of Sale Displays which we lent to garages up and down the country; we talked Halfords – who had become very close to us – into giving it considerable window space in their many shops, yet the line was a total failure. We learned an expensive but valuable lesson. Accessories that are invisible are difficult to sell. Since one cannot see what is under the bonnet, however useful such a gadget may be, it becomes a questionable item.

Another setback was the "Sideler". I am still surprised in retrospect why our engineers allowed us to get involved in the development of this product. It was probably due to the overwhelming enthusiasm of the inventor and his wife.

The "Sideler" appeared, on first inspection, to be the egg of Columbus and a very simple solution to one's parking problems. It was a gadget that was attached to the rear axle of the motor car and through electro-pneumatic operation would lower two trolley wheels to the ground. All one had to do was to drive the nose of the car into a limited parking space, lower the trolley wheels and then perform a quarter circle turn to the edge of the pavement. That was the theory. In practice the additional weight which had to be attached to the rear axle was such that it completely unbalanced the carefully designed stress of the vehicle and the car manufacturers told us that fitting of the "Sideler" would automatically vitiate any guarantee which the car might enjoy.

We must have done something right, however, because our turnover and profits grew. We had formed associate companies in the United States and had a manufacturing partnership in Australia.

Australia had been one of our more successful markets until the Australian Government clamped down protective duties to encourage local manufacture. We advertised in the leading automotive papers for partners with established local facilities who would make our products under licence. We were inundated with over 100 replies ranging from large public companies to small budding engineering firms. Whilst we were going through these, a small, trim man in his forties with piercing blue eyes and a diffident manner walked into our factory at Hayes. "My name is Eric Rainsford. I'm from Adelaide and I am the man you are looking for."

We entered into a partnership with his company – Rainsford Metal Products – which worked on a very simple principle. Initially they would import all components from us and assemble them locally. There were special customs exemptions whereby components could be brought into the country free of duty provided that evidence could be shown that eventually they would be made in Australia. We were only to add a nominal margin of 5 per cent to our UK cost price and the profit would be made by the joint selling company, Tudor Australia Limited. Ultimately, when the bits and pieces were made in Australia, the position would be reversed. The local manufacturer, namely Rainsford Metal Products, would add only 5 per cent to the manufacturing cost, and again the profits would be made by the jointly-owned marketing company. This worked perfectly as long as they imported components because we played the game, but it became a nightmare once they produced locally. The prices which they made were such that the joint company earned hardly any profits whilst their manufacturing facilities grew by leaps and bounds.

I could see that we were tilting against windmills and agreed, after some years, to sell out.

Joint ventures are hazardous undertakings. Big companies like Lucas, Smiths and, of course, the car manufacturers knew this and established their wholly-owned subsidiaries which were controlled from England. They became an integral part of the local motor industry.

Back home we had built up a good team. Gordon Gammon, Ronald Allen and Peter Greig had been with us almost from the outset. They looked after the engineering and buying side of the business. Rudolf Kahn, who went to school with me in Frankfurt, (his parents lived in Golders Green and had often extended hospitality to me when I was a bachelor) had joined me and occupied a senior position. He married one of our secretaries, a charming refugee girl from Vienna and later they emigrated to the United States. Eric Beecham, after his army service, became the Company Secretary. It was the beginning of a lifelong friendship which culminated in our partnership in Butchers Supplies (London) Limited, the Victorinox company.

Those were tough but exhilarating days. We exhibited at motor shows in London, Frankfurt, Amsterdam and Paris – experiences which I would not like to repeat. During the early years I was hoarse after every show. I felt it was my duty to attend to every customer personally. The atmosphere at these exhibition stands, where fans would be whirring, stirring stale air, whisky and tobacco fumes, inevitably brought on a sore throat if nothing worse!

The industry was divided into two types of people – those who liked motor shows, and those who hated them! Laurie Lowenthal and our Sales Director, Keith Taylor, thrived at exhibitions. They were extroverts; they loved mingling, they enjoyed good meals and drinking with "the boys" in the evenings. I was a disciple of Sartre who said, "Hell is other people." All I wanted was to go back to the hotel if we were abroad, and read a good book. Extended conviviality, back-slapping, lavish eating and drinking were my ideas of punishment. And so it came about that over the years I took less and less interest in exhibitions and entertainment of customers, and left this to those under the leadership of Laurie who were good at it and who thoroughly enjoyed it. I ought to add here that even at that time, when enormous demands were placed on our waking hours, I felt that a day which was spent entirely on business was an unsatisfactory one. I do not believe there were many days when I was not engaged for an hour or more in some sort of social or communal activity.

Laurie found his outlet in squash. He had a way of organising his appointments in town to allow him to play squash in the afternoons at the RAC in Pall Mall. Whilst at the time I often felt annoyed about his early departures, I must say that over the years I have come to the conclusion that it has probably stood him in good stead, preserving the health and fitness of a cousin who today, in his seventies, plays real tennis several times a week.

Another minor problem that bedevilled my otherwise close relationship with my senior colleagues was the quality of the motor car I was driving. They quite rightly felt that the bigger and more expensive the Chairman's car, the better would be the cars of the Sales Director, Production Director, Purchase Director etc. I had always felt that the use of a large and ostentatious motor car was all right for those whose ego needed visible support. Mine didn't, and therefore the others had to fall into line. My views were reinforced when, in a weak moment, I agreed that Laurie Lowenthal should run an Aston Martin – a beautiful motor car which only had one fault. It needed a resident engineer in the boot. Its finely balanced twin carburettors were usually out of balance and the slightest mishap would cost a week's wages to repair it.

As the 1960s approached and we became "old timers" in the industry, we occasionally rubbed shoulders with the Big Chiefs, like Sir William Lyons and "Loftie" England of Jaguar, Sir Patrick Hennesey of Ford (who had the technique of leaking unpleasant news by talking in his car to a colleague in the certain knowledge that the driver would pass this on via the drivers' pool), William and Reginald Rootes, Sir Leonard Lord, Sir Miles Thomas and others.

What would they have said if they had lived into the 1990s when not a single car manufacturer in the UK was British owned? For Tudor, disaster and triumph were yet to come.

18

"Into Real Estate"

OUR BUSINESS HAD outgrown the facilities at Benlow Works and I had been looking around for a small factory. I felt that it was very important that we should be our own landlords and this is a maxim which I have maintained throughout my business career, that in a tenant/landlord relationship I much prefer to be the landlord. The two acres that we had our eyes on belonged to Miss Minet, whose family had been the principal landlord of Hayes for many generations. She was the last survivor and did all her business through a general manager known as her Factor, Mr Bartlet. He was the classical elderly retainer of a feudal family. He came to see me.

"I am afraid," he said, "Miss Minet is not so much concerned about the financial aspect of any land sale she may be contemplating as she is to whom she is selling. She wants to be sure that the purchaser is a gentleman."

I was taken aback. I had expected the usual minor wrangling normally associated with the acquisition of a property or site but this particular angle was completely new to me. Was I a gentleman? "What can I do to assure Miss Minet that I qualify under her criterion?" I asked.

"Well," he said, "we have been watching you, and we see you have made some progress and I believe we may be able to do a deal." We paid £12,000 for the two acres and took out a mortgage of £10,400 with the Eagle Star Insurance Company which insisted on life policies in the name of Laurie and myself. As promised, I invited Mr Bartlet to our sparkling, bright new 5,000 sq. ft. factory.

Miss Minet also owned land at the corner of Springfield Road and the main Uxbridge Road on which were some rather dilapidated cottages. The cottages accommodated Miss Minet's former servants. I wanted to buy this land but Mr Bartlet told me that they would not entertain any idea which would prejudice the security of the occupiers' tenure.

I improvised. "I would be perfectly happy to rehouse all these ladies and gentlemen in modern flats, cottages or any other accommodation of their choice, and I can assure you they would have indoor toilets and far better facilities than they enjoy at the present time.

He frowned. "We have had many proposals over the years but so far Miss Minet has turned them all down. However, I will bear your interest in mind, and it is possible that one of these days you will hear from us."

Exactly five years later he reverted to the subject. By that time we had expanded considerably beyond our initial 5,000 square feet of factory space into an area of 20,000 square feet. It was obvious that we were a tight but efficient organisation which paid particular importance to the overall appearance of everything with which we were associated, from cars and trucks to factory and offices. Quite frankly I had forgotten about the Factor when he asked for an appointment.

"Do you remember the conversation we had concerning the corner site at Uxbridge Road?"

"Yes, of course I do," I replied.

"Well, we have been watching you and we are satisfied that you – unlike the other property developers who have approached us – would take care of the interests of Miss Minet's servants. The truth is that our legal advisers tell us that it is awfully difficult to write into a contract precisely what is required. If you will give Miss Minet your word that you will rehouse them the way you promised five years ago then she will be prepared to sell you the land at less than market price."

He sounded like Moses who promised the children of Israel peace and prosperity if they would walk in the way of the Lord. My recently formed company – Groveway Properties Limited – bought the land for £50,000. We went through what in all modesty I can only describe as a model exercise in rehousing tenants in precisely the way in which we had promised. They had the choice of moving to the country or seaside or to be near relatives in more congenial surroundings. By the time we had finished the operation our costs had gone up to nearly £200,000 in 1959 money.

I instructed a B'nai B'rith colleague, Theo Birks, a well-known architect, to draw up plans for this important corner site. We obtained planning permission for a petrol station and an office block of 78,000 sq. ft. I sold the lease of the garage to Shell for £200,000 in return for which they negotiated a fixed rental for the first 42 years. The rental, as far as I was concerned, was pure profit since we had recouped our outlay. I did not have the courage to build the office block on a speculative basis. I have always followed a most conservative line with a vivid imagination of the downside. What could the worst scenario be? I could have an office block which was unlet and which would attract empty rates and bank loan interest. The answer for me was therefore to take less profit and pass the risk element to a third party. I decided to grant a building lease and the company which we ultimately came to terms with was run by a Mr Bosman who had made quite a name for himself in the property, and subsequently in the restaurant, worlds. *The Financial Times* of 12 July 1961 had a picture of the development together with the following report:

Property Investments Consolidation has acquired the building lease of a site on the Uxbridge Road between Southall and Hayes, Middlesex, for the erection of a twelve-storey office block of 78,000 square feet. The total cost of the development will be £450,000 and the main entrance of the building faces Uxbridge Road and has access for cars with space to park 147.

My old Maccabi colleague, Kenneth Brown, acted for me. The leaseholders, PICS, paid me a premium plus 10 per cent of the rack rent. I took a mortgage with the Scottish Widows Insurance Company at 7.5 per cent and all of a sudden I had more than six figures in Groveway's bank account with an assured income.

I remember coming home and saying to Della: "I am 40, you are

30, and if we wanted to we could actually retire now and live on a reasonably good scale."

Another transaction had taken place a few years earlier. The manager of Barclays Bank at Station Road, Hayes, where I had had an account since 1946, rang me one day. Mr Wheeler – known as Spider Wheeler, six foot two, thin, ex-army said, "I think I have something for you. Would you like to come over?"

Twenty acres of freehold industrial land were available at a cost of £20,000. The bank was willing to finance two-thirds. Their particular client was in a hurry to get some money. I bought the land and sold it for £25,000. Had I hung on to it it would be worth at least £10 million today.

The property game fascinated me. I began to study it seriously. With the little experience I had of building Esher House, the Hayes factory and the involvement in Miss Minet's Uxbridge Road site, which led to the building of Hayes Gate House as the new office block became known, I believed that here was an extra-curricular activity which was not labour intensive and not too time consuming.

What it needed was a little flair, friendly estate agents and capital. The banks were only too happy to provide the latter in the 1950s and 1960s. Hayes and the airport area became my preferred location and Farr Bedford my favourite agents. They and the bank came up with propositions on a regular basis.

I selected those where there was a special angle such as difficulties with the local authority, zoning problems, access complications etc. This one-man show became twice as big as Tudor, with its large personnel and infrastructure. We developed factories, offices and warehouses. I eschewed residential property mainly because I could not envisage ever depriving an individual of his home, nor did I want to compete with the specialists in the housing estate developments.

My professional friends – Helmut Rothenberg (accountant), Herbert Garfield (solicitor), and David Stern (architect) asked whether they could join me in one of my ventures. We formed a company and called it Noblefield Properties (Blick Rothenberg and *Noble* and Gar*field*). We bought a residential plot which had been unsaleable because the Ministry of Transport would not allow potential tenants' cars to come into busy Yeading Lane where the site was located. I passed it every day driving to Hayes.

We purchased a dwelling house round the corner, demolished it and solved the access problem via the side street. We promptly got planning permission. We exchanged the now valuable site against an industrial estate in a strategic position in Hounslow, which the local authority needed for town redevelopment. We built an office block in Ealing on a prelet basis and a residential block in East Finchley, Noblefield Heights, and then cashed in our chips.

I also entered into a small number of joint ventures, a euphemism if ever there was one, for the benefit of members of my immediate family to give them start-up capital or a modicum of financial security. One such digression was for the benefit of Pierre Gildesgame. He did not need any money but characteristically, he had rendered a particularly generous act to someone who shall be nameless. I wanted to make an applauding gesture. We purchased a little office building in Essex Street, near the Law Courts, reorganised the tenancies and sold it at a reasonable profit to Michael Laurie who subsequently redeveloped it.

Tudor Webasto, our motor-car sunroof business needed premises in Birmingham. Groveway bought an old factory, pulled down one-third to provide car parking and redeveloped the rest for letting. Unfortunately – and that is the reason why we got the original clapped-out old factory so cheaply – our access road belonged to the Water Board with an unexpired access lease of only 20 years. I tried to obtain an extension to 999 years. The estate manager of the Water Board was a "born again" Christian besouled with missionary zeal. He insisted on meeting me at his home where he and his wife worked hard to convince me that only conversion would save me from hell-fire and damnation. The fact that I was a self-declared Orthodox Jew and committed Zionist only spurned them on to greater efforts. We had a great time discussing eschatological problems. The lease was extended and I am still Jewish.

The 1974 property collapse had no effect on Groveway, whose activities by then had spread into Holland and Australia. The only borrowing we had were long-term mortgages with the Scottish

Widows Insurance Company where the endowment policy premiums and interest were covered by rentals several times.

I entered into several joint ventures with Alec Colman, who, to quote him, was "always willing to have a go". We never had a dispute and we enjoyed working with each other. On one occasion there was an extra windfall which either side could have claimed as "his". We gave that money to Hillel for the benefit of our students.

On one occasion Alec and I were entertained to lunch by the late Bernard Sunley, a man larger than life who ate and drank too much and then went on to fast at health farms. I was warned not to bring a car, to enjoy the bountiful alcohol and to go straight home from Berkeley Square to sleep. This was good advice. After several pre-luncheon cocktails, we entered the dining room, beautifully laid with four different sized glasses next to the gleaming cutlery. We had a jolly time.

Sunley had great vision. He was a buccaneering entrepreneur the like of which they do not make any more. He died in his fifties.

On 8.8.'88 (a memorable date) I wrote to my three daughters in Jerusalem that when shoeshine boys buy shares and gown merchants "go into property", it is time to get out. I sold Groveway lock, stock and barrel, much to the delight of the trustees of our Charitable Trust – a substantial shareholder. The trustees were Martin Paisner, Della and I.

19

Tudor Moves to Wales and Out of my Life: 1961–1973

THE "SWINGING SIXTIES" were followed by the steady industrial decline of the United Kingdom during the 1970s. Union power was in the ascendance. Strikes became a regular feature in virtually all car plants. The mini skirts, the slogan "anything goes" and the squatters who took over empty houses and sometimes even occupied homes while their owners were on holiday, found willing support amongst many members of the public and left-wing politicians.

In 1967 Ford Europe was founded. This enabled the multinational to move its production of cars and components to any of its European plants. It was inevitable that the Unions were up in arms accusing the Ford management in Detroit of playing out the European workers against each other. It is a policy, however, which has continued until this very day and is probably the main reason why Ford has been consistently the most profitable car manufacturer. With the vicissitudes of living under a regime whereby car manufacturers' purchasing officers would change their schedules sometimes twice a week depending on whether or not the factory was on strike for a day or a week or a month – it was very hard to run an efficient factory.

Nevertheless we continued to progress. We had enlarged our factory in Hayes to the maximum of 60,000 sq. ft. on our two acre site. We had branched out into the garden industry by using our know-how of windscreen washers and blown bottle production by diversifying into insecticide sprayers and later on into a whole range of garden tools. We retained the services of leading industrial designers such as Kenneth Grange.

By the end of the 1960s there were only four car manufacturers left in the United Kingdom, three of whom were American-controlled. The Rootes Brothers had sold out to Chrysler, Donald Stokes of Leyland Trucks had taken over at British Leyland, but in spite of all the difficulties the all-time export record of three quarters of a million cars out of 1.6 million production was reached in 1969. This *annus mirabilis* was exceeded only in 1972 when nearly two million cars were produced in the United Kingdom but a much smaller percentage was exported. From that year onwards the motor industry was on the decline.

Bert Walling, the young assistant buyer whom I first encountered in the fateful meeting in Mr Davis' office had by now become Chief Buyer of the Ford Motor Company, assisted by Gordon Kennedy. Bert was later to be "head-hunted" by British Leyland to become their Director of Purchasing, whilst Gordon held a similar post at Chrysler. We therefore had our well-laid network within the major purchasing organisations of the industry and the future looked good.

The Board of Trade told us that under no circumstances would we get any further permission to build in the south-east. If we wanted to expand we had to go into one of the Government-sponsored development areas, which had advantages and disadvantages. The advantages were that the Government would give considerable subsidies. There were reservoirs of labour, and there was no limit to future expansion. The disadvantages were the distances involved, particularly if one bore in mind that the so-called shadow factories which the car manufacturers had put up during the 1960s in order to cope with increasing demand had proved on the whole, thoroughly unsatisfactory. In most cases there was also the additional disadvantage of a split operation if more than one factory was maintained.

We decided to take the unusual step of moving the whole operation into a development area once a suitable location had been found. As soon as it became known that Tudor was willing to move (this was leaked by the Board of Trade with the best of intentions), we were inundated with offers from various parts of the UK – from

Scotland downwards.

Our first choice was Runcorn near Liverpool. I may not have known much about engineering but I did understand land and buildings. So, hopefully, I travelled up to Runcorn and met the officials. They were willing to let us have a maximum of seven acres but only on a leasehold basis. The ground rent, which was fairly low at the beginning, would be reviewed every five years and the review would be based on the increase in the commercial value of the land. "Do you mean to say," I asked, "that if we assist you in making this derelict area into a prosperous one, we work against ourselves?"

"What do you mean?" they replied.

"The higher the value the land becomes because of successful industrialists, the higher the ground rent will be?"

"Well, that's right! Isn't that fair enough?"

"It may be fair enough, but its not for us. In the first place seven acres are not enough and in the second place, we want to buy our land and not be faced with an increasing overhead every five years."

At that time our Board had been strengthened by two important additions. We had advertised for an experienced General Production Manager, and from the many applications which we had received two stood out. One was the Managing Director of a well-known engineering concern, the other was Jeff Thomas, a young consultant, a Welshman with considerable charisma. We found it difficult to make up our minds, and on the recommendation of Ferdinand Metzger, sent both hand-written applications to a graphologist in Switzerland. The answer came back within a week.

"If you wish to employ the first one you will have a steady loyal servant. If you employ the Welshman you will have a rough ride, but he has considerable flair."

We decided to take a chance and employ Jeff Thomas.

Having returned from Runcorn somewhat dispirited, Jeff said to me, "What about Wales?"

"What about it?" I replied.

"Well, it is a fantastic development area!"

"Wales!" I said, "never heard of it. It's miles away!"

"It's only one and a half hours away by train, it's nearer than

Runcorn, and I guarantee that you will have a much better reception there than you had from the Liverpool crowd." Jeff was keen to move us to his home ground, and so it was that he spent a long weekend in Newport and Cardiff, talking to the various authorities prior to my visit of inspection.

The second addition to our Board was Keith Taylor. I had met Keith some years earlier in the waiting room of one of the Cowley factories. His beautiful manners, his public school accent and his penchant for hunting and shooting made him the ideal contact man at the highest level. I said to him at the time that if ever he wanted to work for Tudor he would be welcomed. In the meantime he had set up his own wholesale business but found that he was under-financed. He telephoned me and I interviewed him in my garden. Every year there is one day when flying ants descend upon our swimming pool. That was the very day I invited Keith to join me for a swim. He asked me whether it was always full of fauna. He became our Sales Director and a good friend, although I occasionally asked him whether I could buy the fiction rights to his expense accounts!

When I travelled from Paddington Station to Newport I had little idea what a right royal reception I would receive. Four cars were waiting for me with a number of important officials representing the Monmouthshire County Council, the Ministry of Technology for Wales, Caerphilly Urban District Council, the Chief County Planning Officer of Monmouthshire County Council and the Development Corporation for Wales. It was quite a party! I had not realised until then how desperate the various authorities were to get more industry into South Wales which had not really had too much benefit of the manufacturing boom in the post-War era.

We travelled for many miles in convoy and we looked at many sites. Eager as I was to come to a conclusion I found none that suited our requirements. Too many of them had been mined which would have meant building on expensive piling; others had too many hillocks to level out. By the afternoon it looked as though my journey was unsuccessful.

"Can I just show you one of our model factories," an official said, "to give you an idea of what can be done here?"

I have always been turned on by factories. To me a really well-run industrial unit in an attractive building is a work of art and its humming machinery is music to my ears.

We drove to the Johnson and Johnson factory. This was the English operation of the famous American baby powder company. It was indeed impressive. The Tarmac nameboard had not yet been removed and I made a mental note of the builder's name.

On our journey I had noticed a large expanse of flat land.

"What about that area?" I asked.

"Oh, that's a hundred acre farm. As a matter of fact, the farmer is willing to sell but there is no access so it is no good to you."

On the way back, travelling past the farm, I said, "Supposing we were to buy this land from the farmer, would the Local Authority be prepared to build an access road and a bridge to carry industrial traffic over the river and zone it industrial?"

"That is not a bad idea. We will think about it and let you know."

Within a week I had the undertaking I had asked for and after a short time we found ourselves the owners of 100 acres of land at Ystrad Mynach, some 11 miles at the apex of the triangle with Cardiff and Newport.

We tackled the move like a military operation. Rather than transfer reluctant foremen from London to Wales we brought Welshmen to Hayes in the knowledge that they would be only too keen to return home and make a success of the venture which would bring prosperity to their area. We sold 50 acres of the land to Freddie Strasser of Nova Jersey Knit, a leading Marks and Spencer supplier, who installed the most modern knitwear factory in the UK on the site.

Then followed many intensive sessions with Tarmac whom we appointed as builders. We found them a pleasure to work with. They, too, were motivated by our desire to build the most attractive factory that money could buy. All the ideas and visions which we had over the years of what a really contemporary production unit should look like were put into practice. Basically we built a large hall of some 100,000 sq. ft. where goods inwards could be discharged within a matter of minutes at one end and where the completed product could be loaded on to waiting trucks at tailboard height at the other end. Fronting it would be a separate rectangular block to contain the open plan offices. The two buildings would be connected by two wings, one of which became our laboratory and the other contained the caretaker's flat as well as a comfortable overnight suite for directors and VIP guests. Cecily Lowenthal, Laurie's wife, was in charge of the interior decoration of the flats.

The space between the office block and the factory became a sculpture garden. Some years earlier we had struck up a friendship with the sculptress Naomi Blake, whose works adorn most of the buildings with which I have been associated over the years. They are at North London Collegiate School, at Tudor House, north-west London, at Immanuel College, Bushey and several were to stand in the landscaped area at Ystrad Mynach.

The whispers went round South Wales. "These Tudor people have a crazy governor. He is putting a sculpture garden in the middle of the factory." As a matter of fact it served as a wonderful public relations exercise. Once we were in full swing every important overseas delegation was taken to our factory. Members of the Royal Family came and visited us and on one occasion the Earl of Snowdon spent a whole day with us which proved to be an expensive one. He did not like the colour range of our packaging and thought it lacked unison. As a result we employed the Chief Graphic Designer of the University of Cardiff and our revamped house colours and logos went on all our stationery, packaging, trucks and vans.

The formal opening of the factory took place on Friday, 17 July 1970. The preparations had not been without drama. James Callaghan, then the Home Secretary, whom I had met some years earlier at a B'nai B'rith function at the Guildhall, had become a personal friend. He was the obvious choice to open the factory. He accepted with alacrity. The provision of work in the desolate and abandoned valleys of Wales was then a highly charged political theme and it was of some consequence to a Home Secretary to associate himself officially with a venture which straightaway provided 400 new jobs.

Unfortunately, between Mr Callaghan's acceptance and the

opening of the factory, the Labour Government fell. One day the telephone rang and a young man, speaking on behalf of Reginald Maudling, the Conservative Home Secretary, said, "anything Mr Callaghan promised Mr Maudling will keep. He will be delighted to open your factory." I had to do some quick thinking. Jim was a personal friend. Mr Maudling was an unknown. Mr Callaghan was a Welshman with deep roots in the valleys, and to Mr Maudling this was just another political gesture. I wanted Jim to open the factory.

"Would you mind if we left the final decision for a week or two?"

"Well, it makes it rather difficult because Mr Maudling's diary is filling up rapidly, but if you could let me know as soon as possible it would be appreciated."

By sheer chance I attended a reception at which both James Callaghan and Reginald Maudling were present. I went over to Jim and said, "Let's tackle Mr Maudling now." Jim introduced me and I had the unpleasant task of dis-inviting the new Home Secretary but he was very generous. "If Jim wants to go, by all means let him."

On the great day we hired two special carriages which were attached to the regular London to Newport train; we served a champagne breakfast to some 50 guests who came up from London. It was a distinguished company. When James Callaghan made his speech he said : "There is nothing more tragic in this country than to be an ex-Minister. They take away your car, take away your driver, and all this happens overnight. One day you are the most popular man in the country, the next day nobody wants to know you any more ... except Fred Worms!"

On the following day the local papers were euphoric. The *South Wales Echo* wrote on Thursday, 16 July:

HOW A LONDON FIRM FOUND A HAPPY HOME IN WALES

A successful transplant operation was carried out in South Wales last year and now the patient is in the best of health. This was no medical breakthrough but a big industrial achievement which brought over 400 jobs to the rapidly expanding Rhymney Valley industrial area. In twenty-five years, Tudor

Accessories Limited had steadily increased their output, first in car accessories and later in gardening equipment at their head-quarters in Hayes, Middlesex. In six months, green fields became a 100,000 square foot factory built at a cost of £500,000 and in four weeks the staff and its newly trained labour force completed the move-in and swung into production.

In response to Jim Callaghan's speech I said:

In 1946 we started with half a dozen employees and 1,500 square feet of floor space. In 1961 Stage 1 of our Hayes factory was built, comprising some 5,000 square feet which, over the years, grew to 60,000 square feet. Today we are inaugurating our new factory of 100,000 square feet standing on a site of 50 acres which will ensure that our expansion plans will be catered for for a very long time to come. In 1946 our turnover was £30,000 per annum. Today our Group of Companies, including Tudor (Australia) and Tudor (USA) turn over more than £2 million giving direct employment to some 700 men and women and indirect employment to a great many more.

In looking back over the past 24 years, one aspect deserves particular mention; it can be summed up in three words: Loyalty and Continuity. For nearly a quarter of a century we have had the support of Barclays Bank, Hayes, through the local directors at Windsor. For the whole of this period we have worked with the same legal advisors, Herbert Oppenheimer, Nathan & Vandyk, and for over two decades we have enjoyed the custom of Brown Brothers, Halfords, Gussies, Grattan Warehouse, Littlewoods, BMC, Fords, Rootes, Vauxhall and many other leading names in the automotive industry. This is as good an opportunity as any to say "thank you" to a large number of customers and suppliers with whom we have had the privilege of working and who have shown such patience during the extremely trying period when our operations at Hayes were being phased out and we started with virgin territory in South Wales.

When I use the term "virgin territory" I am not exaggerating.

In April 1969 Tarmac moved on to the site. Within seven months, in November of last year, production began at these works, and by the end of 1969 we were able to phase out Hayes entirely. I would like to express my gratitude and that of my colleagues to the Board of Tarmac, to the local authority and, in particular, to the Board of Trade, now the Ministry of Technology, for the remarkable speed with which they acted, which enabled us to develop this factory within record-breaking time. Let no one say that all Government Departments are run by bureaucrats, unable to make quick decisions. Any time the Industrial Building Section of the Ministry of Technology wants a reference, we shall be very glad to give them a really first-class one.

To my colleagues on the Board; my Joint Managing Director, Laurence Lowenthal, Sir Bernard Waley-Cohen, Keith Taylor, Jeffrey Thomas – to all the senior executives of the company, in particular our local directors, Malcolm Braun, Company Secretary and Bill Pye our General Sales Manager, and to our general body of workers, I would like to say "thank you" for being so patient with me (as though they had any alternative!) during a very trying period. We are embarking together on a most exciting adventure. We are happy to work with the Unions, whose interest in the prosperity of our employees we share wholeheartedly. Already the total number of our workers exceeds the estimate given to the then Board of Trade, and we are today employing the numbers forecast for 1972.

Before our move Helmut Rothenberg, the senior partner of our accountants, rang me. "I have a Mr Henry Kent in my office. He has a company called Car Coverall Limited, which imports the Webasto folding sunshine roof from Germany. He wants to sell his business. Are you interested?"

We bought the business from him and continued to import the components from the Webasto factory outside Munich. The Baier family had by then built themselves a worldwide reputation as the best sunroof manufacturer in the world. The soft folding roof, which we found so attractive in the UK, was duly superseded by the more sophisticated metal sliding and tilting roof which they began to supply to car manufacturers as original equipment. I was somewhat ambivalent about doing business with Germany but was reassured when I found that I was dealing with Mr Baier Junior, a man in his thirties who had never known the Nazis.

Nevertheless, it would be quite wrong for me to say that I entered into this venture with the same alacrity as if we had imported components from France or Italy. In any case, we found the importation process an expensive and lengthy one and when I suggested that we might make the roof in England the idea was warmly received. We brought over a container full of tools from Germany and entrusted Eric Woolley of Walsall Pressings Limited, with whom we had many years of happy co-operation, with the manufacture of the Webasto folding sunshine roof.

After having bought the business we found out the reason why Henry Kent had wished to dispose of it. The man who ran it for him – a typical moustachioed swaggering ex-RAF pilot, had actually cheated him. In granting franchises to various fitting stations up and down the country, he had kept it a secret that he was a 50 per cent owner of the London franchise. When Henry Kent found him out he told him, "I cannot work with you. On the other hand I cannot run the business without you. I am selling out." We decided to keep the chap, but he died of a heart attack not long afterwards.

Since we did not want to finance the acquisition from our own resources, we consulted our co-director, Sir Bernard Waley-Cohen, who had considerable financial connections. "Let's go to my friends the Rothschilds," he said. Stanley Berwin of Oppenheimers acted on our behalf, and N.M. Rothschild (Sir Evelyn's firm) gave us a Convertible Loan Stock. This is an interesting instrument which has the dual advantage of assuring the lender a guaranteed rate of interest coupled with a piece of the action in the event of the business becoming very successful, when the Loan Stock would be converted into ordinary shares. A Convertible Loan Stock would usually yield a lower rate of interest than that of a straight Debenture. Ours was at 8 per cent which was quite a tribute to the Tudor management. Michael Comninos, a director of Rothschilds was our contact Executive. One of the stipulations of the Deed was that our borrowing would not exceed three-quarters of a million pounds without the prior permission of the lenders.

In order to finance the Welsh factory and the land which we had purchased, we arranged to sell the Hayes factory on a leaseback basis to one of the pension funds. We had also agreed with the Eagle Star Insurance Company to give us a mortgage on the Welsh factory. However, technically for a month or so, until all these transactions were completed, our overdraft would be in excess of three-quarters of a million pounds, and our lawyers advised us to seek formal permission from Rothschilds.

"It is a mere formality," they said. Michael Comninos said, "No." "What do you mean 'No'?" I asked in astonishment. "You know perfectly well that the whole matter will be back on the rails within a month."

"The truth is," he said, "that we have been lending money to you too cheaply, and this is a suitable opportunity for increasing the lending rate to 10.5 per cent."

Three years later Rothschilds, participating in the sale of our business made a substantial capital profit.

Two years before the move I had acquired a rather derelict property at Child's Hill, within a few hundred yards of the garage whose manager had shown me the wing mirror in 1946. That site was used for undersealing motor cars, a fashion at the time to protect the exposed metal parts from the grit of the streets with a rubberised mixture. This is done by car manufacturers as a matter of course nowadays, but in the 1960s it was a popular business which needed little capital. With much difficulty Groveway, my property company, obtained planning permission for an office block. We renovated the adjacent workshop, franchised it to Harry Stallwood, our London Webasto fitting station maestro who already had an operation in south London, and moved into the new Tudor Head Office. After travelling to Hayes and back for more than 25 years, working 10 minutes from home was a wonderful relief.

Jeff Thomas was running the operation in Wales; Laurie Lowenthal, Keith Taylor and I would pay weekly visits. Every Tuesday I would drive to Paddington Station, catch the 7 a.m. train, enjoy a breakfast of kippers in the restaurant car and be picked up by

Johnny Morton, our faithful old retainer from Hayes, to be taken to the factory. The half-hour ride offered ample opportunity to listen to the latest gossip and tales of disasters and achievements. By the time I arrived in Jeff Thomas's office I was well-briefed!

I did not like everything I saw. For a start, the production area was not as clean as I wanted it to be. "Jeff," I said, "set an example. We should be able to eat off the floor."

We put waste paper baskets everywhere but we found it very hard to get our Welsh workers to use them. I also objected to the frequent and long sessions which Jeff had with the Union representative in a ritual non-stop shadow-boxing exercise.

Another complaint of mine was that our injection moulding machinery, the pride and joy of our factory – a sophisticated plant which cost many tens of thousands of pounds, broke down too frequently. I protested, "You are not allowing your staff enough time to clean off the sprue. The stuff is hardening quickly and then clings like a barnacle. You should get your workers to remove it three or four times a day." Jeff replied, "Fred, what do you know about production? It can't be done."

I went to Italy to inspect similar factories. On my return I saw him again. "Jeff, every one of the machines in Italy that I have seen is spotless. There are no breakdowns. You are not setting about this in the right way." I did not win.

One day I saw such a surplus mass solidifying on one of the plastic moulding machines that I took a pair of gloves, lifted off the hot sprue and held it in front of Jeff Thomas's face. "What the hell do you think of this?" I demanded. He mumbled some apology. When this extrusion hardened it turned into a kind of giant blue cornflower which I had mounted and which to this very day hangs in the toilet of my offices.

Injection moulding was one of our major operations. Nearly every one of our 200 products had some plastic components and I was determined to find a solution. Wells-Hinton were successful plastic moulders with factories in the south-east and one not far from us in Wales. The owner, Bill Wells, was a burly self-made workman. We bought a 50 per cent interest in the hope that this liaison would have a beneficial effect on our own production. Frankly, it never reached the perfection of the continentals. We later sold our 50 per cent interest when their contribution to our group was no longer meaningful.

Lightning struck on 15 April 1971. Lightning in the form of the first and only strike with which I have been associated in my life. A young girl was warned by the foreman that she was not working properly. In accordance with agreed Union procedure that warning was repeated in writing a month later, and since after a further 30 days the situation had not improved, we had the right to dismiss the defaulting employee. The Works Management observed the procedure scrupulously. When the girl was finally given her cards she burst into tears. "Never mind," said the women on her line, "We'll look after you. Don't you worry."

They came out on strike. To me, this was an affront that struck the solar plexus. After the paternal attitude that we had employed for over 25 years, priding ourselves on our labour relations and the excellent conditions of employment, it was a bitter disappointment.

"Now Fred," said Jeff Thomas "don't interfere. I know how to handle the Unions and the workers. Leave this to me."

"Jeff," I said, "it's not a matter for the Union; the Union is not against us. It is a workers' strike. But I will give you two days. If it is not settled within two days I will interfere."

After five days the strike had become ugly. Everybody had come out in sympathy. Vehicles were stopped from entering the factory precincts; within a short time – rather like a divorce case – the real cause of the strike was forgotten. Journalists came out to interview the workers. "I suppose Tudor are working the knickers off you," one asked jocularly. "That's right," said the spokeswomen for the workers, and she seized upon this brilliant idea. She took off her knickers which were promptly hoisted on a flagpole over a placard – "Tudor are working the knickers off their employees". It became known in the local press as "The Knickers Strike". I advised Jeff Thomas that I was coming down to have a go at settling this dispute. He had become pretty desperate and no longer put up much resistance. A meeting was called.

The local Institute Hall was packed. The employees were unsure of the future; they had lost a week's wages, and they had talked themselves into a truculent, militant mood. The Union representative, Jeff Thomas and I and the workers' representative, sat on the platform. They spoke before me, each one delivering his set piece. I realised that it was no longer a question of working conditions or money. It was an emotional impasse from which both sides needed rescuing.

It was not difficult for me to speak with a broken voice because the aggravation that we had suffered was only too visible in all our faces. I said to the workers that before we had moved to Wales, Jeff Thomas had said to me that the one thing I would find in Wales would be total loyalty. "But Jeff," I quoted, "we have been in Hayes for 24 years, and we have never had a strike. What's so marvellous about workers not letting you down? We are used to that. They are part of the family. You know my door has always been open. You know how many weddings we made possible, loans we made for houses and motor cars. Why should this change?" "Yes, but in Wales you find a special loyalty," he replied. I turned to the workers; "Is this the loyalty we are finding today?"

There were tears and much dabbing of the eyes. The strike was settled there and then on the understanding that we would reinstate the girl for a period of three months whilst trying to find her another job elsewhere. Within six weeks the girl was caught stealing from the canteen and dismissed herself. We did not have another strike but my confidence was deeply shaken. It was another subconscious notch in preparing myself for the ultimate rupture of 25 years' work – the sale of Tudor Accessories.

Keith Taylor, who had his ear close to the ground, warned us in 1971 that it was likely that windscreen washers would become compulsory on all motor cars. We laid down enormous stocks and had a bonanza in 1972 when legislation was passed. That particular accessory had come a long way since we first produced it. The original version was a glorified jam jar mounted in a metal bracket under the bonnet of the car; the jar was connected to a plastic squeezing bulb on the dashboard, and water was discharged from a couple of outsize jets on to the windscreen. The Japanese had electrified the windscreen washer and we were fighting for our survival in this particular field by trying to design a motor and pump that would be smaller and better than the Japanese – a considerable challenge! We bought some of our electric components from a subsidiary of Philips which went into liquidation. We took over three of their top development engineers, locked them away in our laboratory and gave them more or less a free hand to design the best motor and pump. We sent Jeff Thomas to Japan to study the latest production methods and finally produced a combined unit no bigger than a thumb which could outprice and outperform anything known in the world. Within a short time we had a complete monopoly on windscreen washers for original equipment.

At the beginning of 1973 Roland Franklin and his brother-in-law, Ian Stoutzker, directors of Keyser Ullman, the old established merchant bankers, telephoned. Their client, Dutton Foreshaw, wanted to buy us. We met with their directors who had a permanent suite at one of the leading London hotels. They had a Rolls-Royce franchise and lived in great style. I did not think that our philosophy of plain living would marry happily with theirs and we declined the offer. Keyser Ullman collapsed in the 1974 débâcle. Roland and his wife, Nina, emigrated to the United States where Roland carved himself a great new career working for Sir James (Jimmy) Goldsmith. Ian Stoutzker, together with former co-director Guy Naggar, formed a new merchant bank, Dawnay Day.

The motor industry is a small family, and within a short time I was telephoned by one Gerry Mortimer of Smiths Industries. "If you are seriously thinking of selling Tudor, why don't we have a chat?"

Once again my garden, secluded from prying ears, was the venue for a meeting, and within a few days we had worked out a framework which Gerry was willing to put before his Chairman, Richard Cave. Dick Cave, later Sir Richard of Thorn-EMI, was a formidable man. He was a qualified engineer, a brilliant tank commander during the War, a keen amateur sailor and the undisputed Chief Executive of Smiths Industries. We met and he suggested buying us out and paying partly in Smiths shares, convertible loan stock and cash.

There was some tough bargaining, particularly since I insisted on excluding from the sale the 40 acres of Welsh land which were not needed by Tudor, nor was I willing to sell Tudor Webasto because we did not want to deprive ourselves entirely of any industrial involvement overnight. Agreement was duly reached. Two days before the appointed date, Gerry Mortimer rang to say that the Chairman wanted to defer the sale because their share price had fallen. He had been relying on a quotation of 180p and wanted to wait until the price reached that level again.

By that time the idea of ridding myself of the responsibilities of Tudor at the height of the boom was irresistible. I had to think quickly. "I have a suggestion. Go back to Dick Cave and tell him that I am willing to do the deal on the basis of 180p regardless of the share price in a couple of days' time." The sale proceeded as planned during the week of the Yom Kippur war.

Laurie Lowenthal, Keith Taylor and Jeff Thomas were singularly unenthusiastic. They thought we would be better off on our own. They continued working for Smiths within the Tudor framework for a short time. I was the only one who resigned on the spot.

1974 saw the end of the boom, a dramatic rise in the oil price, the crash in the City, the demise of well-known merchant banks, property companies and bankruptcies of many individuals. The motor industry skidded into rapid decline.

According to figures published by the Society of Motor Manufacturers and Trades, UK car production in 1972 reached a peak of 1,921,311 vehicles. The corresponding figure for 1984 was 908,906. Japan's production in 1972 was 4,022,289 and in 1984 7,073,173.

The finger of God had intervened in our favour. By 1980 Smiths Industries sold the whole of their motor division, of which Tudor formed only a small part, to Lucas Industries. Lucas, in turn, managed to survive the storm only because of their important interests outside the motor industry.

20

The Swiss Army Knife and The Story of Butchers Supplies (London) Limited

THE MYSTERY OF my involvement in butchers' knives and the famous Swiss Army penknife is tied up with three families who are closely involved with this venture.

Ferdinand Metzger who brought me to England, came from Mainz, near Frankfurt. He was the prototype of the assimilated German Jew, good sportsman, particularly fond of rowing, a connoisseur of fine wines and dedicated to business. His wife, Berta, also fitted the familiar mould. She came from a wealthy family. She was plain, meek, dominated by her parents and then by Ferdinand. Whether the proverbial bull was called after him or he was called after the bull I will never know, but the similarity is apposite. He was aggressive, prickly and a perfectionist, yet he was probably one of the kindest, most generous men that I have ever met. He was easily moved to tears and had the classical heart of gold. He adored his two daughters, Eva and Ilse.

When they came to England in 1939 with very little money (he left a substantial fortune behind in Germany, some of which was retrieved through restitution after the War), he bought a small house in Putney and carried on business from there. He was an expert in butchers' supplies, from knives to sausages. During the War years when import was at a standstill, he became a consultant to famous firms such as Walls Sausages and taught them good old German recipes. Incidentally, Walls, a subsidiary of Unilever, became enamoured with their advisers of German origin and subsequently bought the business of another close friend of my mother, Richard Mattes, whose Mattessons Products became the trademark of Unilever's meat division.

As soon as Ferdinand Metzger had settled down in Putney he formed his company – Butchers Supplies (London) Limited. Although at that time I had only just begun my Articles, I kept his books and in 1940 he asked me to become the company secretary. In 1946 he took up his pre-War connections, particularly with two Swiss firms; one, a small company called Lico in Grenchen, run by two brothers Liechti, and the other, Victorinox, the world-famous knife firm owned by the Elsener family. Ferdinand Metzger's business grew and prospered until it was no longer possible to run it from his home and so we bought premises in Putney Bridge Road consisting of a shop and ancillary warehouse.

During the War the elder daughter, Eva, on whom he doted, joined the ATS (Women's Army). Sadly she contracted leukaemia and died. Both Ferdinand and Berta were so shattered by this tragedy that they virtually opted out of their already limited activities. It was only commitment to the business, together with the hopes which they pinned on their younger daughter, Ilse, which helped them over this very difficult period. They concentrated their love and affection on Ilse, who had become a dentist.

Metzger was what was called a "fringe Jew". He had very little patience with synagogues or rabbis. Yet he was immensely proud of the State of Israel and on the occasion of his 70th birthday presented an ambulance to Magen David Adom. He was deeply unhappy when his daughter, Ilse, decided to marry a non-Jewish young doctor. However, once he had got over his initial misgivings he gave the couple his enthusiastic support and he bought them a beautiful house. In due course, to Ferdinand's shock and dismay, Ilse converted to Christianity and became very active in the Church. Fortunately neither Ferdinand nor Berta lived long enough to see the break-up of Ilse's marriage. To her utter surprise her husband informed her one day that he had fallen in love with his head nurse and that he was moving out. Today Ilse lives alone, busy with her church affairs and sustained by her son, daughter and grand-children.

As the years rolled by Ferdinand became increasingly worried about succession. By that time I was fairly involved in his business. He took me to Switzerland twice a year on his regular visits to the factories. Thus it was as far back as 1950 that I developed a personal relationship with the Elsener and Liechti families. From 1960 onwards Ferdinand Metzger would say, "Fred, buy the business off me."

"I don't need it, Ferdinand," I would reply. "I've got Tudor and my properties. I'm fully extended. I really don't want it."

I would visit the Metzgers at least once a week. He looked upon me as a son, and in all modesty I can safely say that my visits were the highlight of his week. We would go through the figures in the office and then go back to the house where Berta would wait with coffee and cake. She was a very lonely woman. Their circle of acquaintances was tiny. She, too, was longing to ask me a few questions but the moment she opened her mouth he would slam the desk violently and say, "For God's sake, Berta. Can't you keep quiet for one minute? I never see Fred and for the few moments he is here you are wasting time with him."

My heart would bleed for her and periodically, after watching this performance, I would say, "Look, Ferdinand, you are not being fair. Now it's Berta's turn. For 10 minutes I would like to talk with her without any distraction from you."

He mumbled a grudging consent, retired into the corner, took off his watch and placed it on the desk. After 10 minutes he would call out, "Time's up!" and he would take over once more.

He tried to ensure succession by employing a Mr Jones. This proved an utter disaster, not only because Jones was not really suitable but also because Ferdinand Metzger was not prepared to part with any authority.

Amongst the few items which the Metzgers managed to rescue from their silver collection in Germany was a magnificent nineteenth-century solid silver *chanukiah* – the eight-armed menorah on which are lit the candles at Chanukah time. It is the famous model with eight individual carved lion heads which open up to give access to the wick and oil. Ferdinand Metzger used to say, "Fred, I am going to leave this to you in my Will."

My invariable reply was, "Enjoy it, and use it next Chanukah."

He did not. In 1968 he fell ill. It was literally a matter of life and death. When he miraculously recovered he invited my mother – of whom he was particularly fond, Della, my sister Vera and myself to go to Putney for a special party. He made a little speech, thanked the Lord for having saved him, and amongst much tear-shedding on the part of the ladies and eye-mopping on the part of the gentlemen, handed over the *chanukiah* to me.

"I prefer giving it to you with a warm hand," he said.

It is one of my most treasured possessions.

By that time I had arranged for Eric Beecham to become the auditor of Butchers Supplies. When Eric came out of the army he became a chartered accountant and then joined me. After two years with us, Eric went back into the profession, worked for Barton Mayhew and then decided to go into practice. At that time I had a loose arrangement with one Henry Finck, a chartered accountant with a small clientele. My firm was called Simon Worms & Finck through which I passed the little accountancy work that was forced on me against my better judgement. Eric joined Henry in partnership with the title of Henry Finck and Beecham, to be followed by his independent firm – Beecham and Company – which still exists with a number of partners to whom he sold the practice. It was in his capacity as auditor of Butchers Supplies that he became involved with Ferdinand Metzger who said to me, "Look Fred, this cannot go on. You must buy the business."

We went through the same, well-rehearsed conversation.

"What about that rascal Eric? How much can he earn as an accountant? £10,000 a year? What does he know about accountancy? He is a Frankfurt business boy. Why don't you and he buy it together? You can pay me in cash, and Eric can pay me over a period."

This is what happened. In retrospect it sounded easy. The truth was that those years were really quite difficult. Poor Eric became, once again a trainee office boy in the real German sense of the word. I cannot imagine that in England after the War any other young man would have submitted to this kind of bullying apprenticeship. Part of the agreement was that Eric would gradually wind up his accountancy business, or rather transfer it to his friend, Paul Cohen. That meant that initially Eric spent a few hours a day in his own office, the rest of the time in Putney. Every day Ferdinand would ring me and say, "I can't work with that fellow. First of all he's never here. Secondly, when he comes he jumps about and doesn't concentrate. Thirdly he doesn't listen. I don't know how this is going to work out."

Eric stuck it out and when finally Ferdinand passed away he not only ran the business but built up the penknife side to a figure which Ferdinand Metzger would never have believed possible. The beauty of the arrangement during the last couple of years was that although Ferdinand Metzger had sold the business to us, in practice he continued to run it. We made it clear that as long as he was alive he would be the boss, and as far as the outside world was concerned no one needed to know about the change of shareholding.

He died in harness. His wife, Berta, was so distraught that she took herself to bed. We were afraid she might commit suicide. "Oh Fred, oh Fred," she cried on my daily visits. Della sat with her during the funeral.

"What is going to become of me? What am I going to live on?"

"Berta," I said, "if you went to Harrods every day of the week by taxi and you spent as much as you liked, you would not use up the money that you have got."

I could not convince her. Three weeks later she died in her sleep. The truth was that they really adored each other and she simply could not face life alone.

Eric continued to run the business from Putney. I was increasingly concerned because he had a habit of over-extending himself and falling asleep at the wheel of his car. The daily journey in the rush hour from north to south London was something which could not be tolerated for any length of time. We looked around and found ideal premises within five minutes' walking distance of his Hampstead home and my office. We bought a shell of a building which we converted into offices and stores.

Eric and I have had a remarkable relationship. I doubt whether there is another partnership where there were so few differences of opinion. He and his wife Jean married almost at the same time as Della and I. Although we had separate honeymoons, subsequently we visited the Lake District together and I believe that Jean, who loves to give an impression of being easily shocked, has never really forgiven me for swimming naked in one of those inviting lakes. (It was a really hot day and we had forgotten our bathing costumes.) Eric eats fast, sleeps fast (he says he needs only three hours a night) and drives fast.

Simon Bischheim, Eric's father, was the classical patriarch. He had the good sense to bring his wife, three sons and one daughter to England at a relatively early stage. Our families had known each other in Frankfurt and kept in close touch. The Bischheims bought a modest house in Edgware which became a haven of hospitality to refugee families. My mother and I used to love going there. The old man was well over six feet tall, of military bearing, a good horseman, ex-German army, a true paterfamilias. He died at a ripe old age immensely proud of his children.

Carl Elsener the First started grinding knives in 1884. He also discovered a method of preventing their oxidisation. His wife was called Victoria, and the trade mark therefore became Victorinox which is probably the most respected name any knife in the world could carry today. Carl the First handed the business over to Carl the Second; Carl the Second passed it on to Carl the Third, and Carl the Fourth, in his thirties, is gradually taking over the reins.

The Elsener family originally came from Zug, half an hour's driving distance from Schwyz. Schwyz is the original canton around which Switzerland was founded. The local pride of citizenship is intense. Xenophobia is rampant and newcomers from other cantons are not recognised as equals. Thus it is that the Elsener family, as the largest employers in the canton of Schwyz, who have done more for the area than the rest of industry combined, still go and cast their votes in the canton of Zug. That is the way Switzerland works.

They are strict Catholics. A large percentage of their substantial annual profits goes to the Church. Carl the Third has a brother in the business who confines himself to the production side. Another brother is a missionary and there is a sister who is a nun serving in the Far East. Carl (Charles) has 11 children. He left school at a fairly early age, yet there is little doubt that he is one of the most brilliant engineers that I have ever come across. It is under his benign dictatorship that the business has taken off in a big way and produces more penknives than anybody else in the world. Over the years the factory has grown from a few thousand square feet in a converted series of chalets to the ultra-modern plant covering tens of thousands of square feet in the beautiful village of Ibach. It is fully automated, with robots having taken over much of the highly skilled production processes.

When Charles came to the conclusion that the world was going to face an energy crisis, he hit upon the idea – long before it became popular – of recycling waste heat generated by his machinery. He called in an international firm of experts who prepared plans. He looked at their ideas, took them home and studied them, and then told them that their system would work more efficiently if they would change the dimensions of the inlet tubes, the outlet valves etc. Today he has the most sophisticated, clean air, heating/air conditioning installation anywhere in Switzerland and is virtually independent of outside fuel. The consultants acknowledged that they learned from him. The man is a genius. Periodically he writes to the President of the Swiss Government telling him where he is going wrong and proving his acumen by his own investment success. On the other hand, he relies on the local faith-healer to stop a cut finger from bleeding.

He is also one of the most frugal men I have ever known. He does not own a motor car. In fact, he cannot drive. He detests travelling except on his bicycle. When he took us out to restaurants we were careful to order the cheapest meals lest he felt that we were extravagant. He looks upon Germany, Austria and Switzerland as his home market and supplies the retailers direct from his own regional warehouses.

As the London business expanded, we moved it into larger

premises at Crewys Road, near Child's Hill. Having sold Tudor House, which was virtually round the corner, I moved into Victorinox House. Eric and I travelled regularly to Ibach and became very good friends of the Elseners.

Charles III was concerned about two aspects of our business, continuity and cutting out wholesalers, as he had done in Germany and France. Eric and I did not cherish the idea of building up a large sales force to go direct to the retailers. Since we had reached retirement age we agreed to sell the business in 1990 to a purchaser approved by Switzerland who would fall in with their wishes.

It was a satisfactory sale which allows Eric and Jean to spend much of their time in their beloved Majorca home. We built ourselves small tailor-made offices at the rear of Victorinox House from which we run our investment company and from where I operate to this very day.

21

Bank Leumi and Ernst Japhet

WE HAVE HAD a holiday apartment in Herzliah Pituach near the Sharon Hotel ever since the children were very small. Holidays in Israel became a routine which gave our daughters an early learning and acclimatising opportunity and they looked upon both countries with equal affection. By the early 1970s the square adjacent to the Sharon Hotel had become a noisy exuberant coffee bar and restaurant centre with parking facilities for hundreds of cars so we moved to a new development called Herzliah Crest next to the sand dunes and not far from the Accadia Hotel. To celebrate our move we gave a dinner party and our guests included Ernst and Ella Japhet, Chaim and Aura Herzog, Israel and Rachel Pollak and Aron and Phyllis Sacharov. Every one of the men concerned would play a prominent part in Israel's subsequent history. Chaim Herzog became President of the State. Israel Pollak built up the country's biggest textile conglomerate only to sell it out to Clal at the end of his career and Aron Sacharov made his Sahar Insurance Company into an important firm. He was consistent in his pessimistic forecasts in so far as Israel's politicians and the international insurance market, particularly Lloyd's, was concerned.

Ernst Japhet's career has also been remarkable.

Theodor Herzl, the founder of modern Zionism, came to the conclusion that he needed a major financial instrument to implement his ambitious plans. He founded the Jewish Colonial Trust in 1899 and the Anglo-Palestine Company was incorporated in London in 1902. At that time the Jewish population of Palestine was a mere 50,000. The company changed its name to the Anglo-Palestine Bank in 1930 and to Bank Leumi Le Israel in 1951. The early very strong German/Austrian influence was shown by the original share certificates which bore the legend, "The Jewish Colonial Trust" and underneath "*Juedische Colonialbank*."

Its first General Manager was Z.C. Levontin, a white-bearded patriarch who operated from the branch which was established in Jaffa under the chairmanship of David Wolffsohn.

Voting control lay ultimately with a specially created body under the auspices of the Jewish Agency. Amongst its directors and general managers were some of those whose legendary names are closely involved with the building of the economy of the Jewish State. Until almost the beginning of the Second World War it was the only major Jewish bank in Palestine. Dr Y. Foerder was Chairman from 1957 to 1970 and Dr E. Lehmann followed him and held office until 1977, except for a period in 1974 when Mendes Sachs was Chairman. Pierre Gildesgame and I made the rounds of the leading bankers before every Maccabiah to solicit their financial support and I remember clearly calling on Lehmann, an eminent banker of the German school who ran the bank in a quiet unobtrusive and efficient way. He was followed by an outstanding personality, a man who was to become a star in the international banking world, a man with three generations of banking experience in his blood – Ernst Japhet. Small in stature but with an enormous personality, he was to dominate the Israeli banking scene from the day of his appointment in 1977 until his tragic retirement in 1986.

Ernst Japhet had joined the bank in 1963. In 1965 Dr Foerder invited him to become a joint General Manager but was reluctant to break the news to Dr Lehmann. Finally, Foerder agreed to invite Lehmann and Japhet for lunch. As soon as they had sat down Foerder turned to Japhet and said, "*Sie haben Dr Lehmann etwas zu sagen.*"

Japhet was deeply embarrassed at being put on the spot by his Chairman. He explained the situation simply and quickly. Dr Lehmann turned white with anger at the manner of the announcement and Foerder's lack of courage. "*Herr Dr Foerder, Dass Japhet diesen Posten bekommt ist für mich nicht angenehm, aber fuer die Bank unerlaesslich!*" ("that Japhet gets the job is unpleasant for me but essential for the bank") and he stormed out.

Japhet's policy was one of expansion, to cater both for the business and private customer, to open the maximum number of branches in Israel and abroad and to diversify from pure banking into many other activities. Over the years he secured himself a unique niche in the infrastructure of the country. He was on the board of many charitable institutions, universities, museums, and hospitals and a whole host of other non-profit-making organisations were beholden to him. Finance ministers came and went; Governors of the Bank of Israel followed each other, but the focus of the banking world in Israel was undoubtedly Ernst Japhet. Internationally, too, he developed personal friendships with leading bankers, some of whom had family connections with his ancestors. It seemed that nothing could go wrong for Ernst Japhet, that he would adapt the Bank he ran to continuously changing conditions and that he would be one of the pillars on which Israeli society and the economy could rely.

We are told in Numbers ch. 13, the fourth of the five books of the Torah, that Moses sent out 12 spies to inspect the country which the Children of Israel were to conquer after 40 years' wandering in the desert. Ten of the 12 spies caused alarm and despondency upon their return. They said, "It is perfectly true that it is a land that flows with milk and honey but ... it is a land that eats up its inhabitants."

I have often thought of this quotation when reflecting on the number of outstanding personalities who have been destroyed and driven to despair or even suicide by Israeli society: Jacob Levinson, the brilliant managing director of the Bank Hapoalim who, had he wanted to, could have become Finance Minister, took his life, following allegations that were subsequently proved to have been untrue; industrialists and politicians such as Ofer and Albin who had given their all to the country and who, having taken one false step, were virtually excommunicated and hounded to their deaths.

In 1976 Stuart Young, an eminent chartered accountant called on me. Stuart and Shirley were old friends and in due course Della's brother, Arthur Harverd, was to become a partner in Hacker Young, of which Stuart was the senior partner. It was a small world indeed. That firm was known in earlier years as Hacker, Rubens,

Phillips & Young. The Rubens was none other than John Rubens, who left accountancy to go into the property business together with Barnett Shine, and these two would become great philanthropists. John became Chairman of the Maccabi Foundation and his son-in-law, Michael Phillips, joined his accountancy firm. After the withdrawal of John and Michael from accountancy the title of the firm was changed to Hacker Young. Stuart, on behalf of Ernst Japhet, extended an invitation to me to join the board of Bank Leumi (UK) PLC. I accepted with alacrity because I felt that having had a foot in both camps, that is the business world in England and in Israel for so many years, with my frequent visits to that country (an average of five a year) and my personal friendship with a number of businessmen and politicians I could be of some service.

For many years the English subsidiary had been dominated by one man, Sir Henry D'Avigdor Goldsmid, an aristocrat who ran the bank in a similar fashion to Sir Robert Waley-Cohen's Presidency of the United Synagogue. When I joined the bank the Deputy Chairman and Managing Director was Teddy Joseph who, together with his brother Oscar who was also on the board, had two generations of banking experience in their blood. They had sold their family bank – Leopold Joseph & Sons, but continued to be active in the City. Others on the Board of Directors were my old friend Julian Layton (Major Layton in charge of the Lingfield camp at the time of my internment), Bobby Seligman of Warburgs, Lord Mancroft, Stuart Young, Alex Rosenzweig of N.M. Rothschild, Leonard Sainer, Senior Partner of Titmuss Sainer & Co. and the *alter ego* of Charles Clore and, over the years, a variety of non-Jewish professional bankers who had retired from the joint stock banks.

Ernst Japhet believed in "hands on" management and decided that he would become the Chairman of all the overseas subsidiaries. This involved an enormous amount of travelling and when I got to know him better and we became firm friends I ventured to suggest that this was probably not a good idea. "Important business people tell me in Israel that they cannot get any decisions out of the bank because you are always on a plane and nobody dares to decide in your absence."

"Never mind, Fred," he said. "It is better that there should be strong central management and there is nothing that cannot wait for 24 hours. Anyhow Einhorn and Yekutieli [senior managers] have a considerable amount of authority."

It also became the UK subsidiary's policy to import its general manager from Israel. It was Japhet's way of keeping tight control, a practice that has proved itself over the years provided that there was a strong English Deputy Chairman on the spot.

Japhet's board meetings were an education but one which was received with a considerable amount of strain. He spoke very softly. He referred to all employees – including his fellow directors from Israel – by their family names only. Part-time English directors would be honoured with the title of Mr before their names, whilst those of his inner circle were called by their first names. He enjoyed sticking to certain idiosyncrasies such as referring to the agenda with a German pronunciation with a hard G, although he knew perfectly well that this was wrong. He chain-smoked cigars and for a time consumed considerable quantities of iced sherry.

Stuart Young, whose practice had increased enormously and who was under considerable pressure, also lit one long Havana cigar after another. "Stuart, cut it out," I would say. "You are smoking too much." "It's only my second today," he would reply. "It is actually your third and it is not lunchtime yet." I do not know whether Stuart's tragic passing from cancer had anything to do with this but it was one of the great tragedies of the 1980s at the very time when he had reached the pinnacle of his career as Chairman of the Governors of the BBC and shortly before his brother, David (Lord Young) was to become one of the principal supporters and member of Mrs Thatcher's Cabinet. There is no doubt that our board meetings were in a pillar of cloud rather like the Children of Israel's in the desert, except ours was man-made.

I enjoyed working with Ernst Japhet and later I was invited to become a director of the principal subsidiary in Israel, the Union Bank (Bank Igud) whose board meetings were conducted entirely in Hebrew (unless one of my fellow English directors representing the Diamond Corporation which had a stake in the Union Bank was present).

Although Israel was in a perpetual state of semi-crisis because of the enormous economic pressures, mainly caused by the 30 per cent of GNP Defence Budget, these were crises which on the whole were containable. Governors of the Bank of Israel together with treasury ministers would often use the leading banks to secure foreign currency for the National Exchequer. It was felt that the reputation of the banks and their economic standing was probably more attractive to foreign lenders than that of the State of Israel.

A typical example was related to me by Ernst Japhet. In 1974 Rabinowitz, the then Minister of Finance, called him urgently. "Japhet, the country needs $250 million by next Friday. Try and get it through Bank Leumi."

That was on a Sunday morning. Japhet flew to Frankfurt and secured Dm 100 million from Dr Wilfred Guth, Chief Executive of the Deutsche Bank. By Monday evening he was in New York where, within two days, he raised the balance.

When Japhet returned to Tel Aviv feeling justifiably satisfied with his four days' work, Sapir called on him. Pinchas Sapir, the incorruptible wheeler/dealer had, for many years, been Minister of Finance with quite exceptional powers. He was still the *éminence grise* and the acknowledged king-maker. He stormed in, "You have damaged the country."

Japhet looked up in pained surprise.

"I was rather under the impression that I had saved the country."

"You have given overseas bankers the real figures of our economy. You have ruined us! How you got those loans I'll never know!"

"The answer is perfectly simple. I got them in the name of the Bank because overseas bankers trust me. If once I mislead them I lose my credibility."

Sapir, who was a hard man, replied with grudging admiration, "Bank Leumi is too big and Japhet is too powerful."

Thereafter, at regular intervals, the big banks would be invited to increase their capital and to borrow hundreds of millions of dollars from financial institutions overseas. A large percentage of these borrowings would then have to be deposited with the Central Bank which continued to control and scrutinise all Israeli banks. This was not a recipe for the healthy progression of a young State but it seemed to work and no one was prepared to blow the whistle. It could only work, however, as long as the bank shares continued to go up. Confidence in the infallibility of the banks was the first prerequisite for keeping the balls in the air. It was here that the management of the banks got carried away by their own enthusiasm for the maintenance of the status quo. With hindsight it is easy to condemn a system which was manifestly untenable in the long run. However, those who criticised from the secure base of a Western country with a stock exchange that has its jobbers and brokers do so probably with a modicum of ignorance for what pertained at the time in Israel. The young stock exchange in Tel Aviv had no jobbers or brokers. The majority of the share prices were actually made by the banks and it is no wonder that they recommended their own shares and in fact often reciprocated the courtesy of fellow bankers who bought each other's shares to ensure a continuously rising market.

One year after the B'nai B'rith Award was given to Marcus Sieff in 1982 the International President in Washington telephoned me once again on the very same subject. "Gerald Kraft speaking. This year we would like to honour an Israeli. Any bright ideas?"

"Yes," I replied instantly, "there is one man who has done more humanitarian work than anybody else. Hospitals, universities, museums – Ernst Japhet has helped them all."

At the time Eli Hurwitz, Chairman of TEVA Pharmaceuticals was also Chairman of the Israel Manufacturers Association. A good friend of mine as well as Japhet's, he was most helpful and offered to organise the function. Once again B'nai B'rith charities were to benefit. We sold all available tickets at $200 each for a major function at the Hilton Hotel, Tel Aviv, a remarkable achievement at the time.

Between the nomination and the dinner date, the banking scandal broke and Japhet was right in the midst of it. Some prominent personalities advised us to cancel. Eli and I refused. We held a smaller function at the Bank's head office in Tel Aviv to which the "inner circle" only was invited. Not one person who had paid for the Hilton banquet asked that his money be refunded.

Was the whistle finally blown by a member of the Government or the Bank of Israel or one of the prominent auditors employed by the banks? Not at all. The system collapsed simply because of one man – Yoram Aridor, a self-styled economist who became the Minister of Finance of the Likud. He was determined that his party should have an overall majority at the next election and he embarked on the most enormous Government giveaway in the history of the State. Tariffs were slashed and imports flooded into the country. It was the age of the motor car and the video, the refrigerator and the washing machine. The public realised that this was too good to last and they recognised that vast imports unmatched by exports would lead to a very rapid devaluation of the shekel. Switching into dollars became the fashionable thing and lemming-like the whole country rushed to the destruction of the banking system by demanding dollars.

Since most people who had savings had put these into bank shares, there was a stampede into selling bank shares which no one was willing to buy. The State had no alternative but to step in and bail out the banks. It was not long before recriminations were flying about. Scapegoats were needed and who was more suitable than the managing directors of the various banks? The press had not only a field day or a field week or month but a year of consistent personal attacks into which were dragged the private lives of the banking families. The public was out for blood and the Government had no alternative but to create a Commission of Enquiry. Its Chairman was Judge Beijsky, a survivor of the Holocaust and a man who could be relied upon to "teach those bankers a lesson". I attended some of the Beijsky Commission hearings in Jerusalem and was not impressed. I do not believe that a similar Commission could have operated in England with such a prevalent lynch-atmosphere.

This is an extract from an article which appeared in *The Jerusalem Post* on 18 October 1991 under the headline:

WITNESS: GOVERNMENT DELIBERATELY CAUSED BANK SHARES CRISIS:

The government deliberately brought on the bank shares crisis, Dr Yakir Flessner, who served as an assistant to the governor of the Bank of Israel at the time, testified in Jerusalem District Court yesterday.

He said that on the eve of the crisis in October 1983, acting on his advice, then finance minister Yoram Aridor declined to devalue the currency, knowing for certain this would lead to the collapse of the bank shares.

"We intentionally caused the bank shares crisis," Flessner said during cross-examination by the defense. "Aridor knew that refusing to devalue meant the shares would collapse."

The defense was clearly surprised by his words. "This was the most dramatic moment in the trial," said Dan Sheinman, counsel for Bank Hapoalim.

Other defense lawyers agreed, and noted that the Beisky Commission, which investigated the scandal, "didn't know that the crisis was intentionally brought on by the Treasury."

The defense has contended that neither the banks nor their officers at the time had any intention to commit an illegal act. They have leveled blame on the government, charging it encouraged the manipulation of the shares, then failed to keep its promise to extend credit to the banks to help them get out of the mess they had created.

The outcome was a foregone conclusion. Nearly all the Bank Directors were sacked including some members of the Recanati family who controlled the Discount Bank which they had founded. Amongst the accused was also my good friend Dan Bavly, one of the leading bank auditors in the country. Amazingly, no guilt was attached to the Cabinet Ministers, to the Governor and officials of the Bank of Israel or to the members of the Knesset Finance Committee, all of whom knew perfectly well what was going on and by co-operating with the system gave it their practical blessing. No one complained when the banks produced the foreign currency for the Treasury. Strangest of all, the architect of the disaster, Yoram Aridor, continued as a leading member of the Likud Party albeit with his influence somewhat diminished.

The witch hunt had no limit. All activities of the banks over the previous decades were subjected to close inspection by professionals and amateurs alike who polished their magnifying glasses to find fault. I was moved to reply to a particularly aggressive letter in *The Jerusalem Post* which accused the bigger banks of exceeding their authority by opening branches and subsidiary companies overseas when they should have concentrated on the home market. In my letter I stated that Israel had the choice between becoming a Banana Republic or a second Switzerland. There was no way in which a major banking system could be developed with a tiny resident local population, with a GNP then of some $20 billion and a substantial trade deficit.

So far my personal sympathies had been entirely with the much-abused bankers but subsequent developments cast an extra cloud over Ernst Japhet. Presumably in anticipation of early retirement, he had voted himself a salary with proportionate pension rights of such magnitude that one's first reaction was one of incredulity, followed by astonishment and ultimately by disenchantment. This was capped by a "compensation for loss of office" payment of American pro-portion. Other senior executives of the Bank Leumi were offered salaries and fringe benefits far beyond the recognised scales of the Israeli banking world. It appeared that the authority for these payments was derived from a small subcommittee which had apparently not bothered to report back to the full board. When the figures were made public the board found itself in the embarrassing position of having either connived in an unacceptable arrangement or worse still, of having been kept in ignorance when they should have known. They had let down the shareholders and the public. Israel Pollak and I went to see Japhet. We pleaded with him to scale down the package. He refused.

The militant banking unions who, for years, had claimed that their members were underpaid, found themselves in a triumphant position far beyond their wildest dreams and with the public for a change on their side.

Ernst Japhet was sacked. He isolated himself in New York for a few years before returning to Israel, a tragic waste of a great talent. In July 1991, five years after the Bejski Commission, the trial was held, some 22 defendants were found guilty and punishments were meted out ranging from fines to jail sentences. Japhet's trial took place later and he, too, was found guilty. In February 1996 an appeal was heard, the main charge and the prison sentence were dropped but the fines were maintained.

Eli Hurvitz followed Ernst Japhet as Chairman with a reconstituted board. Alas, this did not last long since the press, fed with "inside information" by all kinds of aggrieved parties continued to attack all those who had been associated with the previous management. Eli, together with most senior executives such as Einhorn, Yekutieli, Buchsbaum and others were made to resign.

Eli's place was taken by Dr Meir Heth, one of the leading academics and economists in Israel, a former Chairman of the Stock Exchange and a former Supervisor of Banks on behalf of the Bank of Israel. He had an enviable reputation. His name was totally unsullied and he was a man of extreme modesty who was never heard to raise his voice. I had been friendly with the Heth family for decades since Meir Heth's father, Nachum, a Haifa lawyer, had been President and later Honorary President of World Maccabi for many years, two posts which I was to occupy in due course. Meir also became Chairman of Bank Leumi (UK) PLC.

The Chief Executive under Dr Heth was Zadik Bino, a brilliant, virtually self-taught banker of Iraqi origin. He had made a name for himself as a general manager of the small First International Bank of Israel (FIBI). Bino was the very antithesis of the Japhet philosophy. In his view banks should stick to banking only and refrain from any extra-curricular activities. He proceeded with tremendous energy to sell off the bank's interests in hotels, real estate companies, joint ventures etc. He was not in the least impressed with slogans such as "Bank Leumi – the bank of the Jewish people." What mattered was the bottom line. If there was no profit in it then public service was of no interest. His personality was so strong that without setting foot in overseas countries, his unspoken requirements were anticipated, marginal branches were closed and in England the bank took an entirely new direction. It closed the majority of its accounts with the public which caused 80 per cent of the work with perhaps 10 per cent of the profits becoming a business bank, eschewing private accounts.

Some of us had held the theory that the banks, after the battering

they had received from the public, would be given every opportunity of earning substantial monies in order to strengthen the bank
shares which the Government would ultimately wish to resell to the
public. Zadik Bino rode on the crest of the wave of predicted
profitability but with consummate timing resigned before that
particular cycle came to an end. Moshe Sanbar, a veteran economist
of Hungarian origin, became Chairman with David Friedmann as
Chief Executive.

David Efrima, the London manager, who suffered greatly under
Japhet's dominance, came into his own when Japhet retired. He now
sat on two cushions at Board Meetings which promoted him overnight from the smallest to the tallest round the table. His period of
office coincided with the property lending boom in the UK, which
resulted in unprecedented bad debts when the real estate market
collapsed.

In the early 1990s Bernard Schreier came on the scene. Born in
Vienna, he came to London after living in Israel for a few years. A
qualified engineer, he built up one of the largest private companies
in England, acquired various interests in Israel including the Sharon
Hotel and, after buying a substantial minority stake in Bank Leumi
UK and Bank Leumi Switzerland, became Deputy Chairman of the
English company. "What does he know about banking? Can he be
of any use?" I thought to myself. Very quickly I learned that we
were dealing with a remarkable personality. Quiet, polite, unostenta-
tious but with an instant grasp for essentials, he provided the
leadership with David Granot, Efrima's successor.

Having served on the board of the Bank for 17 years, I consider
that Granot was by far the most able General Manager during my
period of office which terminated on 31 December 1994 when I
reached mandatory retirement age. I enjoyed these many years
enormously. They widened my horizon and provided an intellectual
challenge of a different nature. Over the years I was responsible for
bringing personal friends and outstanding communal personalities
on to the board such as Ellis Birk, Walter Goldsmith, Jeffrey Greenwood and Bob Glatter. Sanbar and Friedman retired shortly after me
and Granot moved over to the new independent Union Bank. The
chairmanship in Israel was assumed by Eytan Raff, and Galia Maor,

a lady brimful of personality, became Managing Director. Uri Galili, an old friend from Japhet's days, became the London Managing Director. A new era had begun.

PART 3

Jerusalem

22

Into Jerusalem

WITH THREE DAUGHTERS and a growing number of grandchildren living in Jerusalem, I suppose it was inevitable that sooner or later we would gravitate there on a more permanent basis and we moved to the Herzliah Crest within a few hundred yards of the new Marina. This particular block of flats became popular with Anglo-Saxon families. Amongst those who have apartments there are Henry and Wendy Brecher, Harry and Judy Solomon, Brenda and John Katten, Rosalyn and Ian Liss, Peter and Avril Ohrenstein, the Gordon Hausmanns and for a time Stuart and Shirley Young and Michael and Gilda Levy.

"Do your little dance, Dad," the children would call out from the balcony when they saw me cross the square.

Long before Morecambe and Wise, those two immortal comedians, I had developed my own routine which anticipated their hops, skips and arms flailing as they disappeared into the sunset at the end of their act. Not being too troubled what other people thought of my eccentric conduct, I would happily comply and even occasionally get a round of applause from casual onlookers. Today this routine is reserved for one special purpose. Only too often do I see some of my grandchildren in front of their television sets watching some American-produced nonsense. "Rubbish watching time," I call out, and perform my much superior act in front of the box, blocking out the screen. They watch tolerantly, knowing that sooner rather than later the nuisance would stop. One of Noam's friends was kind enough to cheer me on: "Not bad," he said, "at least different from the usual TV garbage!"

The children were quite nostalgic leaving the apartment at the Sharon square. When we moved in some thirty years ago, the area was undeveloped. Della had arrived during a wet desolate month of March to take delivery of the furniture sent from England. She said it was one of the most depressing memories of early Herzliah outside the tourist season. The Sharon was a small family hotel nearby; the square, now a buzzing shopping centre with the ubiquitous car park, was a sandy desert.

When the flats in our block did not sell, Amidar, the Government controlled Housing Agency, put in new immigrants. They did it badly and grudgingly. The old Russian bureaucracy whose principal objective was to displease the customer, reared its ugly head.

On one particular occasion, a Russian woman, a rare immigrant in those days, came crying to us ... "Could we help?" We went over to her flat for which she was given a key by an official who had not bothered to come up with her. The place was filthy. It took us half a day to shovel out the pigeon droppings from the bath and to clean and sterilise it.

There must be many people in the world who claim Teddy Kollek as a special friend and we are amongst them. The man's charisma, his forthright approach, his calculated rudeness, his determination to get what he wants, has made him one of the most successful mayors in the world. Jerusalem is a most complicated mosaic, under the continuous scrutiny of the religious and secular world. It has Jews from 103 countries, 40 different Christian denominations and an Arab population that since 1967 has doubled under the "wicked Zionists" from 80,000 to 160,000. Teddy Kollek has turned Jerusalem from a sleepy small town into the buzzing metropolis which it is today.

On one of his visits to London in 1983 Teddy said, "Fred, I want you to do something for the Jerusalem Foundation." I was aware of the big projects which Teddy was promoting for his City and I replied, "Teddy, I am not in that class. You know of my commitments to Hillel, the Hebrew University etc. Are you sure you are talking to the right guy?"

He answered, "I know perfectly well to whom I am talking. All I want from you at this particular stage is to give me your promise when you next come to Jerusalem you will give me a ring." Little did I know that not only was this the beginning of a long and beautiful friendship but also the principal outlet of our charitable work.

A month later we were on holiday in Herzliah when Nadia telephoned to ask for our help with house-hunting.

We spent two days in Jerusalem, did not like anything we saw and returned to Herzliah. The following morning at 7 a.m. the telephone rang. It was Teddy. In true Teddy style he let fly with a number of swear words and asked what explanation I had. "You didn't keep your promise, you were in Jerusalem for two days; you never phoned me."

"How do you know all this?" I asked.

"I know everything that is going on in Jerusalem. What's your excuse?"

"I was house-hunting for my daughter, but we couldn't find anything."

"Why don't you come to me," he said.

"Teddy, I didn't realise you were an estate agent."

"It so happens that we have a broken-down ruin of a house in Yemin Moshe which belongs to the Jerusalem Foundation. The fact that the ground is made of solid gold is neither here nor there, but you can have it. In fact, I would like you to have it for your family."

Della had complained for some time that she was unhappy that every time we went to Jerusalem and stayed at the King David Hotel she was unable to act out her usual part, that is hosting her children. She did not like the idea that we were always invitees and could not reciprocate home hospitality. So, the plot in Jerusalem became a double family house which was built for Nadia and Alan with a *pied-à-terre* for the grandparents downstairs. The grandchildren absolutely adore our flat. There is a special cupboard which is full of toys for all ages. They come along, zoom in to the special cupboard and sit down and play, often together with Della who has infinite patience with putting jigsaw puzzles or building blocks together.

It is the only house in Yemin Moshe which faces the Bustan, the magnificent public park below the King David Hotel, which has recently been totally redesigned. Yemin Moshe, founded by Sir

Moses Montefiore in 1860 to induce the Jews to leave the Old City and settle outside its walls, is a quiet traffic-free enclave. It has become one of the sights of Jerusalem and during the holidays is a mecca for tourists, hence our high ivy-clad garden walls to ensure a modicum of privacy. We are surrounded by vines, bougainvillaea, orange and lemon trees. There is a small tree with fiery red flowers, our burning bush, whose name no one seems to know – the vegetation is astonishing. I spent the morning one *Erev Sukkot* helping to complete two *Sukkot* for my daughters' families, which we hung with local fruit – artichokes, avocados, passion fruit, melons, grapefruits and grapes.

Sitting in the garden that afternoon I again remembered the 12 spies who were sent out by Moses and, in spite of their fear of the locals, they reported that this was a land of milk and honey. I am seized by a feeling of utter tranquillity and contentment. The Israelis know it as "*Shalvah*", something which has become proverbial because this state of grace is so elusive. The public garden which divides the area from the King David Hotel has scores of old olive trees. I watch two Arabs – father and son – beating the olives from the trees. The son sits in the branches and gently shakes them. The father then passes him a big stick which the son uses judiciously to beat the remaining olives from the tree without damaging them. When the process is finished they move on to the next tree. The olives are then swept together, packed into plastic bags (a concession to the present time) and loaded on to the back of a camel. Jews cannot be bothered picking olives from trees. They get them from the supermarkets in jars. The Jews may have 3,000 years of learning, but the Arabs certainly have more than 3,000 years of know-how on harvesting olive trees.

In 1986, before the Intifada, the late Professor Wollins, a friend and Yemin Moshe neighbour, and I went to Bethlehem one afternoon to buy some olive wood to form the base of a sculpture of a mother and child by Jean Stein, the wife of a leading Herzliah architect, much influenced by the work of Henry Moore. We found a timber yard and saw just the piece of wood we wanted. The Arab merchant would not take any money from us. At first I thought this was the usual preliminary to a happy bargaining session, as our father Abraham had enjoyed when he bought the cave of Mach-pelah. But however insistent I was, I could not move the stubborn resistance of the owner. In exasperation I asked, "Why should you wish to make a present to me, someone you have never met before?"

He replied in stately and slow fashion, "I want to tell you something. I am a Christian Arab. During the last 20 years I have become a rich man. Under the Jordanians we Christians were oppressed. Quite frankly, we have never had it so good since the Israelis have been in charge. You must allow me to make a small gesture."

"But I am not an Israeli," I said.

"You are Jewish, aren't you? That's good enough for me."

Again, in Yemin Moshe we are not short of London friends. Our neighbours include Conrad and Ruth Morris, Ralph and Zehavah Kohn, Valerie and Alan Adler, Charles and Ruth Corman, Stanley and Carole Simmonds and Victor and Lilian Hochhauser, in addition to many American friends including Larry and Marilyn Frisch and David and Jo Morrison. David and Larry are amongst my favourite Jerusalem tennis partners.

Since 1985 we have spent about a third of our time in the Holy City with the odd few days in Herzliah. We simply find it too difficult to leave Jerusalem for family and communal reasons. Herzliah is the holiday apartment for the children's families who use it continuously, particularly during the summer months.

When we come back from Israel the inevitable question from friends and acquaintances is "did you have a good holiday?" The fact is we do not go there for holidays. We live as ordinary citizens, we work hard and often come back to London for a rest. Della has for a number of years been the Liaison Officer between British Emunah and Emunah in Israel, and is involved with the Art

Museums in Israel. I am the Chairman of the Trustees of the B'nai B'rith World Centre in Jerusalem where I work in close co-operation with Shalom Doron and its director, Alan Schneider. I am an active Governor of the Hebrew University and heavily involved in the Maccabi World Union with its headquarters in Ramat Gan, and serve on the Board of Governors of both the Pelech and Efrata Schools and I am closely connected with David Hartman's Institute.

Teddy has also made sure that we are lending a hand in his two principal extra-curricular organisations, that is the Israel Museum and the Jerusalem Foundation. We became particularly fond of the self-effacing Tamar, his loyal wife. When he approached me to help with the last municipal election, my heart told me to give him unqualified support. My head, however, whispered, "No, it's time to retire."

The heart won and Teddy lost the mayoralty. His successor, Ehud Olmert, an ambitious, charismatic politician for whom, it is said, Jerusalem is but a stepping stone for even higher office, spends much time travelling abroad. Before the election he gave me certain assurances.

"That's fine if you are elected," I said.

"Not if, but when," he replied confidently. In due course he phoned me. A note of triumph could not entirely be concealed.

"What did I tell you? Now, here's a new school I would like you to get involved in ..."

When I asked him to speak at the opening of the South American Maccabi Games in the Argentine in January 1996 he readily accepted and delivered a stirring message. Will he collect the garbage and find the time for the minutiae of the Mayor's manifold tasks? The jury is still out.

23

Ayelet Hoffmann's Address to her Class in New York: 1995

This biography is not altogether "auto". The following contribution is from my granddaughter who was 15 years old when she gave her talk. The reason why I include her sentiments in this book is because she expresses precisely, in the unspoilt tone of a teenager, my own sentiments about the mystique of Jerusalem.

As SOME OF you know, this is my first year in New York City and in Ramaz. When my parents told me that we were coming to New York, I had very mixed emotions. On the one hand, I resented having to leave my friends and home in Jerusalem. On the other hand, I appreciated the experience of spending a year in one of the greatest cities in the world. Both of these emotions were justified, but throughout this year I also realised that a year away from Israel gave me the opportunity to use the distance from my home in order to see my normal, usual, everyday life in an unusual and unique way.

I would like to speak not about the Jerusalem of books and poetry, but the Jerusalem I know.

When I first think of Jerusalem, I see faces. The faces of my friends, who I've grown up with. My next thought is of places. The little balcony in my elementary school where I sat with my friends during recess; the road which I walk at least twice a day to go to school, and to Tzofim [Scouts] – my youth group; the hundreds of steps in my neighbourhood – Yemin Moshe. Sometimes I see an image of the Laromme Hotel, or Ben-Yehuda St, but often, my first association, is of some obscure bench or patch of grass where I sat talking to a friend until 3 or 4 in the morning.

I was born in Jerusalem, and except for a year in Ann Arbor, Michigan, I grew up in Jerusalem. To me, that was Jerusalem – my home. Sure, on Yom Yerushalayim I would draw pictures of huge stone walls, and I would sing words written a quarter of a century ago, but once I was finished singing those words, Yom Yerushalayim as a special day was over.

The first time I actually remember thinking that I would probably live in Jerusalem my entire life was when I was nine years old and I returned from a family trip to Tel Aviv at the beginning of July. It was hot and clammy, and Tel Aviv was brown and withered. The beach was sticky and humid, so we stayed there only briefly, and then drove back to Jerusalem, but the ride back with the oppressive heat wasn't too pleasant either. I remember getting out of the car and feeling the cool Jerusalem wind and looking at the crisp green of the trees against the white stone. I sort of felt the tension, which I hadn't realised was there, drain out of my body, and I thought fleetingly: this is where I belong. It wasn't an actual thought, it was more like intuition, but it was there.

That same year, my class took a trip to the Chomot – a walk on the walls of the Old City. I was walking at the back of our class with a boy named Ze'evik. Now, we were only about 10 feet above the ground, but Ze'evik was extremely afraid of heights, and he crawled along the Chomah and cried hysterically. I remember sympathising with Ze'evik because I am also a little afraid of heights, but I also remember feeling even sorrier for him because he couldn't get up and look around at the beautiful view which I, too, was seeing for the first time from the walls of the Old City.

A couple of weeks ago, in Mrs Taub-Weinstein's Tenach class, I had to memorise a *pasuk* from *Yisha'yahu* [Isaiah]: "And it shall come to pass in the end of days that the mountain of Hashem's house shall be established at the top of the mountain and shall be elevated above the hills and all the nations shall flow to it."

When I read this *pasuk* my immediate association was of Shavuoth. Every year, my father wakes me up at four in the morning and we walk in the pitch black of night to the Old City. As we near the Kotel [Western Wall], and I'm just beginning to wake up, dawn is breaking, and suddenly thousands of people in white shirts and blouses can be seen approaching the Kotel. Now, I admit that often I think of the Kotel as just a stone wall which everyone makes a huge fuss about, but to see – in the light of dawn – such a huge number of Jews, is literally awesome. And feeling part of it is even more amazing. It doesn't matter if occasionally I find Judaism hard to understand, or if at times *halachah* seems irrelevant. Being together, in the light of dawn, on the ground of an historically and architecturally magnificent – and to me, even magical place – is absolute euphoria.

It lasts only a split second, and then I see a friend from school, and I'm back in the Jerusalem of everyday. But for the fifteen minutes it took for me to memorise that *pasuk*, I was wondering what Jerusalem really is – is it the magical Jerusalem which you've all heard about time after time, and which I occasionally experience, or is it a modern and prosaic Jerusalem, in which I go to school and Tzofim?

And, as can be expected, I've come to realise that it is both. In a way, many of you who visit Jerusalem only once every few years, are lucky because you get to experience the magic of Jerusalem. But in a way, Jerusalemites are even luckier, because even though they are oblivious to this magic most of the time, they experience it subconsciously, and they are part of that magic. I feel that I am the most fortunate, because when I go back to Jerusalem in a few weeks' time, I will have the best of both worlds: capturing the magic that you feel when you visit, but knowing at the same time that a part of everything I do is Jerusalem.

24

Della's Experiences During the Gulf War: February 1991

THE CRISIS IN the Gulf deepened; first the meeting between the Iraqi Foreign Minister and James Baker collapsed, then the UN's Perez de Cuellar and Saddam Hussein failed to reach agreement. A gut feeling that had been slowly welling up suddenly hardened. Since my children refused to leave Israel in its time of trouble, I had to be with them to give whatever help I could and to show my solidarity with the State. I had planned to go to Israel anyway whilst Fred was skiing in Switzerland but on the Monday before the start of the War I made up my mind at 8.30 a.m. to go immediately. By 9.30 I was on my way to the airport.

It was indeed touching to see the lift of morale and warm welcome my arrival produced, not only amongst the family but also amongst the wide circle of their friends. I knew absolutely that I was in the right place at the right time. A blessed feeling that I don't think I had often experienced came over me.

I was soon fitted out with my gas mask by courtesy of our Chief Rabbi elect Dr Jonathan Sacks, who kindly picked it up for me. He was spending a six months Sabbatical in Jerusalem and was staying around the corner in Yemin Moshe. His children went to school with our grandchildren.

I seemed to develop a hunch when trouble was brewing and was not surprised when I turned on the radio in the early hours of Tuesday morning, to hear reports of the first bombing. The War had started. There were many disturbed nights. I always slept at one of my daughters' houses. Once I was caught on my own when the sirens went and that was quite scary. Anyway, I wanted to help out with the grandchildren. Of course there were some tears at first. There were difficulties with putting gas masks on the little ones who had just been woken from a deep sleep. Caroline had particular trouble with her two-and-a-half-year-old daughter. At times they had to fight with her to get her into the special plastic gas-proof crib. She was terrified of these "strange creatures" with gas masks, trying to push her into something awful.

It is hard to describe the relief throughout the whole country when the anti-missile Patriots arrived and then when the warning time for missiles to land was increased from 90 seconds to five minutes. We soon learned that Jerusalem was relatively safe. Nevertheless, there was always a scramble to get into the sealed room in case Iraq's aim was not too good. There was the tensing up as one listened for a bang, then the relaxation as one realised that it was not in our area, and then the further relief when one heard it had only been a conventional warhead and not a chemical one!

Relativity thus can change one's perceptions. I thought of bombing during the Second World War and remembered that we *only* had to fear the possibility of a mustard gas attack and not the horrific array of chemical weapons that are now available. We were given a special information book about these with such chilling details as "some gases are odourless and cannot be seen, so keep a lookout for signs of birds and animals dying all over the place"!

Anyway, we soon got used to spending time in our sealed rooms and the sight of eight-year-old grandchildren engrossed in the fantasies of C.S. Lewis' Narnia books and turning the pages with the gas mask extension of their nose I will never forget. The kids easily beat me at "memory game". I can tell you, it's not so easy to concentrate through your mask, crouched under the bathroom basin – the only free space – while wondering what was going on outside!

The days were trying because the children could not go to school, could not go outside much because parents were reluctant to let them go further than a few yards in case of an alert, and then the much-needed rain came pouring down turning everything into mudbaths. Rain is scarce in Israel so they do not provide proper drainage but I think the Almighty planned this rain in order to dilute the poisons if they came. But did He have to send the burnt out remnants of a Soviet satellite on to the outskirts of Jerusalem, making that one of the many nights with three alerts?

I was impressed with the way Nadia, Hilary, Caroline and their husbands handled the situation and calmed the fears of the children. They discerned their unspoken worries and discussed them. Thus Alan was aware that five-year-old Matan thought that Israel was going to lose the War, so he sat down and explained how strong Israel's forces were, how she had never lost a war, and how this time so many other countries were trying to keep the War away from Israel and so on.

I was touched the way the grandchildren expressed their relief and pleasure that I was sleeping with them. They made sure I was comfortable in the sealed room and they helped me with the mask. They were the best experts because they had been well drilled in school.

One day there was an early alarm at 6 p.m. We had become blasé. Until then everyone had returned home by nightfall but that afternoon Nadia and the boys were swimming and Alan was at a meeting. Eleven-year-old Ayelet phoned down to me in my flat to ask if I had heard the siren. When I realised she was alone I whizzed upstairs to find her calmly sealing the room with the usual tape and wet towels. She later confided to her mother, "I was only checking if Grandma was okay. I wasn't worried. I didn't need help."

Claire Kevehazi had come to stay with Hilary because Jerusalem was supposed to be safer than Tel Aviv. Michael and Gene in Givatayim had sustained quite a lot of damage – windows, walls, furnishings etc. Ruth and Barry Fluss in Haifa also had windows blown out. Claire was a great morale booster, always busy helping with household tasks and full of stories and jokes.

"*Tehillim*" is the Hebrew for Psalms and "*Tillim*" is the Hebrew for missiles. During one alert when everyone was glued to the radio and there was much talk of "*Tillim*", one woman who could not understand Hebrew well shouted, "Be quiet everyone, things must be serious, I think they are suggesting on the radio that we should all say *Tehillim!*"

Instead of the traditional Yom Kippur greeting of "*Gemar Chatima Tova*" (May you be sealed in the Book of Life), people were saying "*Gemar Atima Tova*" (May you be sealed safely in your room.)

Ben-Gurion never managed to get Israelis to flock to the Negev but Saddam Hussein did!

One afternoon I was umpiring a football match between my grandchildren when a dispute broke out between players. I called out, "Carry on, that was just a misunderstanding." They looked at me in horror. "We thought you said that was a missile landing!"

Israeli society is really geared up to help the children. The morning after the first alert the TV announcer said, "Well, that was quite a night," and the whole country collectively giggled. Then he said, "Let's do some keep fit to relax. What's that, you little one in the corner? Too tired? Could you manage to move just your little finger?" And so the whole country started with the little finger and progressed from there. They had wonderful discussion programmes with children as panellists, top brass and politicians answering their queries and psychologists calming their anxieties. I was also impressed how, during the first two weeks whilst the children were confined to home, kindergarten teachers made a point of visiting all their pupils at least once in their own homes.

I'll conclude with some thoughts. I pondered about the old problem of Jews in the Diaspora on dual loyalties. I rushed out to Israel as soon as trouble appeared on the horizon but whilst there my family often laughed at me because whenever various Gulf spokesmen were interviewed on TV I always stood up for the British. "Aren't they the best? How I like their stiff upper lip and their British understatement." I could not reconcile myself to the excitable American and Israeli TV compared to the quiet professionalism of British TV and radio I am used to.

Fred joined us during the last week of the War. He was a very bad example to the children by not putting on his gas mask. He said that since he had a choice he preferred to rely on the incompetence of Saddam Hussein's long distance aim to the certainty of half suffocating in his gas mask. He was duly barred from the "safe room" for which he was deeply grateful. He, at least, got a proper night's sleep! By that time, anyway, the danger had passed. Saddam Hussein had shot his bolt.

25

The Jerusalem Foundation, the Israel Museum and the Cochin Synagogue

TEDDY KOLLEK FATHERED both the Jerusalem Foundation and the Israel Museum which have proved equally brilliant concepts. The Jerusalem Foundation made it possible to carry out projects which were far beyond the capacity or even the dreams of the small impoverished town which Jerusalem was when Teddy became Mayor. The $400 million raised during the last 30 years for 1,400 projects transformed the face of the city and made it into the blooming metropolis that it has become, with its many parks and play areas for children, its cultural establishments, sports and recreation areas, health centres for Jews and Arabs, etc.

Under the directorship of Ruth Cheshin, assisted by her principal lieutenants, Alan Freeman, Yossi Fisher and Jane Biran, the Foundation remains an independent charity. The ubiquitous Harry Sapir lends gravitas to the finance committees of the Jerusalem Foundation, Israel Museum and Hebrew University. Amongst leading London activists are Alex Bernstein, Lord (George) Weidenfeld, Martin Paisner and, most importantly, Vivien Duffield. Vivien has carved herself a unique reputation both in London and Jerusalem. The Clore Galleries and the redevelopment of the Covent Garden Opera House in which she played a leading part are amongst her London contributions, whilst in Jerusalem the Clore/Duffield Foundations have financed important projects including the Teddy Stadium and the Citadel Museum of the History of Jerusalem.

Della and I have been actively involved for many years. In April 1992 we were awarded the Jerusalem Medal "for unceasing support of Jerusalem". This medal was created by Jacques Lipchitz for "Benefactors of the Holy City". It depicts Samson struggling with the lion seen against the background of the Western Wall of the Temple with the palm tree symbolising Judah. The reverse features a menorah with the Hebrew words for "Pray for the peace of Jerusalem" (Psalms 122 v 6).

The founding of the Israel Museum in 1965 was an act of enormous courage. People at the time thought that Teddy was out of his mind. Israel was in great financial difficulties; every public organisation was desperately short of cash and Teddy decided that Jerusalem needed a museum. He said, "My friends tell me one should not build a museum in times of crisis. On that basis the museum will never be built."

Most people now recognise that even allowing for Teddy's optimism, what has been achieved in the last three decades is absolutely phenomenal. His museum in Jerusalem is recognised as one of the greatest in the world, and unlike Tel Aviv which is basically an arts museum (founded in 1932 by Mayor Dizengoff), it is a multi-layered phenomenon ranging from archaeology, ethnography, ancient and modern art, numismatics and its youth wing with its hands-on facilities for children, to the famous Nogucci sculpture garden and the Shrine of the Book.

The organisation, known as the British Friends of the Art Museums of Israel, was started in 1966. Its progenitors were Alex Margulies, Doris Morrison and Pierre Gildesgame. When Pierre assumed the Chairmanship in 1968 he invited Della to join his committee. She has been a member ever since and over the years has involved me in the Museum's manifold activities. It has become very close to our hearts.

In 1993 the Israel Museum held an important Rembrandt exhibition which included the famous painting of Moses holding the two tablets of the decalogue. Next to the painting was a notice stating that it was not clear whether Rembrandt had painted the first set of tablets, which were smashed by Moses when he saw the children of Israel dancing round the golden calf, or whether these were the second set. I said to Yitzhak Rogow of the Israel Museum who showed me round, "I don't see the problem. The tablets are clearly the first ones, which he is about to smash."

"How do you know that?" he asked.

"Because there is a very slight variation between the wording of the first and second tablets. You can read the text very clearly [in Hebrew]: 'Thou shalt not bear witness against your neighbour with an outright lie' – 'B'eid shoker', whereas on the second tablets it says 'B'eid shove.' Shove is a more subtle way of misleading people; it is not an outright lie; there is a fine nuance between the two words."

"Are you sure of your facts?" he asked. "Let's go and find a Chumash." And so off we went to his office to examine the Pentateuch. We looked at Exodus ch. 20, v. 17 – and then at Deuteronomy ch. 5, v. 18, and saw the variation in the text.

"Eureka, you have given us the answer." A happy Yitzhak went to the intercom to spread the news amongst his colleagues that Moses' tablets were not identical and that the notice beside the picture could now be updated.

The conclusion – experts in one field may be naive in another.

In 1994, in an impressive ceremony, Della and I were made Honorary Fellows of the Museum. The platform party consisted of Dan Meridor, Ayalla Sacks-Abramov and Michael and Judy Steinhardt. Teddy introduced us and Lady Sieff, the present Chairperson of the British Friends who became a Fellow in the following year, read the citation. It says so many wonderful things about us that I am reluctant to publish it here. Other recipients of the Honorary Fellowship at the time were my old and valued friend Yekutiel (Xyl)

Federman, the owner of the Dan Hotel Group who was my Habonim *chaver* 60 years earlier and Arturo Schwartz, the famous Italian art collector and benefactor. An earlier "Honoree" was Romie Shapiro who, together with his wife Blanche, devoted himself to the Museum and added the chairmanship of the Bezalel Academy of Arts to his communal portfolio.

The Cochin Synagogue became our principal contribution to the Museum. In 1990 when Della and I were celebrating three family anniversaries, we asked Teddy Kollek what we could do for the Israel Museum.

He replied, "I would like to pray in a Cochin Synagogue."

"*Bevakashah* – be my guest," I said. "When are you going to India?"

"No, no," he said, "not in India, I want the synagogue to be brought to Jerusalem."

Teddy's pipedreams are usually translated into reality. Today, the Kadavumbagam synagogue stands proudly in the Israel Museum. It was dismantled in Cochin by experts. All its component parts, particularly the magnificent wooden ceiling, were numbered and the wood was dried out in a special kiln that was built near the Shrine of the Book in the Museum complex, since Jerusalem weather conditions are very different from the monsoon climate in south-west India. It was the first time in the 30-year-history of the Israel Museum that the roof was raised to accommodate a permanent exhibit.

The origins of the Jews in the Cochin area on the Malabar coast go back some 2,000 years. It is said there were Jewish communities there, possibly before the arrival of the first Christians, and certainly before the fourth century. There were well-settled communities in the eleventh century when the famous Jewish copper plates, which are now stored in the Paradesi synagogue, were produced, spelling out special rights for the Jews.

The Cochin Jews were divided into three categories: the white Jews who came from Europe and western Asia, the black Jews referred to as slaves who were converts, who originated from the indigenous population, and the *Meshuhrarim*, their descendants who were formally freed by their white masters, often because they had inter-married and produced brown children. In 1505 when the influx of Spanish and Portuguese Jews fleeing from the Inquisition began, one Francisco Pinhero brought Torah scrolls and other Jewish books to Cochin.

In 1540 an anonymous applicant wrote a letter to one of the leading rabbis of the time, Rabbi David ben Solomon ibn abi Zimra who resided at Cairo.

An enquiry has been made from India from the island of Cochin where there are about nine hundred heads of households. Of these one hundred are Jews by origin and of (Jewish) stock, and they are meyuhhasin (Jews of attested Jewish pedigree). The rest are descendants of male and female slaves, and they are rich and devout and charitable. The meyuhhasin do not intermarry with them and call them slaves, and on this account they have contention and quarrels without end. Among these rich persons are some who are called partial slaves. Some are (descendants of) Jewish traders who came there from the land of Turkey and from the land of Aden and from Germany and Caucasia, and they brought female slaves and begot from them sons and daughters and manumitted them because they had borne them (children) or because they were satisfied with them and their service; they manumitted them in their land with the status of Jews. Others did not manumit them, but when they went away the slaves fled; the master, in order not to be delayed from his journey, had paid no heed, and had left him and gone – and after the master had gone, (the slave) remained with the status of Jew with the others and there is no one who would rebuke him, and he remained on his own.

Unfortunately, just as in the twentieth century, when Hitler and his armies pursued Jews who had fled from Germany into neighbouring countries, so the Portuguese, after having expelled their Jewish population, conquered the south-west coast of India in 1498, introduced a milder version of the Inquisition and remained there for 170 years. The local princes, however, were friendly to the Jews who had proved useful citizens with international trading connections. They enriched the area where sophisticated merchants were conspicuous by their absence.

The Rajah of Cochin proved particularly helpful. In 1525 he made the generous gesture of donating the land adjacent to his palace to the Jews, and over the next 100 years, three synagogues were built on this land later called Jew Town. He also appointed the leader of the Jews as their official spokesman under the title of Mudaliar. The first of these was Baruch Joseph Levy, a white Jew who nevertheless felt impelled to build a special synagogue for the black Jews, and that indeed is our Kadavumbagam synagogue which was completed in 1544. His son, Joseph Levy, built the magnificent Paradesi synagogue immediately adjacent to the Rajah's Palace. This elaborate building, exclusively earmarked for white Jews, still stands today in Cochin and has become, rather like the Prague Altneushul, a great tourist attraction. The 400th anniversary of the foundation of the Paradesi synagogue was celebrated in Cochin in 1968. The then Prime Minister of India, Mrs Indira Gandhi attended.

It must be understood that the synagogues of south-west India were not the large edifices put up in many European countries which would have horrified the Cochin Jews. Their synagogues were for the extended family and rarely had accommodation for more than 80 people.

By 1663 the Dutch became the masters of south-west India and the next 125 years were truly a golden era for Cochin and its Jews but the relationship between the white and the black Jews remained a tenous one. There were clearly defined rights beyond which the black Jews dared not aspire. For example, there was free mixing on Simchat Torah, but a black Jew could not be called up at the Paradesi synagogue.

In the 1950s the bulk of the Cochin Jews emigrated to Israel where they joined kibbutzim and moshavim, mostly in Galilee and the Negev.

Cochin Jewry was dominated for 50 years by one Satto (Shabtai) Koder, an immensely wealthy man whose hospitality and generosity became renowned. He was the Kadoori equivalent of Cochin. Just as the Kadoori Family in Hong Kong owned the ferry and the electricity corporation, so the Koder family in Cochin owned the ferry and the electricity corporation. I knew the Kadooris having been their dinner guest in Hong Kong as early as the 1960s.

Our daughter Hilary, who visited Cochin on her honeymoon, recalls with awe and affection the magnificent reception which they had for the whole of the *Pesach* period in the Koder household with its many servants and its very strict observation of the laws of *kashrut*. Since there were none of the usual Jewish shops which our New York or London households take for granted, the Koder family prepared for *Pesach* three months beforehand.

Professor Ben Segal, the eminent historian, who has written a book about Cochin, told me that when some 20 years ago he travelled to India, Lord Mountbatten, the last Viceroy of India, said to him "If you are going to Cochin, don't forget to give my best regards to Satto Koder."

Koder died in 1994 from diabetes. His daughter Queenie and her husband Sammy Hallegua still live in Jew Town.

There was a wonderful atmosphere of celebration and excitement at the formal opening of the synagogue in the Israel Museum in June 1995 at which 400 Indian Jews from Bombay and Cochin participated. The staff of the Museum said that they could not recall any other occasion when there was such an electric atmosphere. Satto Koder's nephews, Sammy and Napa, who live in Israel attended the occasion.

Our Indian friends sang, danced and performed some ritual rhythmic movements – all wonderfully evocative. When they actually saw the synagogue some burst into tears. It was not just a homecoming for them but it was a far more splendid interior than they remembered.

When Della and I first saw the beams, slats and doors some four years ago before they were acclimatised to the Jerusalem air, we were very disappointed. We wondered quietly whether it had been worthwhile going to the expense of importing what seemed to be dirty pieces of wood all the way from India. Apparently it was the custom to whitewash the interior of the synagogue every *Pesach*. The whitewash, under the grime and dirt produced by the subsequent commercial activities when the synagogue was used as a warehouse, gave it a most disappointing appearance.

Its phoenix-like resurrection and restoration is due entirely to the experts at the Israel Museum whose X-ray equipment had disclosed the magnificent colours and designs last seen in their pristine beauty perhaps one hundred years ago. Inch by inch the colours were restored by experts who spent 10,000 hours on this labour of love. The present generation of Cochinis saw a synagogue in Jerusalem in which they had prayed in Cochin but which had improved so miraculously that it seemed that they had God's special approval for the move. An important symbol of a once remote and now defunct community has found a permanent place of honour in Jerusalem, a fate which its founders in 1544 would not have imagined in their fondest dreams.

In addressing the Indian Ambassador, who participated enthusiastically in the opening festivities, I said, "When, on our festivals, we recite "Hallel", a song of praise for the Lord, we sing: *Hodu Lashem Ki Tov*. Perhaps the far-seeing composer of this encomium wanted to give thanks not only to the Lord, but also to India." "*Hodu*" is the Hebrew word for India. It also means "Praise (the Lord)." The quoted sentence can have a double meaning: "Praise the Lord for he is good" or "India is the Lord's for it is good"! (and has always been to the Jews).

In 1995 we helped to bring over the artefacts of another disused synagogue in neighbouring Parur and the magnificently carved Torah ark, bimah and Eliahu's chair were formally consecrated in June 1996. Three metres high and five metres wide, the ark is dated 1891, although parts of it were taken from an older design. It is replete with Jewish symbols – there is a vision of the prophet Zachariah, a menorah with two olive trees on either side, dripping on to the seven branches of the menorah, and elaborate Hebrew inscriptions carved by master-craftsmen whose skills, sadly, have long since died. The synagogue is now complete.

In December we visited Cochin, the Paradesi Synagogue and Queenie and Sammy Hallegua. We had tea at their house which is situated in Jew Town, between the Paradesi Synagogue and the Rajah's Palace. If we expected the same warm reception which we had from our Cochini friends in Israel, we were soon to be disillusioned. Sammy Hallegua is the uncrowned king of the remaining 20 Jews in Cochin. He is a powerful personality, fluent, persuasive with an intellectual's forehead and with uncompromising views. "The money you gave should have been spent locally for the preservation of our heritage."

"Are you suggesting," I asked "that the interior of the Kadavumbagam Synagogue, which had deteriorated into a dirty warehouse, should not have been transferred to Jerusalem? Are you aware of the intense pride which 2,500 Cochinis in Israel have felt in their ethnic identification, which has been crystallised for the first time since their immigration, by the relocation of the Synagogue within the Israel Museum?"

"I am not in the least interested what they think in Israel – what I do object to is your additional acquisition of the bimah, aron and furniture of the Parur Synagogue."

"You do not think that a properly furnished synagogue, seen by many thousands every year, will do more for the history of Cochin's Jews than a small relic in Parur, which few people visit?"

"No, I do not," he stated firmly.

"Where are your children?" I asked. "In America," he replied.

"Will they come back to Cochin?" "No, definitely not!"

I persisted in my questioning. "Who pays for the upkeep of the magnificent Paradesi Synagogue?"

"Our community – you saw what a terrible job the authorities are making of preserving the Indian heritage when you visited the Rajah's Palace. We prefer to do it ourselves."

Indeed, I had expressed my shocked reaction earlier at the neglected state of the Palace and its gardens, which looked like a garbage collection area.

". . . and how much longer can the community survive?"

Aye, there's the rub.

Della mentioned to Sammy that we had recently visited Nevatim, near Beersheva, where a considerable number of Cochini Jews had settled successfully. They had built themselves a synagogue which reflected both their original Indian heritage and contemporary Israeli architecture. Next to the synagogue they had created their own little museum. Just as the children of Israel had responded in the desert to the appeal to make contributions in cash and in kind to the new portable Tabernacle, so the Cochini Jews from all over Israel brought forth ancient artefacts and lamps, gold-laced garments, scrolls and various religious appurtenances. Shmuel Kadmon, Council Mayor of the Greater Beersheva district, together with our host, Yizhak Elihu who had welcomed us, were immensely proud of their achievements. Shmuel Kadmon said that this Indian Heritage Centre, would become the nucleus of the local authority's drive to attract more tourists to the Negev.

Sammy and Queenie listened attentively and liked our suggestion that the Israel Museum should sell double tickets for admission both to the museum in Jerusalem and to Nevatim. They agreed that the commemoration of the long and distinguished history of Cochin Jewry was now assured. We parted as friends. But who will take care of the Paradesi Synagogue in the next generation? Unless some special "Friends" organisation can be formed on an international basis, it will suffer the fate of the adjacent Rajah's Palace.

Our nostalgia for Cochin does not include one particular telephone call. We had travelled by ship from Bombay. I waited especially until we landed in Cochin before making local calls. There was a telephone kiosk on the harbourfront with a lady attendant. I made a couple of calls, costing together 50 cents (US).

The following morning Della phoned Sammy Hallegua from the ship and had a friendly chat with him. It cost $135! The fact that we were anchored within a mile of the recipient of the phone call was irrelevant. The signal was beamed to the satellite first and that's a luxury to be avoided if possible. There should be a hazard warning next to a ship's phone!

26

The Hebrew University of Jerusalem

THE HEBREW UNIVERSITY was officially opened on a barren hillside of Mount Scopus in 1925. Lord Balfour, he of the 1917 Declaration, delivered the inaugural address. In 1954 the Givat Ram campus was created.

Until 1967 the University was cut off from West Jerusalem but after the Six Day War when Jerusalem was reunited, Mount Scopus returned to normality. In 1971 the Rothberg School for Overseas Students was opened. The ageless, dynamic Sam Rothberg, who has collected millions for the University, is still actively involved. The University operates from four campuses, with 23,700 students, 1,400 faculty members, 12 libraries and a $285 million budget which represents an ever-increasing challenge to Hanoch Gutfreund, the eclectic President and his financial advisers.

The International Board of Governors meets annually in addition to which there are periodic meetings of various sub-committees. I see my principal role on the Board as one of stressing the Jewish content of the "University of the Jewish people", in laying greater emphasis on Jewish studies, in attracting more students with *kippot* and in allocating more resources for these seminal activities.

The British Friends of the Hebrew University of Jerusalem is one of the largest fund-raising organisations within the ambit of Anglo-Jewry. During the years of my involvement its chairmen have included Professor Albert Neuberger, Ellis Birk, John Sacher and Michael Gee. Since Stephen Goldman was appointed Chief Executive ever increasing amounts have been sent to Jerusalem, culminating in £4.3 million during the 1995 calendar year.

I chair the Students and Academic Committee; our principal aim is to send students from the UK on a variety of courses to the Hebrew University. I am blessed with excellent committee colleagues i.e. Judy and Judge Clive Callman, Lady Mary Marre, Kenneth Alberman, the Chairman of the Union of Jewish Students and a changing team of academics. Michael Barnett, our professional Student Affairs Co-ordinator, visits Jewish and non-Jewish schools regularly to enlist participants for our various study courses. There is an arrangement between a number of British universities and the Hebrew University whereby the third year of a BA degree in certain Jewish subjects is spent in Jerusalem partly financed by the British university. The extent of our activities is largely dictated by the availability of scholarship funds. A five-months' course, known as the British Australian Summer Programme, in the gap years between "A" levels and university, involves an outlay of $8,000 and for a full-year course $12,000 are needed for fees and living expenses – sums which cannot readily be found by many parents. This remains an ever-growing challenge.

The Hebrew University has more out-of-town students than any other university in Israel. Its 7,000 beds in a variety of dormitories include accommodation which was obsolete 20 years ago and almost double that number is required. This is why in 1990 Della and I built state of the art dormitories which, alas, fill only part of the yawning gap.

At the end of 1995 Della and I provided the money for the acquisition of a remarkable work of art with which we can whole-heartedly identify. It is a sculptured bimah, some 4 metres high, by Hadass Ophrat. The bimah seems to float ethereally above its stepped base and was inspired by the famous Abuhav Bimah of Safed with its mystical connotations. We are adding a *Ner Tamid* – an everlasting light. To be associated with this imaginative project gives us particular pleasure because it is another symbol of the university's increasing interest in traditional Judaism. The bimah will be on permanent exhibition outside the Hecht Synagogue over-looking the Old City – it has been dedicated to the memory of Yitzhak Rabin.

27

Efrata and Pelech Schools

Lest anyone thinks that the problems of Jewish education are confined to the Diaspora, and that the residents of Israel are well catered for, that their children will have Jewish identity stamped upon them not only by the mere fact that they were born in Israel, but through the education they receive then I am afraid that they will be faced with considerable disappointment.

One of the basic problems with Israeli education is that the system is divided into two streams, the secular and the religious. Quite frankly, I cannot happily identify with either. The secular stream has put *Yahadut*, that is the identification and knowledge of our Jewish heritage, to one side. The Bible is looked upon as an unreliable guide book full of legends of mythical ancestors.

The religious stream, on the other hand, has been captured by the right wing. Teachers who more often than not come from the Yeshivoth do not as a rule confine their instructions to the religious angle but subtly introduce politics so that children who are poured into one of the two streams are – dare I say it – brainwashed from a relatively early age. What is missing is Maimonides' classical middle – the much-despised central Orthodoxy. It was, therefore, with considerable pleasure that we discovered the Efrata school in Baka, until recently a rather deprived area of Jerusalem next to the German colony.

The Efrata primary school was founded by Anglo-Saxons. It is nominally affiliated to the religious stream but follows its own programme. Its educational direction can be compared with that of the United Synagogue in England. Pupils are accepted from non-religious homes; parents are involved in the syllabus and they took it upon themselves to keep the school going whilst there was a mandatory teachers' strike in the early 1990s.

One of the interesting side effects of the Efrata school is that Baka became a highly desirable residential area. Upwardly mobile young couples gravitated there and property prices rose steeply simply because parents wanted to send their children to Efrata which, being Government subsidised, had to confine its intake from the local area only. I am happy to say that six of our grandchildren are or were pupils of Efrata and this is one of the reasons why we became closely involved with it.

Another school which is quite outstanding is Pelech, a High School for modern Orthodox girls. It was founded in 1965. Ten years later the redoubtable Alice Shalvi became its principal and for over a decade the school gained the highly coveted title of an Experimental High School which is the equivalent of three Michelin stars for a restaurant. It is recognised today to be one of the best girls' schools in the country. Its curriculum, teaching and management are all geared towards educating the girls to total commitment to Judaism, whilst at the same time inculcating tolerance, openness and respect for the pluralism of Israel's modern society. The girls are expected to do army service and often distinguish themselves in various élite units.

Pelech is a comparatively small school with 220 pupils. It is operating as a pedagogical laboratory which has succeeded in demonstrating the compatibility of modern Judaism with the traditions of the Talmud and the *halachah*. A course was established some three years ago entitled "Education for Work". This introduces pupils to science-based industry and research institutions which are vital for the development of Israel's economy.

Whilst the overall objectives of North London Collegiate and Pelech are not dissimilar, their physical facilities could not present a greater contrast: North London Collegiate, set in its acres of magnificent green belt country, with its stately buildings, laboratories and covered swimming pool representing the best of the public schools on the one hand, and Pelech, in a worn-out residential house with few basic facilities at the other extreme.

Because of the acute shortage of space, Pelech girls are also taught on a balcony which is covered with corrugated iron. In summer it is unbearably hot and in winter the rain drums on the roof. One can only admire the girls who are able to concentrate under those very trying conditions.

After some years, Efrata became the victim of its own success. Classes which hopefully should have been limited to no more than 20 to 25 children, grew to 30 and it became essential that the school be expanded. I was approached by the Parents' Committee to see whether I could be of assistance. At that time, in 1987, Yitzhak Navon, the former President, who was a particularly dear and close friend, was the Minister of Education and Culture. He explained that much as he would like to help, there was a desperate shortage of school facilities throughout the country and particularly in the Jerusalem area. The only way to deal with the Efrata problem was if outside financial help could be provided. I asked him whether he would be good enough to chair a meeting of the various interested parties at which I would endeavour to promote the idea on the basis that finance would be found.

And so a series of meetings took place in Mr Navon's office which were attended by representatives of the Ministry of Education, the Municipality, the Parents' Committee and the heads of the three schools who had either a direct or potential interest in the campus. The Pelech school had secured a small foothold on the Efrata campus with the building of some laboratories. A large building was occupied by Nitzanim school for handicapped children and of course there was the Efrata school itself. After long and difficult negotiations we came to the following conclusion: The Ministry of Education together with the Municipality would provide a new building for Nitzanim; the building used by Nitzanim would become the new campus building for Pelech – a fantastic upgrading of their facilities – and a new wing would be added to Efrata.

In 1990 Della and I celebrated what we called our 170th anniversary; Della was 60, I was 70 and we had been married for 40 years. We wanted to mark the occasion by special contributions to four Jerusalem establishments which were particularly close to our hearts. We took financial responsibility for the Efrata expansion and for moving Pelech into its new building after upgrading it to their requirements; we built dormitories which were desperately needed by the Hebrew University and we agreed to bring over the synagogue from Cochin.

By the end of 1995, the extension to Efrata had been in use for three years and we have added the Gildesgame Playing Fields. This particular campus is one of the most attractive in Jerusalem and hopefully, in 1997, the move of Pelech will take place.

The present Headmistress of the Pelech School is Shirah Breuer. Her husband is from the famous Breuer family, an evocative name in the annals of traditional Orthodox Jewish education particularly for those who, like me, were educated at the Breuer (Samson Raphael Hirsch) school. I believe that my Old Frankfurt mentors would have approved.

28

The B'nai B'rith Bridge

IN THE SPRING of 1987 Teddy Kollek rang me at our house in Yemin Moshe. "Fred, I want you to come over right away. I have something which I think will be of great interest to you."

"What is it, Teddy, can you give me a clue?"

"Yes," he said, "I think I have found a site for the B'nai B'rith World Centre that you have been looking for."

B'nai B'rith has had offices in Jerusalem which were established in 1980. It was a symbolic gesture of this world-wide Order in its identification with King David's City as the undivided capital of the Jewish people.

This was a critical time in the history of B'nai B'rith; numbers were declining, its influence was beginning to wane. A major centre in Jerusalem with exhibition, teaching and training facilities could re-establish B'nai B'rith as the world's leading Jewish membership organisation.

I asked Teddy whether it would be all right to bring Avigdor Warsha with me. At the time Avigdor was the Executive Director of the BBWC. Teddy showed us a map of the cultural mile which starts at the Jaffa Gate and travels down the Hebron Road along Yemin Moshe past the Sultan's Pool, the Arts and Crafts Centre and the Scottish Church. Immediately below the Scottish Church is a large area which the Rothschild Foundation was going to build on but had decided against it – this was the plot that had now become available. Teddy pointed out that it was possibly the finest site in Jerusalem, overlooking the walls of the Old City, and an opportunity which would not come again.

I put the proposal before our colleagues in Washington and Gerry Kraft, the International President, flew over to Jerusalem to get personally involved. He was enthusiastic about the idea. "Look Fred," he said, "I am an expert in building; I have put up lots of shopping centres in the United States, this is my cup of tea, leave it with me."

Gerry sat in his suite at the Hilton with the architects from early in the morning until late in the evening discussing plans in their minutest details. Fund-raising was to be undertaken by the tried and tested veteran, Jack Spitzer. My recommendation was that a building costing no more than $3 million should be erected, that a similar sum should be set aside for an endowment fund to secure the future of the centre, and that fund-raising should start immediately. Gerry seemed confident that these monies could be found by B'nai B'rith on a world-wide basis. I reminded him from time to time during the lengthy months whilst the plans were being studied and submitted to the Municipality that prompt action should be taken, but then Gerry's father died, his term of office came to an end and he withdrew from the project. I think the reason he had lost interest was because the estimated building costs had crept up to $9 million, a figure that was completely out of our reach.

Gerry Kraft was succeeded by Seymour Reich as International President. This period happened to coincide with the stock market collapse and the great property crisis. Seymour said to me fairly and squarely, "There is no way we can set aside funds from B'nai B'rith – funds that we haven't got, and unless you can get the monies together we will have to forget about the whole scheme."

I made it perfectly clear that I was not an international fund-raiser and that if the intrepid Jack Spitzer could not do it, nobody else could. Jack, by that time, had actually received promises for something like $3 million but that sum was now totally inadequate.

Teddy Kollek, watching from the sidelines, said "Am I going to be disappointed by B'nai B'rith?"

Teddy, Seymour Reich, Avigdor Warsha and I met at the Hilton Hotel and Teddy said, "Before we go any further I would like to get an undertaking from you to give the Municipality a planning gain. By planning gain, I mean the building of a bridge across the Hebron

Road." (The Hebron Road is one of the busiest and most dangerous roads in Jerusalem. It separates Yemin Moshe on the one side from the Cinémathèque on the other side, and one takes one's life in one's hands when crossing it.) The cost of the bridge would be $300,000.

Seymour Reich said, "Completely out of the question, we have not got the money and we are not going ahead with the project in any case."

I felt that here was an opportunity of redeeming the good name of B'nai B'rith, in the full realisation that the major building project was going to be aborted.

I said to Teddy, "The bridge will be built."

Seymour glared at me and said, "Have you gone out of your mind, Fred?"

"No Seymour, the bridge will be built."

"Excuse me, gentlemen, could I just have a private word with Fred?" asked Seymour.

He took me outside, "Unless you take personal responsibility for the bridge, I want you to call it off here and now because we are not going to support you from Washington."

I replied, "I will take personal responsibility provided that I can use the special fund which we set aside from the Japhet Award Dinner, which should cover some of the cost. The rest I guarantee."

The bridge today is a magnificent structure which soars high over the Hebron Road, has steps and ramps for prams and wheelchairs and – most important of all – bears a large legend "The B'nai B'rith Bridge". At its formal opening ceremony, wet cement was laid out at the Yemin Moshe end into which Teddy, Helen Reich (Seymour's wife who tragically has since passed away), Jack Spitzer, Joseph Domberger, Murray Shusterman and I impressed our hands. Teddy gave me a large photograph on the back of which was written – "To Fred Worms, without whom this bridge would not have been built".

29

Jerusalem's Supreme Court Building

DOROTHY (DOLLY) DE ROTHSCHILD ran the family Endowment Fund – Yad Hanadiv – with a firm hand. The Fund had financed the building of the Knesset, the Open University of Israel and a variety of other splendid and imaginative causes. In 1984 she sent a four-page handwritten letter to Prime Minister Shimon Peres setting out her thoughts on the construction of a new Supreme Court Building and offered to finance it. She quoted Isaiah 1: 26 "And I will restore your judges as at first, and your counsellors as at the beginning. Afterwards, Jerusalem shall be called the city of righteousness and a faithful city."

We had met this remarkable and energetic lady through her connections as Patron/President of the B'nai B'rith Stepney Community Centre. She seemed to us the epitome of the *grande dame*, a lady who knew her mind, who did not suffer fools gladly, a perfectionist who expected results. Della and I were amazed when Miriam Rothschild wrote to us that as long as Dolly's husband, the redoubtable James, was alive she rarely opened her mouth and played the part of the dutiful wife. They had no children.

Alas, she died before the Supreme Court was completed. She left £98 million to her favourite relative, Jacob (Lord) Rothschild, who became Chairman of the Trustees of Yad Hanadiv. In the summer of 1992 Jacob sent a four-page letter to Della and me, detailing the four-day programme and inviting us to be his guests at the opening ceremony of the Supreme Court. Thus we found ourselves part of a distinguished group of 80 families including 23 Rothschilds from England and France who travelled to Israel.

I had known Jacob Rothschild for many years, long before he inherited his title from his father, Victor, and have always admired his relaxed, almost languorous, attitude, his razor-sharp mind, his ability to listen with seemingly total concentration and his facility to move with ease in the arts and financial worlds.

At the request of the Israel Museum I had invited Nicholas Serota, Director of the Tate Gallery, to visit Israel as our guest two years earlier. It was only now that he was able to accept the invitation and we found ourselves in the amusing situation in which Nick was sitting in Club Class whilst Della and I and the rest of our friends for whom central booking was arranged, sat in the tourist section.

The opening party took place in the great hall of the Tel Aviv Museum which coincidentally celebrated its 60th birthday. The Federman family of Dan Hotel fame were our hosts and supplied a gourmet meal for 500 guests. The highlight of the evening was the opening of the Leon Bakst exhibition. Bakst, the Russian Jewish artist had painted a series of panels based on the fairytale of *Sleeping Beauty*. These panels were commissioned by James de Rothschild who requested that he, his wife Dolly and other members of the family be featured in the paintings. He was to be Prince Charming but Dolly, who at the time was a modest young girl, refused to be the Sleeping Beauty and chose instead to be one of the good fairies. The paintings had hung in their flat at St James's Place in London. Jacob had made an arrangement whereby they would be on loan to the Tel Aviv Museum until such time as they could be hung permanently in the refurbished Waddesdon Manor which he had inherited, and there they are on display today in their pristine beauty in a room designed to show them to perfection.

The formal opening of the Supreme Court of Justice was an historic event, bearing in mind that the Jews have had no such building since the Second Temple was destroyed in the year 70 AD. The guests included the President, the Prime Minister, the Cabinet, the Judges of the Supreme Court and the movers and shakers of Israeli society who managed to be included amongst the fortunate invitees. It was a memorable and moving ceremony.

The building had taken eight years from the concept in Dolly's letter to Shimon Peres until its opening on 10 November 1992. The architects were Ada Karmi-Melamede and Ram Karmi, a brother and sister team. Every single stone in the building was hand hewn. It took 30 workers two and a half years just to cut the stones. In the opinion of some, the Supreme Court building has become one of the new wonders of the world, the Taj Mahal of Israel. Age-old tradition blends successfully with modern technique. There is an enormous glass curtain which opens up a panoramic view of the city of Jerusalem. Karmi-Melamede described the internal space. "It is a courtyard of motionless silence. The stone quarried from the earth and the water reflecting the sky symbolise truth and justice. (Justice reflects from the sky and truth grows out of the earth. Psalms 85: 12.)"

The biblical custom of dispensing justice at the gates of the town is maintained by the symbolic gatelike entrance to each courtroom.

The following day Lord Rothschild received the Jerusalem Medal from Teddy Kollek in a ceremony at the Crown Theatre. Jacob made a moving speech on the theme of his growing commitment to, and identification with, Jewish values, a subject close to my heart which I had discussed with him on a number of occasions. Sir Isaiah Berlin, who sat next to me, gave me a significant look and said, "Who would have thought so 20 years ago!"

30

A Fashion Model in the Family

IT IS FRIDAY, 24 September 1993 – the eve of Yom Kippur, the most solemn day of the Jewish year, the 25-hour fast, the day of penitence and prayer. Jerusalem traffic has virtually ceased; everybody is at home making leisurely last-minute preparations. The telephone rings. Della picks it up.

"It's Bob here."

"That's nice of you to phone. Fred – Bob Glatter wants to speak to you," said Della, preparing to hand the phone to me.

"No, Della, I want to speak to you," said Bob. "First of all, well over the Fast ... "

"Thank you, Bob – and the same to you and Shirley."

"... and congratulations, Della, for being one of the 10 best-dressed women in the Jewish world."

"Oh, come on, Bob. This is not the time for practical jokes."

"Would I joke on *Erev* Yom Kippur! I am perfectly serious. In today's colour magazine in the *Jewish Chronicle* you are No 9 following, amongst others, Gail Ronson, Barbra Streisand, Barbara Amiel, Nancy Kissinger and Estelle Wolfson. Esther Rantzen comes after you at No 10."

It was perfectly true! In due course we received the colour magazine which forms part of the Worms Memorabilia.

The denouement came when our chic Nadia saw it. She hooted with laughter. "You, mummy?! There must be a printing error – although you do look lovely in the picture."

"They ought to know that it is 80 per cent Marks & Spencer with 20 per cent local boutiques," replied Della, who had fasted well.

3 1

My Favourite Synagogue

HAD DR JOHNSON been Jewish, he might have said: "Every man should have two shuls, if only for the purpose of an alibi."

Apart from Norrice Lea in Hampstead Garden Suburb, I have three other shuls – one in Highgate, which is my "bad weather" standby, one in Herzliah Pituach and the other in Jerusalem. Over the 30 years we have had a home in Herzliah, I have seen the shul grow from a temporary minyan into a prestigious synagogue, with custom-made furniture, a plethora of *sefarim*, air-conditioning, stained-glass windows and a specially marked seat for ex-President Chaim Herzog.

However, that is not the shul I want to write about. My favourite is a distinguished but modest building in Yemin Moshe, Jerusalem, an area which encompasses Mishkenot Shaananim which was founded by Sir Moses Montefiore in 1860 for the benefit of the poor. Its character has changed many times over the last 100 years. The shul was built in 1898 and here we have its first English connection. One Israel Levy, resident in London, sent a cheque for £213 8s od to Chief Rabbi Hermann Adler who passed it on to Rabbi Salanter of Jerusalem. It was an act of faith backing the first Jewish settlement in Jerusalem outside the Old City.

In 1947–8, during the War of Independence, Yemin Moshe became the front line and one of the shul members, Avraham Michael Kirschenbaum, was killed by a sniper's bullet near the building. There was a prolonged hiatus between 1948 and 1967 when Jerusalem was divided and the neighbourhood became a no-go area. A pathetically primitive pillbox is still preserved in our garden as a memorial to those traumatic years. It was only in 1972 that the present community began to take root.

The English connection has been maintained. My own family has had weddings, a *brith* and a Bar Mitzvah there. The Alan Adlers, Victor Hochhausers, Leo Grahames, Conrad Morris, David Winemans, Charles Cormans, the Kalmans and their families even unto the third generation are members, with sons or sons-in-law leading the services.

From the United States we have the writer, Herman Wouk, and from South Africa Mendel Kaplan (former Chairman of the Jewish Agency and now Chairman of the Jerusalem Foundation).

After 1972 the area was largely allocated to artists who thrived in this quiet green oasis which developed into a Jewish mecca during the three foot festivals (which should be renamed the three car festivals) when half Israel came to visit their studios, to picnic on the lawns and to enjoy the view. Many artists made themselves rich by selling their properties.

The houses, clinging to a steep slope, are built on seven stepped terraces with the Sultan's Pool concert area in the valley. My shul stands on the lowest terrace. It bears the grand name of *Beit Yisrael* but it cannot accommodate more than 90 men and 55 women. It is an architectural jewel, a single-storey bungalow, some 25 feet high with two-thirds of the elevation taken up by windows which are almost always open.

Usually the birds sing, the luxuriant shrubs try to climb in, the sun shines from an azure sky and the view is the greatest in the world as the panorama of the Old City walls, the citadel and the Tower of David confront us with their eternal stillness.

Nothing compares with *davening* in *Yerushalayim*. The golden stones, the pure air, the indefinable *Shechina* make it mandatory for us to rush there on the High Holidays and the *Chagim*. I would like to qualify this endorsement. Would I say the same if I were to attend the magnificent choral services in the Bet Haknesset Hagadol, the vast synagogue built by Sir Isaac Wolfson, which last just as long as they do in the Diaspora? I fear not. At the Samson Raphael Hirsch School, Joseph Breuer challenged us to endeavour to concentrate throughout the *birkat hamazon* (grace after meals). Have you ever tried it? It sounds easy. It is not. How much greater is the problem when services go on for three or four hours. The Almighty, surely, prefers two hours of concentration to three-four-hour-long services made "beautiful" by the *chazan* with or without choir, repeating the words, performing, scaling the heights of the octaves and making one's mind wander until the elusive *kavana* (devotion in prayer) has slipped away and one thinks of mundane affairs.

At Yemin Moshe there is no danger of that. Non-professionals take it in turn to lead the service. Some of the younger members touch me deeply with their sincere, straight-forward rendering of our prayers which appear to adopt a fresh meaning. Occasionally we may have a guest who fancies himself as a star performer. Nasal vibratos, extracts from operas etc. are discouraged. The community simply takes over by singing the well-known local *nusach* (traditional tunes) until the miscreant, who will not be invited a second time, is back on the rails.

And for reading the Torah, we had Reb Shmuel. He was 93 when he passed away. His thunderous voice had, alas, suffered somewhat from old age but his *layning* was still a religious experience. When he read from the Torah his watery eyes lit up (he did not wear glasses), a didactic finger waved through the air, emphasising this or that point in the text. There was the feeling that a direct descendant of Moshe Rabenu was imparting the wisdom of the law to us.

Later, when he made *kiddush*, Reb Shmuel stabbed his index finger at you, involving you personally in the commandment to observe the *Shabbat*. You, your son, your daughter, your servant and the stranger wihin your gates, and the pointing finger moved from one to the other until a final jubilant sweep of the arm encompassed the whole congregation.

Born in the Ukraine and educated at yeshivot in Moscow, Reb Shmuel had eliminated the *ou* or *oy* sound. *"Vayemer Meyshe"* was his version of *Vayomer Moshe*. Strangely enough, my Yekkish prejudice against East European "mispronunciation" did not apply to Reb Shmuel or anybody else in this shul. People pray with all kinds of accents and vowel variations; Russian, Polish, Litvak, German, English, American, Sephardi, Ashkenazi – nobody minds in the least. Our pathetic Diaspora prejudices, where one or the other pronunciation is frowned upon in certain quarters and actually "drives some members away", appear laughable in this shul. In *Yerushalayim* we feel that the Almighty pays more attention to the still small voice regardless of the accent than to those who, by their conduct, imply that only their particular version will produce the right resonance in heaven. Amongst our present volunteer readers from the Torah is Dr Jonathan Halevy, Director of the Shaare Zedek Hospital, who never makes a mistake.

At 10.15 on *Shabbat* our little community gets together for *kiddush*, an important social event where friendships are cemented. I walk up the few steps to our home in our traffic-free enclave elated by a *Shabbat* spirit which is so serene and poignant that it defies description.

"Oh, how the City that was once so popular remains lonely like a widow. All her friends have betrayed her. They have become her enemies. All her gates are desolate. Her adversaries have become the head."

Thus is the mournful chant of *Echah* (Lamentations) which the Jews have read for countless generations. Many disasters have taken place on the 9th Av but, until the Holocaust, none equalled the traumatic damage to the Jewish psyche as the destruction of the First and Second Temples. Yet, how can we, in this day and age, read *Echah* with the same conviction as we read it some fifty years ago? Is Jerusalem not a booming City? Are not the Jews in full control of a united, prosperous town? How can one describe a metropolis which suffers from perennial traffic jams as a lonely, abandoned one? Her gates are not desolate. Are there not vast crowds milling around the Jaffa and Damascus Gates? The highway from Tel Aviv to Jerusalem carries thousands of travellers every day in an unending flow. Far from being abandoned, the City is resonant with humming activities.

The church bells are ringing, the muezzins are calling from their mosques. The hotels are full. It is difficult to get a room. Representatives of many religions and peoples are crowding the streets. What is the relevance of *Tisho B'Av* in a City that is no longer destroyed but is greener, greater, more vital and, perhaps, more religious than it has ever been? Why more religious? Because there are more Yeshivot and houses of learning than at any time in Jewish history. What is the meaning, therefore, of *Tisho B'av* at the end of the twentieth century? Has it not been overtaken by *Yom Hashoah*? Is the Holocaust with its mind-boggling genocide, the loss of six million, not a calamity beyond comparison with all the accumulation of disasters which happened on *Tisho B'av*?

The Second Temple was destroyed because of *sinat chinam* or causeless hatred. Now at the end of the twentieth century there is hatred not only between Jew and Arab but a growing chasm between Jew and Jew, the *Charedim* and the secular, the political right and the left, between the haves and the have-nots, and most worryingly there is the dichotomy between Israel and the Diaspora. Yigal Amir, a student at Bar Ilan University, after assassinating Prime Minister Yitzhak Rabin, claimed to have heard the voice of God as interpreted by certain rabbis who placed their version of the *halachah* over the law of the land. As long as we have religious leaders whose inflammatory rhetoric divides the people, whose call upon young soldiers to disobey army orders causes doubt and dismay, as long as the name of the Lord is invoked by these misleaders, and until we follow Rav Kook's dictum that we should cultivate *ahavat chinam* – causeless love – we need *Tisho B'av*.

The golden light of *bein hashmashot* (between the sun and the moon, i.e. dusk) lasted only some 10 minutes. The *minchah* (afternoon) prayer had been completed and we sat in our Yemin Moshe shul awaiting the arrival of nightfall before we could start our *Erev Rosh Hashanah* prayers. There was a quiet buzz of conversation in the synagogue. The men wore jackets out of deference to the cool Jerusalem evenings. Some wore ties. The boys had changed from open sandals to Reebok sneakers.

Herman Wouk, immaculately attired in blazer and grey flannels, studied a page from the Talmud. "Can you learn a *Daf Gemore* [a page from the Torah] by yourself?"

"My grandfather learned with me every day but it helps if I am familiar with the *mesechta* [section]."

The President of the shul came over, pressed my hand and said two words. "*Maftir Jonah.*" I was delighted with this honour but later that week he telephoned me.

"I don't know how to put this. I am embarrassed. You are, of course, perfectly free to say no."

I was intrigued.

"Let's have the question."

"Herman Wouk would very much like *Maftir Jonah*. It seems that a long family tradition has to be maintained."

As a matter of fact, I had already given some thought to the reading of this *Haftorah* and how to interpret the different voices. God – Jonah – the sailors – the reading of the Royal Decree calling for repentance ... but now there was an opportunity to perform a last-minute mitzvah, one which might tip the heavenly scale of forgiveness for my sins in my favour.

"No problem. If he sets so much store by it, he must have it."

"You will, of course, take morning *Maftir* instead," he replied, much relieved.

On Yom Kippur *minchah* Wouk read the story of Jonah and the Whale expeditiously, unemotionally and faultlessly.

Three days after my return to London a parcel arrived by special delivery. It was a new, leatherbound, special edition of Herman Wouk's *This is my God*, the book that has been responsible for so many *Baalei Teshuvah*, or born-again Jews, returning to their faith. It included a handwritten special dedication to me from the author, which I treasure greatly.

I quote from page 106 of the book:

I would not give up for anything, my remembrance of the

mournful auction chant of the *shamas* [beadle]: *"Finif tollar um shlishi!"* Five dollars for the third reading! Nor do I want to forget the historic auction one Yom Kippur afternoon nearly forty years ago, in a synagogue in a Bronx cellar, when my father outbid men with far more money (though they were all poor struggling immigrants) for the reading of the Book of Jonah. One by one the competitors dropped out as the bidding went up past a hundred, a hundred twenty-five, to the incredibly magnificent sum of two hundred dollars, bid in one devastating leap by my father. I can still hear the crash of the sexton's palm on the table, and his shaken happy shout, *"Zwek hunderd tollar um maftir Yena!"*

My father made this tremendous and costly *beau geste* because his own father, a *shamas* in Minsk, had had the prerogative of reading the Book of Jonah, and he was determined to keep the custom in the family. He did, too. In that synagogue nobody ever seriously bid against him for the honor again. To this day my brother and I read the Book of Jonah at Yom Kippur services wherever we can. We have done so in places as far apart as Chicago, Hawaii and Okinawa.

I was glad to help to maintain his family tradition which has been carried on faithfully since. Herman and Sarah Wouk have become great friends. I consider his two books *The Hope* and *The Glory* relating the history of the State of Israel during its first 40 years amongst the best researched historical novels, that I have read. We have a joyous reunion every year in Jerusalem during the high holiday period.

32

My Credo: Religion versus Charedim

RELIGION SHOULD BE practised in moderation.

Al tiyeh zadik harbe, Al titchaham yoter (Ecclesiastes 7: 16) "Do not be overrighteous and do not set out to be too clever" – is an injunction that is often ignored by some of our co-religionists. The wise old Kotzker Rebbe put it another way, quoting from Genesis: *Ve'anshe s'dom raim vechataim – lehashem meod*, which traditionally translated reads: "And the men of S'dom sinned exceedingly before the Lord."

"Wrong translation," said the Rebbe; "this is what it means, 'And the men of S'dom sinned – but exceeded before the Lord'."

When correct conduct between man and his fellow becomes secondary to the minutiae of religious practice, then it is an offence before the Almighty.

The immobility of the *halachah* during modern times is an oxymoron or, as the Talmud puts it, *Tartai d'satrai. Halachah* is based on the Hebrew word to walk, to make progress. *Chazakah* means immobility, traditional unchangeability. One has the impression that the rabbis confuse the similar sounding nouns.

The absence of a rabbinic will since leaving the ghettos of central Europe has left the *Charedim* (ultra-Orthodox) in a time warp, incapable of facing the challenges of modern times and condemning their Judaism to be acted out in a laager mentality, eschewing exposure to the scientific and technological challenges of the twentieth century. If Moses the law-giver and Moses Ben Maimon (Rambam) came down to earth, they would be astonished, if not appalled, by religious practice carried out in their names. The

Rambam stated that Greek philosophy was an essential part of his studies and Samson Raphael Hirsch insisted on secular education alongside Torah learning.

Instead of love and compassion for *Klal Israel* (the whole of the Jewish people), our *Charedi* brethren often demonstrate a militant intolerance of their fellow Jews, of the State of Israel and indeed, of each other, whilst reserving a special brand of xenophobia for the goy. This would not matter all that much if their influence was confined to Stamford Hill, Mea She'arim, Boro' Park or Bnai Brak but, alas, it is all encompassing through their manipulation of succeeding Israeli governments. The unfortunate proportional representation voting system in Israel makes it virtually impossible for any party to have an absolute majority. Coalitions invariably include the ultra-Orthodox, a small tail that wags a large dog. The result is that the *Charedim* give religion a bad name. To paraphrase Lord Acton, "Politics corrupt – religious politics corrupt absolutely."

Thus it has come about that the quiet tolerance of the *Yishuv's* secular majority has turned into hatred of the Black Hats who, to them, symbolise the Jewish religion.

They are upset by their financial shenanigans carving out large slices of the national budget for their Yeshivoth and Kollelim; their refusal to serve in the army; the interference of non-resident rabbis in the electoral system, offering blessings for the "correct" vote or curses for the wrong one, their contempt and delegitimisation of any other form of religious expression; their reliance on their despised neighbours for the maintenance of the infrastructure of the State and its basic services; their internecine feuding placing each other in *cherem* (excommunication) e.g. Rav Schach, the 96-year-old sage of the Ponevitch Yeshivah, said that the nearest thing to Judaism was the Lubavitch religion; such declarations as made by Rabbi Peretz that a train accident in which a number of children were killed was God's punishment for women serving in the army, etc.

The irony is that in biblical times, the *kehunah*, the priesthood, was always strictly separated from the secular kingdom, as specified in the Torah. When the Hasmoneans' descendants tried to combine the two, it led to the destruction of the Second Temple and our 1,900 year dispersion.

One of the greatest sages of our time is Rabbi Adin Steinsaltz, who is translating the Talmud into modern Hebrew, English and Russian – a giant undertaking equating the mammoth task of that great exegete Rashi. In his book, *Strife of the Spirit*, he states that the tragedy of our age is that there is not a single outstanding religious personality who carries any weight outside his own defined circle. The implication is that we cannot expect any changes in the *halachah*, in our lifetime, however much they may be overdue.

Do the *Charedim* work for *Klal Israel* by trying to involve the secular majority in our wonderful traditions, the rhythm of our festivals, the sanctified difference of the seventh day, the *Shabbat*? No. When they venture outside their closed circle, they battle against those religious Jews, who choose to express their faith differently. The delegitimisation of anything left of their particular *halachah* is the single greatest contributor to our tragic division.

We Jews are privileged to belong to a faith which has spawned two other great religions whilst keeping it free from icons, wafers and Holy Ghosts. We recognise that we shall never know or break the mystique of the great unknown *"Ehyeh Asher Ehyeh"* (I am what I am). Even a moderate understanding of our philosophy would eliminate the craving for cults of those who are put off by religious fanaticism and look for greener pastures.

It has been said that the worst moment for an atheist is when he feels grateful and has no one to thank. Pluralism inside the religious camp is not a curse but a blessing – *Klal Israel* is the objective. But there is another side to the problem. Eighty per cent of the *Yishuv* send their children to the secular school system. This, as at present constituted, remains an unmitigated disaster. I may justifiably be accused of prejudice against secular Judaism, which I consider an oxymoron, but no one can doubt the impartiality of the Shinhar Commission set up by the Israel Government. Following the publication of its report on this very topic, it emerged that Talmud and Jewish Thought are not taught in 99 per cent of secular schools.

Only 40 students out of 214,000 took university degrees in Bible Studies, thus creating a Caananite population whose Jewish affiliation is expressed through blood, soil and nationalism. High School students equate religion with the "Black Hats" who represent the negative qualities of the ghetto Jew from whom they wish to distance themselves as far as possible. *Ma'ariv*, the Israeli newspaper, reported in March 1996 that nearly 90 per cent of Israeli adults do not know the Ten Commandments, whilst some 40 per cent could not name the five books of Moses.

Amnon Rubinstein, who was Minister of Education until June 1996, is not a religious Jew. He has recognised, however, that the present state of affairs threatens the very Jewishness of the State of Israel. In his book *The Zionist Dream Revisited* he wrote, "The great majority of secular Israelis have no such [Jewish roots] memories. Jewishness is remote and vague. It invades an otherwise totally profane routine on rare dramatic occasions: birth, marriage, death. Their ignorance often becomes embarrassingly apparent when they travel abroad and realise how isolated they are from the routine of a Jewish community and how unknown the religious service is to them."

The children from the secular schools, for whom exposure to the Bible, if any, is that of an unreliable guide book with interesting legends, are deprived of their 3,000-year-old heritage which should enrich modern society. Fortunately, the Shalom Hartman Institute has been commissioned by the Minister to retrain teachers of Jewish Studies within the secular public high school system towards a new approach to the Jewish tradition. This could make a crucial difference.

I have seen Israeli youngsters in different parts of the world sit in astonishment at a traditional Friday night meal. They had never witnessed the kindling of the lights, the *kiddush*, the *birkat hamazon*, all in their mother-tongue. They loved it and they felt deprived. Their parents had pre-empted their choice of lifestyle.

From Moses to Moses to Moses, we had Judaism by osmosis. This stopped with Moses Mendelssohn and the *Haskalah*, after the protective shell of the ghetto was peeled off. It would be the greatest irony if, instead of the Torah coming out of Zion, the Diaspora – like Babylon in the olden days – would be the provider of *Torah Im Derech Eretz*. Maligned as it is, for me the Rambam's middle way, *Derech Hayashar* remains my credo.

33

Parents versus Children

ONE FINE DAY Della and Nadia were sitting on a bench near the King David Hotel discussing Nadia's wedding arrangements. They were surrounded by screaming kids. The noise was deafening. It was impossible to conduct a normal conversation. Della, in her best Hebrew, asked the children to be quiet. "*Sheket bevakashah.*" It made no impression whatsoever. After several more unsuccessful pleas Nadia said, "Watch this Mum." When a screaming little girl jumped past her, Nadia got hold of her, shook her and talked to her sharply. The children withdrew. Della was appalled. "What's happened to my gentle North London Collegiate daughter?" "This is the only way you can prevail in this country with kids," said Nadia.

Whilst I have my reservations about the one-time political movement, Yesh G'vul (lit. There are Limits), I have no such reservations in so far as the upbringing of children is concerned. Every child must know the boundaries beyond which bad conduct cannot be tolerated. A sharp word on the right occasion can save many a harassed mother hours of anguish. Children need to feel unconditional love coupled with firmness. Of course, it would be wonderful if never a harsh word was spoken, if the conversation was always gentle, and the children co-operated without making a fuss, did their homework without being prompted and went to bed without being asked. Alas, real life is not like that. Children will continuously strain at the leash and test the frontiers of their parents' and teachers' authority. If no firm line is established, children will become confused and ever more demanding.

I believe strongly that children appreciate a firm but fair hand. I remember when Ayelet and Noam were still small they came downstairs (we live below the Hoffmanns in Jerusalem) to play with

Della's special toy assortment. I would take them on one side and say, "Now look kids, if you want to play down here you are very welcome. No tantrums. The tantrum department is upstairs." It worked like a charm. I do not believe that they were repressed and let their parents suffer from the restrictions which they suffered downstairs. On another occasion I smacked Noam's bottom symbolically as it were. He looked at me in amazement, ceased doing whatever was annoying us and when it came to lunchtime insisted on sitting next to me.

There are now new buzz words – "democracy in the family", "consulting six-year-olds who have an equal vote". Of course, they have an equal vote when there is a choice of entertainment on offer, but at the end of the day there must be a line of authority which will be flexible as they grow up. Over the years we have seen food fads established and demolished. Spinach is good for you; spinach poisons you; margarine has side effects which were previously unknown, etc. The same applies to the theory of child education. From Dr Spock to Rudolf Dreikurs, whose book Hilary gave me to read, old axioms are being given new garbs. My credo remains that children must feel that they can totally rely on the support of their parents, that there is a firm anchor which will not shift and which will always be there to lean on.

A free-for-all leading to unlimited indulgence is the quickest recipe for the unhappiness of all concerned. Parents who are short-tempered, suffer from loss of sleep and go from day into night like harassed zombies, must look into their management of the children. We can learn from the ultra-Orthodox who have a large number of children where mothers push the latest offsprings in a twin pram, whilst the older children ranging from two to 15 follow her on a *Shabbat* walk in Mea She'arim. There is no screaming, no shouting, no squabbling. The mother looks serene. She must have done something right.

Grandparents are told that they are out of touch, particularly when their children are professionals in this particular field. Nadia, is a psychologist, Hilary is a social worker and family therapist and has considerable experience with all types of children, and Caroline is a schoolteacher with a remarkable flair for keeping classes of 40 disciplined. They are, therefore, all well-qualified to practise their theories with their own children.

I remain convinced that children, to whom rebellion is a natural process, expect to be disciplined when agreed lines of conduct have been breached. When King David suffered the grievous disappointment with his son Adonijah who rebelled against him, he cried out in anguish, "Did I ever chastise him?" The tragedy was that he did not.

PART 4

Communal Involvement

34

Maccabi

ORGANISED JEWISH SPORT began only at the end of the last century. For 3,000 years, ever since the young David hurled a stone at Goliath and King Saul threw a javelin at his son Jonathan, games for the sake of health and enjoyment were not part of the Jewish way of life. There was a time when sport nearly caught on under Greek and Seleucid influence. Alexander the Great had the good sense not to interfere with the religions of his subjects. His occupation of the Holy Land, on the whole, was benign. The upper classes, including the High Priests, rather enjoyed the civilised way of life of the Greeks. Their sports competitions, performed by men in the nude, startled and then appealed to the local population. Young Jewish men quickly aped the Hellenistic customs, participated enthusiastically and some went so far as to have a reverse foreskin operation in order to look the same as their Greek competitors. It was the equivalent to hunting and shooting in our time. Then and now the chances of Jews who participate in these sports not assimilating were remote.

However, when Antiochus began to slaughter Jews and desecrated the Temple, Matathias the Hasmonean and his son, Yehudah Hamaccabi (The Hammer) led a daring rebellion which is commemorated in our Chanukah festival. It is not surprising that in the light of this experience the rabbis and Jewish leaders developed an aversion against sports which they considered mischievous, goyish activities. Their prejudice was justified by the conduct of the Roman conquerors whose penchant for setting lions against gladiators and slaves against each other, as spectacles in their stadia was dramatically in opposition to the ethos of Judaism and, indeed, newly emerging Christianity.

In subsequent centuries sport became the privileged pursuit of the leisured classes, particularly the land owners. There was little opportunity for Jewish merchants to joust. Once the ghettos were established and the rabbis ruled supreme, the most one could hope for was to follow Maimonides' injunction to teach one's child to swim, not in order to engage in competitions, but to preserve life. There were, however, exceptions to the rule. Jewish sources refer to ball games, fencing and horse-riding in Spain and Provence during the Middle Ages. The *Shulchan Aruch* (Caro's guidebook to the Jewish way of life) published in the sixteenth century, discussed whether ball games were permitted on *Shabbat* and Yom Tov. It must have had some contemporary relevance since in the same century Rudolph II forbade fencing competitions between Germans and Jews. At the end of the eighteenth century, the young Jew, Daniel Mendoza, became boxing champion of England. It was the beginning of a phenomenon where ambitious young men from an under-privileged minority background fought their way to recognition and higher living standards, just as at the present time black people predominate in this field.

Max Nordau rationalised our shortcomings when he coined the phrase and called for "Muscular Judaism" at the second Zionist Congress in 1898.

> Our history tells us that Jews used to be strong and muscular, but for a long time we have been concerned only with physical self-denial. In the narrow streets of the ghetto we forgot to exercise and stand straight. The weight has now been lifted; our will is free. No one will now prevent us from attending to our physical recovery ... the more Jews achieve in various branches of sport, the greater will be their self-confidence and self-respect.

Nordau was a man full of contradictions. He was the classical specimen of the *Haskalah* Jew. His father was an Orthodox rabbi called Sudfeld (Southfield). When Max was 18 he rebelled against religion, called it a big lie, and devoted the rest of his life to pamphleteering against it. He became a doctor and journalist. At 50 he was already an *éminence grise*. He never engaged in sport himself. He changed his name to Nordau (Northmeadow) to annoy his father and married out. Dedicated to Herzlian Zionism he became a co-founder of the World Zionist Organisation.

When he made his famous clarion call for physical fitness Nordau was not really such a revolutionary as was generally thought. As a result of the Enlightenment in nineteenth-century Europe, Jewish students at German, Austrian and Czech universities had already felt the need to equal the sporting prowess of their fellow students. They were barred from the student fraternities which engaged in duelling. It was illegal to duel against a Jew or to accept a challenge from a Jew. It was not surprising, therefore, that in the 1880s and the 1890s there was a proliferation of Jewish Student Societies at such universities as Berlin, Heidelberg, Munich, Prague and Vienna. They were the precursor of the Jewish golf and yacht clubs which were formed in Anglo-Saxon countries a few decades later.

The first Jewish sports club was founded in Budapest in 1888 followed by another in Constantinople in 1894, mainly used by German and Viennese Jews, who were living there at the time. The Bulgarian club in 1897 was the first one to use the name Maccabi. Bar Kochba Berlin was formed in 1898 and thereafter the pace accelerated. By the beginning of the First World War there were scores of Jewish sports clubs in Germany, Hungary, Switzerland, Yugoslavia, Russia, Poland and in Palestine where the first club was formed in Jaffa in 1906. In 1903 a roof organisation called *Die Juedische Turnerschaft* was created. When the first modern Olympic Games took place in Athens in 1896, six Jewish athletes won 13 medals for the various countries which they represented. The First Maccabiah (World Jewish Olympics) took place in Palestine in 1932, the Second in 1935. At that time Lord Melchett, scion of the Mond family of ICI fame, born a Christian with a Jewish father but reconverted to Judaism, led the parade into Tel Aviv on a white horse. He was to become Honorary President of the Maccabi World Union, the first of my predecessors from the UK which included Professor Brodetsky and Lord Nathan. The 1935 Maccabiah was known as the Maccabiah of the *aliyah*. Certificates (immigration permits) were hard to come by. The German team was chosen mostly from athletes who wanted to settle in Palestine and who simply forgot to go back to Germany. Long before the Nazis came into power, the MWU had enshrined in its aims and objects the upbuilding of *Eretz Israel* as a major objective.

In 1921 the Maccabi World Union was founded in Carlsbad, Czechoslovakia. The names of the various Maccabi Clubs – Maccabi, Bar Kochba, Hagibor – honoured the ancient Jewish warriors who were the first to stand up in defence of their people. Many of these clubs prospered and produced world-class competitors. An example was Hakoah Vienna. It was founded in 1909 and dominated Austrian sport until the Nazis closed it down. When their football team went to New York in the 1920s it attracted the largest spectator crowd on record. Its weight-lifting, swimming, water polo and football achievements were only equalled by those of Bar Kochba Berlin on the running track.

The headquarters of the Maccabi World Union, which had been in Berlin since 1929, were transferred to London in 1937. By that time the Maccabi World Union consisted of more than 40 national organisations, with a membership approaching 200,000. Alas, the clubs in the very countries from which the movement originated were doomed to extinction, as the Nazi jackboot first trampled on German Maccabi, then in rapid succession the Austrian, Czech and Polish clubs were closed down. In 1947 there was a traumatic meeting in Basel attended by the survivors of the camps, the emaciated remnant of the millions who had perished.

The headquarters were transferred from London to Tel Aviv and in 1956 Kfar Ha-maccabiah (Maccabiah Village) was founded on some 20 acres of green belt land outside Ramat Gan. Its original purpose was to accommodate the overseas athletes who came in ever-increasing numbers to the Maccabiot, which were to take place in the independent State of Israel at four-yearly intervals. Nowadays, Jewish sport worldwide has become synonymous with Maccabi. Maccabi sports clubs have been re-established in Russia and her former satellite countries. Regional games take place in Europe, Australia, Canada, USA and Latin America between Maccabiot.

The Maccabiah Village has become a multi-million dollar enterprise with its large hotel complex, 16 tennis courts, four swimming pools, squash and gymnastic halls, convention centre and cinema. It houses the headquarters of the Maccabi World Union and Maccabi Israel and is the jewel in the Maccabi crown.

One of the Talmudic rules of logic is known as *meclal leprat* (from the general to the particular). Having painted the general background to the history of the Maccabi Movement, I will now deal with some of the highlights of my own passionate, lifelong involvement.

As soon as I came to England I joined Maccabi Association London at Compayne Gardens, known by its acronymn MAL. I believe that the immediate post-War years were of such vintage quality that a true description sounds like hyperbole. Never before or since has a single club had the ability of attracting so many outstanding personalities at the same time. To a large extent this was due to the charisma of Pierre Gildesgame, "Mr Maccabi", who, over the years, became one of my best friends, my teacher and role model who, next to Joe Gilbert of Hillel fame, has probably had more influence on my life than anybody else.

I have a brochure produced in 1937 for the opening of the MAL Building. It reads like a Jewish *Who's Who* with Lord Melchett as Honorary President and Professor Selig Brodetsky as President. Amongst the Vice-Presidents were Mrs Rebecca Sieff, Barnett and Elsie Janner, Norman Lasky, Simon Marks, Colonel N. L. Nathan, MP (later Lord Nathan), the Marquis and Marchioness of Reading, James de Rothschild, Viscount Samuel, Leon Simon, Isaac Wolfson and Lionel Schalit. E. F. Freud of the famous family was the architect.

Another great personality who served on the Executive of MAL was Conrad Abrahams-Curiel, Managing Director of Associated Weavers – one of the largest carpet manufacturing concerns in the UK. He was the epitome of a gentleman with a touch of class, a man who was as comfortable and relaxed with the youngsters of MAL as he was on his yacht.

Other Executive Members were Jack Salmon, founder and owner of Jax Retail Stores, Jack Steinberg, Alfred Morley, Jack Mundy,

Harry Shapiro, Reuben Turner, Bernard Saphir, Aubrey Scott – who alas died tragically young – Cyril Blausten, Fred Oberlander, the outstanding wrestling champion who came to London from his native Vienna, Jack and Bryna Richman who started the famous MAL Theatre Group, Eric and Beryl Rayman, Ken Gradon and Sidney Farleigh to name but a few. I was "Cultural Director" and regularly clashed with Fred Oberlander, the Sports Director, over the use of the hall. It is not surprising that with such talent many more Maccabi Clubs were formed in Great Britain and Ireland to become the Maccabi Union. In due course Pierre Gildesgame became Chairman and later President of the Maccabi World Union. John Rubens, another good friend, became a great benefactor both to British and World Maccabi.

Following in the footsteps of my predecessors, Pierre and Lionel Schalit, I became Chairman of the European Executive. MWU is divided into territorial organisations – Europe, North America, Latin America, South Africa and Australia.

Europe, where the seeds of the movement had been sown, had a miraculous recovery during the post-War years. Maccabi clubs slowly re-established themselves everywhere except in the Iron Curtain countries where that miracle was delayed for another 40 years. In 1950 we celebrated the Third Maccabiah, the first one to be held in the State of Israel, under quite extraordinary circumstances. The two-year-old country was poor, with a primitive infrastructure, a small population and an appalling cuisine. The Israelis were the biggest consumers of Norwegian fish fingers in the world and we lived on them during the Games.

I was deputed by Pierre to go and see Louis Pincus, an eminent ex-South African lawyer, who, at that time, was Chairman of the nascent El Al to negotiate a special deal to fly our Maccabiah team from England to Israel. As a product of Habonim I expected Israeli leaders to live in a kibbutz style and walk about in open-necked shirts. When I met him in his suite at Claridges I was horrified to see him in a pin-striped suit. He was most helpful and over the years we became firm friends.

During the next 30 years it was my privilege to meet every Israeli President, Prime Minster and Chief of Staff either in connection with the Maccabiah or on B'nai B'rith business. Amongst the principal "Machers" was Pinchas Sapir, the Minister of Finance, who ran the country with his little black book. He said to Pierre and me at the time, "I can spare you ten minutes." We spent two hours with him, he wrote one of his little *peteks*, his personal notes, which cut Gordian knots through bureaucratic delays and, like a passe-partout, opened doors for us in miraculous fashion.

Moshe Sharett became a personal friend. He died a bitter man who detested Ben-Gurion. "He made me wash dishes," he said.

"What do you mean by that, Moshe?" I asked.

"I had nothing else to do but to help my wife at home. He would not let me in." Ben-Gurion was notorious for his ambivalent attitude to some of his political colleagues.

One of the 1950 Maccabiah accommodation centres was a tent village on the beach at Tel Aviv where the Hilton stands today. I, as one of the leaders, had the privilege of being quartered with a Tel Aviv family and it was my good fortune that it was the Bavlys. Bavly père was the founder of the famous accountancy firm which my friend, his son Dan, carried on until his retirement in 1995, and Bavly mère was the chairperson of Hadassah in Israel. They lived in some comfort in Gordon Street where the toilets only flushed until 10 in the morning due to water rationing, but there was an atmosphere of restrained optimism.

Jewish independence at the time was intoxicating. The Maccabiah was due to open in the then primitive Ramat Gan Stadium on the second day of *Sukkot*. The three Jewish foot festivals are kept for two days in the Diaspora but only for one day in Israel. Some Israelis say, tongue in cheek, that this is a punishment for Jews who live in the Diaspora. My family and I have long given up keeping the second day since we invariably spend the Festivals in Israel. However, in 1950, my ultra-Orthodox brother-in-law, Ken Graðon and I set out to march from Tel Aviv to Ramat Gan in a temperature of some 95 degrees. Through the generosity of Marks and Spencer who had supplied our uniforms, we wore white flannels, a blue blazer and a smart straw hat. The blazers were made in a heavyweight material which, in that temperature, felt like a fur coat. Every other car stopped to offer us a lift. When we declined politely explaining that it was Yom Tov, they thought we were crazy – and perhaps they had a point!

Since 1950 this great Jewish sports festival has grown enormously. Thousands of sportsmen and women stream into Israel every four years, bringing with them tens of thousands of tourists presenting an ever-increasing logistic and financial challenge. How many great and wealthy countries in the world would be prepared to hold Olympic Games every four years in the same location? This is precisely what Israel has been doing and I never cease to marvel that despite my forebodings that the next Maccabiah cannot be as good as the last one, the Games get better every time.

I have been a member of the World Executive since 1950 and after Pierre Gildesgame's tragic death followed in his footsteps and became World President in 1982. This must be distinguished from the elevation to Honorary President which followed in 1994. *The Jerusalem Post* of 2 May 1982 wrote:

The election last week of industrialist Fred Worms as the new president of World Maccabi to succeed the late Pierre Gildesgame, is certain to herald new approaches to Maccabi's work in 35 countries.

Worms, 61, a footballer for Maccabi in his youth in Germany and later in England, is addicted to Jewish education.

"I am not among those leaders within Maccabi who see sporting prowess as an absolute value. That was a concept of the ancient Greeks. For Maccabi in the Diaspora sport should not be an end in itself, and I shall devote much effort to promoting increased Jewishness and Jewish education stressing the centrality of Israel," Worms told *The Jerusalem Post*.

He expects to be personally active in recruiting talent from within Israel's universities to further his aims. "That kind of work is my cup of tea," Worms said. The choice of Worms as World Maccabi Union president would have delighted Pierre Gildesgame, who was killed in a hit-and-run road accident outside Lord's Cricket Ground in London last year. For almost 50 years Worms followed in the footsteps of his great friend, Pierre Gildesgame; he is now executor of his estate. In many ways the two men were very much alike.

In the 1950s the Maccabi World Union headquarters were accommodated in two rooms in Nachmani Street in Tel Aviv – a noisy thoroughfare which made meetings a torture. Without air conditioning, closed windows proved intolerable and open windows meant that the traffic noise ruined conversation. Apart from the need for better headquarters, there was also the four-yearly problem of accommodating the Maccabiah athletes from overseas.

In 1955 Ramat Gan was a small insignificant suburb of Tel Aviv but it had one tremendous asset – its Mayor Avraham Krinitzi. He was one of the "old school" of the LaGuardia type. He was not particularly interested in committees which proliferated as they do in all municipalities, but he got things done. He was a "hands-on" mayor who travelled with the town architect and the town gardener through his domain every morning between 6 and 8 a.m. looking at the latest developments. He created play areas, a national park and flower gardens, and made Ramat Gan into the attractive garden city which it is today. He, together with his deputy, Shalom Zyssman, were also important members of the Israel–Maccabi hierarchy.

The Chairman of the MWU in 1955 was one Aron Netanel, a prosperous industrialist, small of stature but dynamic and determined. Between them they managed to obtain from the Israel Land Authority 80 dunams (20 acres) of land which was to become the Maccabiah Village. A board of directors was formed with Krinitzi as Chairman, Aron Netanel, Lord Nathan, Pierre Gildesgame, Shalom Zyssmann and amongst others Avraham Tori, a lawyer and myself. In 1996, Tori, well into his eighties, and I are the sole survivors. Tori deserves this description in more sense than one. His book, *Surviving the Holocaust, the Kovno Ghetto Diary*, edited by Martin Gilbert, became an important source book for Holocaust researchers.

Having got the land our troubles started. We had no money for buildings and I was asked by my colleagues to approach Mordechai Stern, Chairman of Rassco, a Government controlled building organisation. Stern had a good look at those who stood behind the project and offered to put up buildings which would be paid for in due course, whatever that meant. Accepting his generosity was the first mistake we made. It taught me one thing – whilst paupers cannot be choosers, on bargains you lose your money. The buildings, put up cheaply without quality control, caused us no end of trouble and over the years had to be virtually reconstructed.

When we returned to England Pierre and I and a few others organised a dinner for the benefit of the Maccabiah Village. With the Duke of Edinburgh as the guest of honour we raised the phenomenal sum of £80,000 which could probably be multiplied more than tenfold to bring it up to present day figures, and this was the first genuine cash injection into the Maccabi Village Company.

Since an accommodation centre cannot be run for the purpose of using it only once in four years, and then only for a month or so, it was necessary to find a formula whereby it would earn its keep. We hit upon the idea of making the Maccabiah Village a hotel enterprise and sports centre. In later years we added a Convention Centre, built special halls for functions and seminars and finally, and most beneficially, created a country club.

I am skipping many years of pain, agony and debt with these few sentences. We employed professional managers who were either inefficient or plain dishonest. On one occasion I discovered a porter taking half a cow out of the kitchen and loading it into a van. At that time our managers were two brothers who had their own hotel enterprise and who fed their guests with our food!

Two factors turned the Maccabiah Village from a running sore into the tremendous success it is today. The first was Michael Kevehazi's *aliyah*. My cousin Michael joined Maccabi and after emigrating to Israel he came to the conclusion that our Israeli/Maccabi colleagues had formed a clique. "Will they ever give me a chance to do a job of work?" he asked in desperation.

Well, Pierre and I saw to it that they did and once Michael took charge of the finances of the village we entered into a new era. At that time only half the land had been developed by us. During the crisis years when we had not known where next week's wages would come from, I said to Krinitzi, "Look, our land has become very valuable, let us sell a dunam or two to get out of debt."

"Over my dead body," he said. "In Israel you buy land, you never sell." He was right and I was wrong. We developed the then surplus land into a beautiful country club with tennis courts, swimming pools, squash hall, gymnasia etc.

Krinitzi was tragically killed in a road accident when he visited his country cottage in Zichron Yakov. Before his death he wrote his Hebrew autobiography and with a great flourish handed me a signed copy. In telling the story of Ramat Gan and its resistance to the Turks and to the English and his determination to make it the most beautiful city in Israel, he refers to a few characters. One he describes as a *Luftmensch* which is German/Yiddish for a man of no substance, a bluffer, but which literally translated means "a man who lives on fresh air". Later on when the English translation of the book was produced which he also signed for me I was interested to see that the translation for *Luftmensch* was airman (pilot).

These are the highlights of some of the Maccabiot. The 1950 Maccabiah was opened by President Chaim Weizmann. There was a tinge of sadness in the hearts of some of us because of the absence of Professor Selig Brodetsky, the Maccabi World President.

Selig Brodetsky left England in 1949, in order to assume the Presidency of the Hebrew University, a great honour and a climax to his distinguished career. Of poor East End origin he became a senior wrangler at Cambridge and one of England's leading Zionists. He was President of the Board of Deputies, held many other posts and was known as the peripatetic professor running from London to Leeds and back. Somehow he never made it in the establishment of the new State of Israel. Chaim Weizmann, in his book *Trial and Error* did not refer to him at all and when Brodetsky finally, after returning to England, wrote his autobiography, the once ebullient optimist had become a very bitter man. When Ken and I visited him in Jerusalem prior to the 1950 Maccabiah in order to extend an official invitation to him to be a guest of honour we had an enormous shock. The cheerful man with shrewd eyes and brilliant smile had shrunk into a shadow of his former self. What had happened?

"It's a land that kills its inhabitants," – he greeted us with the quotation of the 10 out of the 12 spies sent by Moses to Canaan. He was deeply unhappy with the total lack of co-operation from the dispersed campuses of the Hebrew University and their local professors. It must be remembered that at that time Mount Scopus was on the Arab side of Jerusalem and the University had make-shift arrangements in a variety of buildings all over Western Jerusalem. Brodetsky was used to the discipline of an English campus where faculty members would listen to the master of the college. What he found in Israel was chaos, indiscipline, lack of finance, and no cohesive central authority. His health suffered badly, he was too ill to attend the opening of the Maccabiah and a year later he returned to England a broken man. Pierre and I who financed the cost of his autobiography wanted him not to publish after we read the proofs but he insisted. He was a great man who should have written his life story five years earlier when he was full of *joie de vivre* and optimism.

The Fourth Maccabiah in 1953 was opened by the second President of the State, Yitzhak Ben Zvi. Twelve countries were represented and 890 sportsmen from overseas marched into the Ramat Gan stadium with first-time appearances from Brazil, Chile and Australia.

The Fifth Maccabiah in 1957 is identified with the creation of the Maccabiah Village and the remarkable gymnastic display from four-times Olympic gold medallist Agnes Kelety, formerly from Hungary. Agnes and her husband, Bobby, are neighbours of ours in Herzliah and even in 1996 we still see her going for her daily run and swimming some 20 lengths in the pool in our garden complex.

The Sixth Maccabiah in 1961 was the first one recognised to be an organisation of Olympic standing – and an official regional sports event under the International Sports Federation. One thousand athletes from 27 countries were accommodated partly in the new Maccabiah village sleeping in dormitories some four or six to a room under conditions which would not be acceptable nowadays. Two family traditions were carried on; Philip Oberlander, the son of Olympic Champion Fred Oberlander, won a gold medal in wrestling and Michael Wittenberg, son of another Maccabiah champion, won a gold medal in weight-lifting. Dick Savitt of Wimbledon fame won two gold medals in tennis.

The Seventh Maccabiah introduced a 15-year-old swimmer – Mark Spitz. He won three gold medals and went on to win seven gold medals at the infamous 1972 Olympic Games in Munich. Tom Okker, another international tennis player, began his career on that occasion and subsequently won a gold medal at the Olympics.

Prior to the 1965 Maccabiah, I met Yitzhak Rabin. He was then the young dashing Chief of Staff whom Pierre Gildesgame and I approached to seek his permission to allow army parachutists to land as part of the opening ceremony of the Games. Over the years I met Rabin on many occasions, including the period when he was rather a diffident Ambassador to the United States. We were on first name terms. His murder sent an arrow into the psyche of the Jewish people. His name will go down in history as one of the great heroes of war and peace, whose courage and vision changed the face of the Middle East.

The Ninth Maccabiah stood in the shadow of the 11 Israeli athletes who were murdered at the Olympic Games in Munich the year before. The Maccabiah torch was brought into the stadium by an American-born Israeli basketball star, Tal Brody, who later as captain of Tel Aviv Maccabi led his team to win the European Championship.

The Tenth Maccabiah in 1977 hosted more than 2,700 athletes from 33 countries. Fifty-five Maccabiah records were broken including those established by Mark Spitz.

The Eleventh Maccabiah in 1981 was dedicated to the memory of Pierre Gildesgame – "Mr Maccabi". Three thousand five hundred athletes from 30 countries participated and 35 new records were established.

The Twelfth Maccabiah in 1985 held during my presidency of the Maccabi World Union featured 4,000 athletes from 40 countries. Thereafter we incorporated social and cultural events, such as international children's painting competitions on the history of Jewish sport etc. Hungary and Romania participated for the first time.

The Bar Mitzvah Maccabiah (the 13th) in 1989 included teams from the Baltic countries whilst the Russians, to tumultuous applause, marched into the enlarged Ramat Gan stadium in 1993.

This was also the first time that our cherished South African colleagues took part officially in their Springbok uniforms. For many years, this corner of the world, which has brought forth a dispropor-tionate number of outstanding Jewish athletes, was banned from official participation. That country's apartheid laws had made their sportsmen and women into pariahs and our *chaverim* had to suffer under this pernicious system. We partly overcame these difficulties imposed upon us by the International Olympic Organisation (IOC) by forming *ad hoc* teams but these were unsatisfactory compromises which caused heartache and heart-seaching. We thank the Almighty that these troublesome days are over.

During my years as World President, the Chairman of Maccabi World Union was Dr Israel Peled, the Mayor of Ramat Gan. Immediately after the Mexico Olympics in 1968, Dr Alec Lerner, the son-in-law of the late Lord Marks, a director of Marks and Spencer and a devotee of the new State, had made *aliyah*. He agreed to act as a stop-gap Chairman of Maccabi World Union on condition that he would not be detained long. In fact the king-makers at the time, Pierre Gildesgame, Chaim Wein and Yitzhak Caspi, were very anxious to have a "real" Israeli and not a new immigrant as Chairman and there were two suitable candidates. One was Mena-chem Savidor, the other was Israel Peled.

Savidor's eloquence was his undoing. He was one of the old-fashioned Zionists who harangued his audiences in a theatrical way, dealt in hyperboles and, in spite of his great abilities, had all the vanities of a man who thinks highly of himself. He became the Speaker of the Knesset and when I invited him to one of our Hillel fund-raising affairs to be our guest of honour he accepted with alacrity, but he was bitter that he never made the Chairmanship of Maccabi World Union.

One of the reasons which prompted us to nominate Peled was the desirability of having the Chief Citizen of Ramat Gan in our camp. With the rapidly expanding Maccabiah Village, the granting of quick planning permission for our continuing extensions was essen-tial. From that point of view Peled served his purpose well. He and I differed on a number of occasions. To me the non-political status of the Maccabi World Union was sacrosanct, unlike other sports bodies in Israel, which are financed by political parties. Peled, however, was a political animal as all mayors are to some extent, and when election time came he bedecked the Maccabiah Village, which by then had become the headquarters of the Maccabi World Union, with the flags of his party and identified us in the eyes of some members of the public as a subsidiary of the Likud.

The relationship between a President and a Chairman is, by its very nature, a delicate one. The President must recognise that the Chairman is the Chief Executive of the Movement, whereas the President is the custodian of its conscience. It was only on rare occasions when I felt that matters of vital principle were involved that our disagreements were brought before the Executive. There were also tensions between our respective successors, Michael Kevehazi who became Chairman of Maccabi World Union, and Marcos Arbaitsman from Sao Paulo who followed me as World President. Since 1994 Uzi Netanel the son of the famous Aron Netanel, the co-founder of the Kfar (village), has been the World Chairman and he has, I hope, worked out a suitable *modus vivendi* with the President, Ronnie Bakalarz, from Colombia.

Whilst the principal aims and objectives of the Maccabi World Union remain the promotion of sport, we look upon this as a means to an end. To us, an outstanding footballer who uses his Maccabi Club merely for the sake of enjoying the sport but otherwise divorces himself from Judaism, is not an ideal Maccabi member. We want a combination of sporting prowess and Jewish identity. The latter cannot be achieved without an adequate education. We have a unique opportunity not open to other organisations. We appeal to youngsters who are not prepared to join Jewish youth clubs or who do not want to be involved in anything which smacks of idealistic aims and objectives. However, once in Maccabi we try to introduce them to their heritage. Leadership seminars have taken place in Israel at the Kfar Maccabiah and in Jerusalem but for years our efforts were haphazard, disorganised, lacked continuity and long-term planning. Frankly, we did not have the right material in the ranks of our honorary officers, nor did we have sufficient funds to start up our own education organisation. Indeed, why should we when there were so many specialist bodies in the field?

When Avraham Infeld became an emissary from Israel in London, and served on the Hillel Executive, I recognised a man of outstanding ability. Born in South Africa, from a secular household, he became one of the most erudite and charismatic educators with a flair for attracting young people. After his return to Israel he started his own organisation, Melitz, which has assembled a team of brilliant educators. Amongst its products are Jonathan Kestenbaum, the head of the Chief Rabbi's Office in London. I brought Melitz into Maccabi and now Melitz is the official accredited body which looks after the education portfolio of the Maccabi World Union. It has been a great success; Infeld has travelled to Latin America and he and his team have given new meaning to Maccabi education. The special packs which they made up for our new members in Russia containing as they did videos, explanations of Jewish holidays, and the history of Zionism, all in Russian, were an eye-opener to the Jewish Agency and have been copied widely since.

Following the completion of my term of office as World President, I was elected Chairman of the Board of the Maccabiah Village Company, a $20 million enterprise, and together with our general manager, Yoram Eyal, followed later by Giora Bar-Dea, was able to preside over the continued expansion of the Kfar and consolidation of its finances. Having served a maximum term of eight years as Chairman I was elected Honorary President of Maccabi World Union, only the fifth man to hold this position.

After Pierre Gildesgame's death we decided to create in his name a museum depicting the history of Jewish sport and the Maccabi World Movement in the Maccabiah Village. I became Founder Chairman and we raised the necessary funds from Pierre's English friends and admirers. We made a video film with the professional help of Geoffrey Preger and created an archive of talking heads i.e. leading Maccabi personalities over 70 years old from all over the world, whose local Maccabi memories can be recalled at the touch of a computer button. Apart from the display of historic trophies, photos and other memorabilia, we have an important resource archive of the history of Jewish sport under the capable administration of computer expert Rivkah Steinitz. The Museum's founding curator was Arthur Hanak who had made a lifelong study of the subject. After his demise Rivkah Rabinowitz took over the reins which she holds firmly to this very day. Judge Yitzhak Braz is the Chairman of the Museum Committee whilst I continue as Chairman of the Trustees.

A major extension of the Museum is under way, to make it more attractive to children of school age. Our ultimate aim is to create an ongoing seminar centre on Jewish Sport. Geoffrey Preger, Melitz and senior personnel from the Israel Museum are engaged in formulating plans which, hopefully, will bring these ambitious ideas to an early realisation. I shall be happy to conduct any of my readers over the new museum from 1997 onwards.

In 1982 we introduced the equivalent of a "Distinguished Service Medal", *Yakir Maccabi*, for select leaders of the Movement who had reached the age of 65. Shimon Peres handed me my medal in 1986 in the course of a festive ceremony during which the contribution of the Awardee was shown on a large screen. At the time I was somewhat embarrassed by it all and Della and the children have never forgiven me for not inviting them to the function.

35

Jewish Education

I THINK I CAN safely say that not a working week has passed during the last 50 years in which I have not given some time to the various educational organisations with which I have been associated, ranging from Maccabi to Hillel, and from the Governorship of North London Collegiate School and Immanuel College to the Pelech and Efrata Schools and the Hebrew University in Jerusalem.

Jewish education is a matter about which I feel strongly, and if people are not careful I am liable to go on enthusiastically about the subject at great length. Having had a thorough grounding in the Jewish sources during my 10 years at the Samson Raphael Hirsch School in Frankfurt, which in retrospect was really a mini yeshivah with quite outstanding secular teaching, I was puzzled by the ignorance of my contemporaries when I first came to England. In later years I found at Hillel that our students were on the whole keen young people, motivated, dedicated and reasonably well-educated in general subjects but Jewishly virtually illiterate. Why? Let us examine the educational scene in the early 1970s.

A minority of Jewish children in the UK attended Jewish schools, but many did not reach the standards which could in any way compare with pre-War continental levels. Some 8,000 youngsters went to the Hebrew classes of the London Board (United Synagogue) and a much smaller number to the classes of the Reform and Liberal Synagogues. The rest had no exposure whatsoever to Judaism. It was a very unsatisfactory state of affairs. Those who attended the Sunday morning Hebrew classes were often taught by inexperienced teenagers; they learned a small paragraph of Genesis by heart, they read with great difficulty, stuck it out reluctantly mainly to please their parents until the age of Bar Mitzvah or Bat Mitzvah and then closed their books with a great sigh of relief. They only reopened them with some diffidence on their bi-annual visits to the synagogue during the High Holidays.

This portrait may seem a caricature to the Orthodox, committed families of Stamford Hill or Golders Green, but it is not an untypical profile of the Anglo-Jewish youngsters during the first three post-War decades. My own prejudices were unfortunately confirmed in no uncertain manner when my oldest daughter, Nadia, a bright girl, eager to learn, joined a Hebrew class at the age of six. She was reluctant to go the following Sunday so I went along with her and had permission to sit in. I never sent any of my three daughters to Hebrew classes again. They were taught by me and by a series of outstanding private teachers ranging from the late Dr Meir Gertner to Rabbi Isaac Bernstein. In their early teenage years they became leaders in Bnai Akiva, and when at the ages of 18 each one went on *aliyah* they had no difficulty in integrating themselves into Israeli society either from the language aspect or as far as our biblical and historical heritage was concerned.

I realised that this extremely expensive process could not possibly apply to the majority of the community's children and having analysed the situation, I wrote a 30-page manifesto in March 1976 called *Facing Facts: Is it within the power of the Community to arrest the crisis in Jewish Education?*

I was greatly encouraged in this by Chief Rabbi Jakobovits. He had spelled out in his inauguration address that his most important aim was to raise the standard of Jewish education. He founded the Jewish Educational Development Trust (JEDT) in 1971 with a publication, *Let My People Know.* Unfortunately, initial promises made by a number of philanthropists were slow in coming in, and after five years the Chief Rabbi was somewhat disenchanted with the progress that had been made. I had come to the firm conclusion that without adequate finance there was no way in which we could raise the level to an acceptable standard. *"Ein Kemach ein Torah"* – a maxim quoted in the *Ethics of our Fathers* which, freely translated, means . . . "without material assistance there can be no learning". The very future of our community was at stake.

Years earlier I, amongst others, had written to Arthur Koestler that his prognosis that Jews should either emigrate to Israel or assimilate in their countries of residence was unrealistic and that history would prove him wrong. It was clear that apart from *aliyah*, the most important service which the Jews in the Diaspora could render to the State of Israel was to ensure their own survival, to remain a supportive link both for future *aliyah* and to give political, moral and financial support. Dr Emil Fackenheim, the great educationalist/philosopher, summed it up succinctly, "The Holocaust can only be understood by denying Hitler his victory. Our creative, thrusting survival is our duty. Go forth and multiply." His assumption was that the multiplied would remain Jewish.

I thought at the time that the only body which had adequate machinery to raise the funds for Jewish education was the Joint Israel Appeal. For many years after the War the leadership of the JIA was in the hands of the Marks, Sieff, Sacher and Wolfson families i.e. the captains of commerce of M & S and GUS provenance. By the 1970s the younger generation, led by Trevor Chinn, Cyril Stein and Stuart Young (who became disenchanted and resigned), was rapidly assuming control of what had become a self-perpetuating hierarchy. The JIA was a sophisticated fund-raising body with a large staff, national coverage and many specialist fund-raising committees. I maintained that if only 10 per cent of the funds raised by the JIA could stay in this country and be channelled through a revitalised JEDT then one could engage in long-term planning, found new schools, train better teachers and pay them salaries that would make their profession a desirable one. In short, one could begin to compete with the efforts made in Australia, America and South Africa by local communities.

I quote from the introductory statement of my booklet:

Our experience in the last few years has shown a rapidly diminishing commitment on the part of the Jewish student. This problem has been highlighted by the Sacher Committee which has dealt extensively with the scene on the campus. The leadership malaise amongst the students is the direct result of their tenuous affinity with Jewish matters. This is not surprising when one looks at the pitiful number of children who receive any Jewish education after the age of thirteen. Statistics of the London Board show that less than fifty have a Jewish education of more than three hours per week after the age of fourteen. This from a potential of some ten thousand in the age group of fourteen to seventeen. The obvious conclusion is therefore that remedial action must be taken at a very much earlier stage.

I had drawn freely on the publications of Chief Rabbi Jakobovits' *Let My People Know*, Professor Prais' *Sample Survey on Jewish Education in London 1972/73*, Dr Braude's report *Survey of Jewish Day Schools in the United Kingdom and Ireland*, and the Annual Report of the London Board of Jewish Religious Education prepared by its Director of Education, Tony Brown.

I continued:

Jewish education in the Diaspora is on a par with the up-building of the State of Israel as far as the allocation of resources is concerned. These sentiments have been stated on many public occasions by many members of the Israel Government. This has been placed formally on record during the various emergency conferences that took place in Israel during November and December 1975.

To implement these directives a complete reappraisal in the allocation of communal funds is required.

Jewish education in the United Kingdom compares very badly with other English speaking countries. In the United States, with a Jewish population approximately fifteen times the size of that in Great Britain, more than three hundred million dollars per annum is spent. Proportionately, we ought to allocate ten million pounds. In fact it is a small fraction of this figure. The relative percentages in South Africa and Australia are higher than those of the United States.

A separate fund-raising machinery to provide such large sums year by year is doomed to failure. It would probably be counter-productive if its fund-raisers were to stress the relative importance of Jewish education compared with the needs of Israel. It has already been said that "one million more or less for Israel is marginal, to a country with a four billion dollar deficit" – whereas "one million more or less for Jewish education in this country would be the difference between success and failure". Such arguments, however undesirable, would inevitably arise if a separate fund-raising organisation were to be set up.

On 4 June 1976, the *Jewish Chronicle* carried a leading article on my proposals highlighting their call for the revitalisation of Jewish education with the injection of substantial funds by the JIA and the drawing together of the finest educational brains, resources, ideas and personnel. The article supported my contention that without such action the only committed Jews in 30 years' time would be the extreme right wing. In the "Personal Opinion" column of the same issue the following item appeared.

The Worms Plan for Jewish education should appeal even to the ledger-heads in the community, for, to put it at its crudest, today's school-children are tomorrow's JIA subscribers, and without an effective level of Jewish education there will be no Jews and no JIA. Not everyone, I may add, would regard that as a calamity. There are people who, though devoted to Israel, regard the Diaspora as an anachronism and would like to see it phased out and, indeed, they give money to Israel for that very reason. It would thus be wrong and, possibly illegal, to divert any significant proportion of JIA money to domestic causes. Mr Worms therefore suggests that subscribers be invited to earmark a proportion – say 5% of their money – for Jewish education. I regard this as an invaluable suggestion, not only for the funds it might yield, but because it would serve as a virtual plebiscite on Jewish education. A money shortage is but one of our difficult-ies. Before one launches upon an ambitious scheme to revitalise Jewish education, one must first feel assured that the community wants it.

The response was electrifying. For some months the *Jewish Chronicle*'s correspondence columns were filled with protagonists and antagonists of the scheme. Whilst Stuart Young, who was then still the Joint Chairman of the JIA, was reported in the issue of 11 June to have confirmed that the JIA was discussing my plan, the Chairman of the Jewish Welfare Board, the late Lionel Leighton, expressed his concern that domestic charities would be left out in the cold if the JIA embraced Jewish education.

In another article on 18 June the *Jewish Chronicle* wrote that funding of Jewish education would give to the JIA the opportunity to bring together independent and committed individuals to consider the purposes of Jewish education and to insist on constructive programmes and the avoidance of waste and duplication.

Overseas support came from Philip Klutznick who was probably the outstanding American Jew of that time.

> ... Whilst I am not a great believer in foretelling doom, since in our history somehow events have proved such predictions as exaggerated, nevertheless, I am vitally concerned with reducing the prospects of extinction by increasing the prospects for Jewish education ...
>
> ... what is essentially at the core of the depressing evaluation of much Jewish educational activity in many countries is the absolute lack of resources both fiscal and manpower to perform the kind of task that will fit in our modern society.
>
> I am delighted that so important a publication as yours endorses an approach to improvement. I am delighted, too, that my good friend, Fred Worms, has helped to focus attention on this very critical problem.

Professor Prais, whose survey of the educational history of a sample of teenage London Jewish children I had drawn on in writing my paper, also sent a letter to the *Jewish Chronicle* in support of providing a solid financial basis for Jewish education to give it a proper priority, as did Pierre Gildesgame:

> Fred Worms' crusade on behalf of better Jewish education was

fully underscored, if any aditional evidence was needed, by the survey which appeared in your issue of May 28, revealing the appalling ignorance in the ranks of children attending Jewish schools, most of whom have hardly ever heard of Dr Theodor Herzl. Similar enquiries on kindred Jewish subjects would doubtless yield equally disturbing results.

Money alone is not likely to solve this problem. The setting-up of an emergency educational committee, on the pattern laid down by the late Lord Sieff immediately after the Second World War, and the availability of a permanent fund, responsibly managed and allocated, will at least afford an opportunity to educationalists to apply these to the raising of the level of education with the help of teachers whose training would be geared to a programme of specialised tuition.

The Survival of Anglo-Jewry as an identifiable community will depend on its human quality and degree of dedication to Judaism and its aspirations. A generation of inadequately-educated individuals is hardly likely to produce the leadership we so sorely need.

If the leaders of the JIA here and in Israel are really worried about succession, then the "price" they are asked to pay by Fred Worms for better education is low compared to the heavy losses in vigorous fund-raising manpower which we are likely to sustain and which will deprive Israel of the moral and financial support she will need for many years to come.

On 24 September 1976, under the heading "The Last Jews", the editor called for a sense of communal purpose to improve Jewish education for both children and their parents – that without such determination the Jewish community would wither under the inroads of assimilation, intermarriage, and even more so, through sheer ignorance of anything worth passing on to the next generation. I cannot recall any other subject to which the *Jewish Chronicle* returned in successive editions. For the fourth week running the editor devoted his leading article to the subject.

The Joint Israel Appeal has set itself the tremendous task of raising £1 million through this year's Kol Nidre appeal ... It is in no sense to negate the urgency of the appeal if, in the same breath, cognisance is taken of the ongoing debate over the use of some portion of JIA proceeds for educational purposes in this country. Had Anglo-Jewry a "community chest", education would undoubtedly be one of its priorities. But there is no such general purposes fund [nor] the readiness on the part of our major fund-raising organisations to surrender some part of their independence in order to make this feasible.

The question then arises whether some form of co-operation can be achieved with the JIA, or whether our stretched resources are to be burdened with the establishment of yet another fund-raising organisation. The answer surely lies in co-operation. But the solid objections of some JIA leaders are also worthy of consideration. It is not merely that they are fearful of diminishing the funds remitted to Israel. They demand to know exactly what educational purposes are to be served by a diversion of JIA income. It must also be acknowledged that, however shortsighted the view, education as a fund-raising endeavour is held in far less esteem than assistance for Israel.

At this stage ... no one knows precisely how many Jewish day schools this community needs, how many teachers, what aids will advance the low level of much Sunday School teaching, the number of youngsters who will want to go on to more advanced Jewish studies ... or how much any one or all of these requirements will cost.

In December 1976 Michael Sacher was given the B'nai B'rith Award for outstanding communal services. He reiterated his stand that the JIA should concentrate entirely on collecting funds for Israel because this was what the contributors expected from it. In the intervening months the question of Jewish education had become the foremost debating subject wherever concerned Jews came together. A number of them wrote to say that if the JIA would not co-operate then they would bypass it and earmark their contribution for Jewish education direct, sentiments which were deeply deplored. They had missed the point. We did not want to diminish funds for Israel. We wanted the JIA machinery to help us raise funds for Jewish education.

The controversy came to a conclusion in June 1977. Much work was done behind the scenes by Chief Rabbi Jakobovits and Moshe Davis with the leadership of the JIA who finally agreed to co-operate. A seminal letter appeared in the *Jewish Chronicle* on 17 June:

> We are concerned about the continuation of Jewish education in this country. We believe that it has a vital role to play in the survival of our community and thus in the fulfilment of our support of the State of Israel. We must enhance the quality of education, ensure a sound continuing basis for the existing network of schools and, where possible, establish new schools in areas where they are needed.
>
> We pledge our participation in a campaign to fund the Jewish Educational Development Trust, particularly in the light of its revised and enlarged programme. This will in no way detract from our efforts, both individually and collectively, on behalf of Israel.

The letter was signed by Lionel Becker, Michael Blake, Henry Brecher, Rabbi Sidney Brichto, Stanley Burton, Rosser Chinn, Trevor E. Chinn, Norman Feingold, Stafford Fertleman, Warren Fox, Bernard Garbacz, David Hyman, Brian Kerner, Peter Levy, Henry Lewis, Alan Millett, Ben Pollard, David Pomson, Harold H. Poster, Michael M. Sacher, J. Edward Sieff, Cyril Stein, Fred Worms, Stuart Young.

In its leading article under the heading NEW DEAL FOR EDUCATION the editor wrote:

> Jewish education throughout Britain – whether in day schools, or kindergarten, synagogue or withdrawal classes, is promised a new deal in plans announced today by the Jewish Educational Development Trust.
>
> A planned programme of Jewish educational development, including teacher training at various levels, has been made

possible by the decision of the top leadership of the Joint Israel Appeal and other communal leaders, to pledge their personal support for the considerable funding which will be necessary. JIA funds will not be involved in any way, but the JIA will lend its expertise in the administrative sphere.

No price tag has been attached to the cost of helping existing schools and classes to expand their Jewish educational facilities or for the provision of new ones, but it is reasonable to estimate that something in the region of £750,000 will be required in the first year alone for the support and extension of existing facilities and that a similar sum will be needed in following years for these purposes.

We had won the battle but it was not at all clear whether we had won the war. The JIA involvement for some time remained tenuous and whilst we had the blessing, and to some extent, the personal support of some of its leaders, the revitalised JEDT owed its success largely to the energy of Stanley Kalms (now Sir Stanley). Stanley, a man of restless energy, had built the Dixon Group from a couple of photographic shops inherited from his father into one of the largest retail organisations in the UK with considerable interests overseas. A man with a large heart and a short fuse who hides considerable intellectual ability under a rough pragmatic exterior, he believes that a committee of two is 50 per cent surplus to requirements. The revitalised JEDT, Jews' College, and the creation of the Sinai/Sobell Primary School in Kenton were largely due to his drive and enthusiasm.

Many members of the community were concerned with the reluctance of the JIA bride to enter into any form of liaison with Jewish education. In particular Dr Abraham (Bram) Marcus, who had left medicine to make his fortune in highly specialised medical publishing, felt that too great a proportion of the community's resources went to Israel. He and I decided to get the facts and we set up a committee and invited Ellis Birk, who was then Chairman of the Jewish Welfare Board, David Lewis, Chairman of the Jewish Blind Society, Peter Levy, one of the principal creators of the Sternberg Centre and Robert Glatter, the Honorary Treasurer of the

Hillel Foundation to join with Bram and myself. We invited Bernard Garbacz to use the resources of his firm to conduct a research project which came to some exceedingly interesting conclusions. These were published on 17 December 1984.

It showed that 60 per cent of charitable funds raised by Anglo-Jewry went to Israel via the JIA and other Israeli institutions such as universities and museums, compared to 12 per cent spread thinly on the many organisations which engaged in Jewish education in the widest sense. It was not surprising, therefore, that with such blatant underfunding the community's decline was continuing.

36

The Jewish Education Development Trust and the Charles Kalms–Henry Ronson Immanuel College

SIMON CAPLAN BECAME the director of the Jewish Education Development Trust in January 1985. Stanley Kalms had brought him to London from the Board of Education in Glasgow to make him his principal assistant for Jews' College and the JEDT. Together with Rabbi Jonathan Sacks they were responsible for the phoenix-like resurrection of a desultory Jews' College.

I am obliged to Simon Caplan for the loan of the records compiled by him on which I have drawn in writing this chapter. Extending to well over 100 pages, they could form the basis of a Ph.D. thesis, but he is quite right to delay publication of the full text. It records the clash of personalities involved, the rivalries between the leading players and their ambivalent attitude to the President of the Trust, Chief Rabbi Immanuel Jakobovits. By 1995 the wounds had not healed. Stanley Kalms, the most powerful activist at the time, has not resumed his important and seminal work within the Anglo-Jewish community and others have fallen by the wayside.

The Chief Rabbi invited Kalms to become Chairman of the JEDT and thus was created a partnership that was fraught with difficulties alternating between close and creative co-operation and periods of mutual distrust. However, on one thing they were *ad idem* – namely that in order to bypass the slow moving existing communal bodies, the Trustees of the JEDT should consist of the principal movers and shakers who would not only be instrumental in securing funds but would be in a position to carry out the Trust's policy.

The co-operation of the JIA leadership was essential and Trevor Chinn, Cyril Stein and Gerald Ronson joined the Board of Trustees. Other Trustees were Rabbi Jonathan Sacks, Judge Finestein, Ronald Metzger (Treasurer), Sir Harry Solomon, Morris Serlin (Property), Conrad Morris and Peter Levy.

I was given the portfolio of Part-time Jewish Education, largely dispensed by the Sunday morning *chadarim*, which I found thoroughly frustrating because there was no money to implement my plans and the teachers were mostly untrained young volunteers.

In 1984 the JEDT, in conjunction with the Torah Department of the World Zionist Organisation, commissioned a feasibility study to examine the possibilities of the creation of two schools, proposed in *Let My People Know*. At that time Jules Kornbluth, Chairman of the Governors of the Independent Jewish Day School in Hendon, a modern Orthodox primary school, together with his wife Elaine were amongst the principal protagonists leading a pressure group for a modern Orthodox secondary school in north-west London.

Michael Cohen, the Director of the London Board of Jewish Religious Education, a United Synagogue body, Menachem Levine of the Torah Department, Dr Stephen Miller, Head of Department of Social Science and Humanities at the City University, London and Simon Caplan produced a report, the upshot of which was that the atmosphere was right for the establishment of the two schools but that the one in north-west London should receive priority.

During the Eighties, the Trust concentrated on the promotion of promising young people to play a leading part in Jewish education in the UK. Professor Seymour Fox of the Hebrew University created the concept of Jerusalem Fellows, who, after intensive training in Jerusalem over a period of years, would return to the Diaspora to assume senior posts in Jewish educational establishments. Amongst them were Alistair Falk, now Headteacher of the Solomon Wolfson School in Ilford, Michael Gillis who became Headmaster of Mount Scopus College in Melbourne, now working in Jerusalem, Jonathan Kestenbaum, who joined Melitz before he became Director of Chief Rabbi Sacks' office in London, Simon Caplan, Dr Alex Pomson, also at the King Solomon School, Ann Korn at the Sinai School and Johnny Ariel who works for Melitz.

The JEDT in due course participated in an offspring of the Jerusalem Fellows, namely the Educators' Fellowship of which Syma Weinberg (Jewish Continuity), Rosalind Goulden (Headteacher of Kerem School) and Jean Shindler (Headteacher of Mathilda Marks Kennedy School) were distinguished graduates. Furthermore, the JEDT established the National Bursary Committee and sponsored a number of outstanding young educators such as Jonathan Cannon (now Head of Jewish Studies at Carmel College).

Undoubtedly the finest achievement of the JEDT, however, was the creation of the Sir Michael Sobell Sinai School in Kenton, a primary school which has proved a great success and later, Immanuel College.

Whilst there was an ecumenical approach on the part of the Trustees, Chief Rabbi Jakobovits was determined that the ethos of *Torah im Derech Eretz* should apply to the new secondary school. This slogan was coined by Rabbi Samson Raphael Hirsch, the founder of the eponymous school in Frankfurt some 140 years ago. Like Maimonides, he valued a modern, secular education alongside study of the Torah. There was a consensus that the school should aspire to become a model of excellence along modern Orthodox lines. The issue was complicated by the opposition of the United Synagogue whose Honorary Officers had suddenly woken up to the fact that it would not be under their control and could become a serious competitor to the Jewish Free School in Camden Town. This was headed by the combative Mrs Jo Wagerman who campaigned against so much money being earmarked for just one educational establishment.

The other major obstacle was the lack of a suitable site. The search during the 1985–8 period happened to coincide with the property boom years. As soon as a site came on to the market residential developers who, at that time had virtually unlimited banking support, would be on the scene and snap it up. The catchment area was north-west London including Hendon, Golders Green, Edgware and possibly as far out as Borehamwood, Bushey or Elstree. Green belt sites were examined only to be reluctantly turned down because of planning difficulties. The Orange Hill School in Edgware came on the market. Negotiations for its acquisition, which had proceeded satisfactorily, were disturbed by the intervention of the Governors of the Hasmonean Boys School. In the event the local authority used this as an excuse to withdraw the site altogether.

The ultimate acquisition of the Rosary Priory School in Bushey where Immanuel College is located, was an on and off saga, complicated by the fact that it was within a green belt area. The site, of some eight acres, which was subsequently increased by the purchase of an additional four acres, belonged to a convent which continues to operate to this very day immediately adjacent to the school. The advantage was that there were already a number of buildings *in situ* which, after some further expenditure, could be used. The disadvantage was that it contained a Victorian folly – Caldecote Towers – a "listed" building suffering from dry-rot and other problems, which would have to be repaired as a prior condition to obtaining planning permission for new classrooms.

Stanley Kalms bought the property for £3.7 million. At the time he was labouring under the impression that the overall cost of the school would be some £6 million. No one at that stage had any conception that the ultimate outlay would be substantially in excess of that figure.

Frenetic activity ensued. Action committees were set up and it was even hoped that the school could open by September 1989 – a wholly unrealistic target. I quote from Simon Caplan's papers:

Kalms acted in characteristic fashion. Morris Serlin was asked to revive the professional building team which had successfully completed the Jews' College development. On the educational front, Kalms turned to another Trustee – Fred Worms. Worms, a well-respected Yekke, a product of the Samson Raphael Hirsch School in Frankfurt, a "dati" Jew with a solid intellectual Jewish background and a clear and powerful advocate of tolerant centralist orthodoxy, was something of a rarity in the high church anti-intellectual atmosphere of Anglo-Jewry.

He and Kalms had often clashed across the committee table but Kalms recognised in him a man who would stick unswervingly to his principles, who could be trusted not to allow the project to be manoeuvred by inches towards the right and equally to stand up to the pressures and challenges of the Reform contingent within the body of the Trustees. Worms was to chair the Professional Advisory Committee.

Dr Jonathan Sacks wrote a paper on the principal objectives of the school, a seminal document which was received with acclaim. Ronnie Metzger, the treasurer of the JEDT, was to keep the finances in order and Kalms himself would lead the fund-raising with the assistance of Conrad Morris.

My committee consisted of Gabi Goldstein, a high-ranking civil servant in the Department of Education and Science. Aged 48, with vast experience in religious and secular education, he seemed to us the obvious choice for the Headteachership. Denis Felsenstein, another senior educator, was a former Deputy Head of JFS, a head teacher of a non-Jewish school and a senior inspector for one of the largest educational authorities in the country. Aged 62, he had reached the comfortable stage in his life where he worked as an independent educational consultant. He was a member of my synagogue and a Garden Suburb neighbour for many years. Philip Skelker and Clive Lawton were both professional educators. Both had held the post of Headteacher of King David School in Liverpool. Philip took over the headteachership of Carmel College and Clive Lawton, in due course, became the Chief Executive of Jewish Continuity.

There was also the ubiquitous Dr Stephen Miller, without whose demographic expertise no committee of this type was conceivable, and Meir Fachler, who had made *aliyah* but who had come back to this country to help us. Jules Kornbluth, Johnny Weil, Dr Caroline Lindsay, Seymour Saideman, a leading lay leader who would later become the President of the United Synagogue and, most importantly, Dr Jonathan Sacks made up the rest of this extremely hard-working team which was well co-ordinated by the enthusiastically involved Simon Caplan.

We had a well-nigh impossible task. We should really have convened two years earlier. We were expected within a period of six months to define the ethos of the school, to deal with its admission policy, single sex or coeducational conundrum, define the extent of Jewish studies, the parent/teacher relationship, the staffing policy, the pupil intake, site utilisation and curriculum development. Apart from this we were also charged with the appointments of a head-teacher, a head for Jewish studies, other senior teachers and the possibility of creating a sixth form within a couple of years of the school's establishment.

In hindsight I can only marvel at the chuzpah which we had in tackling this enormous agenda within the very narrow time limit. Miraculously it worked. We sat in almost non-stop sessions for a period of eight months. All our recommendations were accepted unanimously by the Trustees. We brought over my old friend, Professor Michael Rosenak of the Hebrew University, one of the world's leading pedagogical experts, who stayed for some months to advise us. The headteachership was offered to Gabi Goldstein. Gabi was ambivalent. He was being discouraged by his wife who felt that at that point in his life he should not take any chances with what seemed a perilous venture. We therefore advertised and had many applications but none were really suitable. One *Shabbat*, after conclusion of the service, I said to Denis Felsenstein, my neighbour in the Norrice Lea Synagogue, "Congratulations, Denis, you are going to be the new Headteacher of the Bushey School."

"You must be joking, Fred. I am 62, I am enjoying what I am doing. There is no way, at my stage in life, that I am going to take on this enormous responsibility."

"Well, think about it," I said.

He did and he accepted. This was probably the crucial point in the creation of the school. I doubt whether any other person would have had the combination of know-how, patience, perseverance and determination that Denis has shown over the last five years. He has made the school into what is generally recognised as an outstanding, if not sensational, success. He has built a loyal and devoted teaching staff around himself, and on his retirement in 1995 had secured continuity of the well-established ethos of the school through Myrna Jacobs, his former Deputy Headteacher.

However, all this was in the future, and we still had to go through

Above Fred Worms with Nachum Goldmann and Gerald Baron Cohen; *below* with Yitzhak Rabin.

Above With Menachem Begin;
below Shimon Peres presenting Fred
Worms with the Yakir Maccabi
Award.

Right Rabbi Adin Steinsaltz, President Ezer Weizman and Fred Worms; *below* with the Rothschilds at Mayer Amschel's tombstone, Frankfurt 1994.

Above Building the B'nai B'rith Bridge between Yemin Moshe and the Cinématheque, Jerusalem; *below* fixing the mezuzah on the Cochin Synagogue door, Israel Museum 1995.

Above Caroline and Nitzan's wedding 1985, with Yitzhak Navon and his son; *below* dedication of Mifgash Gildesgame with Teddy Kollek and Martin Paisner.

Above Caroline and Nitzan with twins Roi and Barak, and Sigal; *below* Ayelet, Matan, Tal, Nadia, Noam and Alan.

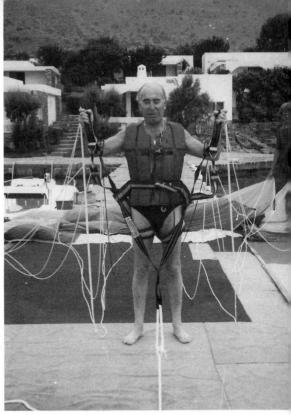

Above left Hilary with Kineret, Maor and Ma'ayan; *above right* parasailing in Crete; *below* with Aunt Claire Kevehazi at the Meta Worms Gardens at the Maccabiah Village, Ramat Gan.

גן
מטה וורמס
META WORMS
GARDEN

Above Della and Fred at Giza; *below* Teddy Kollek and Martin Weyl presenting a carved lotus flower at the Cochin Synagogue opening ceremony.

a series of crises between August 1989 and February 1990. When Stanley Kalms realised that the cost of the school would be millions more than previously estimated, he resigned. He felt let down. Originally the bulk of the school's finances was to be provided by the donations of one million pounds each from the Ronson Foundation, the Kalms Charitable Trust and a JIA contribution of approximately £1.5 million. In consideration of two of the major donations the school was to be known as the Charles Kalms–Henry Ronson Bushey School, or Charles Kalms–Henry Ronson Mount Scopus School. It was only after considerable pressure from those of us who wanted to commemorate the Chief Rabbi's vital involvement that the name of Immanuel College was agreed upon.

The resignation of Stanley Kalms, the principal power house, the dynamo, the Chairman of the Jewish Educational Development Trust, looked at the time like a mortal blow. The Trustees were considering the cancellation of the whole project – selling the site, taking a loss and going back to the status quo ante. Gerald Ronson, in particular, felt that the Kalms acquisition was a major mistake and that for less money he could find a better site.

There followed an interregnum during which survival was precarious. The Chief Rabbi said he would continue to lend his support only if the Chairman of the Governors was approved by him personally and proceeded to nominate me. I turned him down instantly and stated that under no circumstances would I be prepared to be involved for an indefinite period in view of my many other commitments. The most that I would do would be to hold the fort until a suitable candidate was found.

So it was that whilst its very existence was at stake Denis Felsenstein, Simon Caplan, Serlin, Metzger and I maintained the exacting routine preparations for the opening of the school. Denis's calm, pragmatic, unflappable attitude served as an example. He was requested to attend Trustees' meetings, which had now reverted to Hamilton Terrace after the power had shifted from Stanley Kalms to Lord Jakobovits, who had been elevated to the peerage in the meantime.

Michael Phillips was appointed successor Chairman of the JEDT. Michael had the great advantage of being *persona grata* with all camps. He had no pedagogical pretensions but was an able administrator who would not willingly associate himself with a failure. In the event, he provided an invaluable bridge between the JEDT and its successor organisation, Jewish Continuity, and it was he who was responsible for the setting up of the Committee of Enquiry into the general state of Jewish education in the country, which culminated in the Worms Report (see Chapter 37).

Henry Knobil's inspired appointment as Chairman of the Governors was another key to the ultimate success of the school. Henry, who had recently retired from full-time business activities was the ideal man for the job. As an ex-Marks and Spencer Executive, he had established his own textile concern and had a flair for human relations and a reputation as a man of deep religious convictions based on modern Orthodoxy. He threw himself into his task with enthusiasm and he has led the Board of Governors of Immanuel College for a period of five years with unflagging zeal and triumphant success.

In the meantime Gerald Ronson continued to look for a site but finally had to agree that there was really no alternative to Bushey. Michael Levy, who had only recently joined the JEDT, came up with a formula that was finally accepted. He suggested that the Trust make itself responsible for the bulk of the commitments on the understanding that the Chief Rabbi, together with a number of Trustees, raise the remaining three million which were needed to complete the project.

Some of us had our reservations that the Chief Rabbi, with or without help, would be able to find such a vast sum which so far, in spite of the intensive efforts of Conrad Morris after the departure of Stanley Kalms, who has since received his Knighthood, had proved so elusive. However, by that time everybody was so exhausted that the formula was adopted. All this now appears ancient history.

By 1995 the school had become a classic success story with 300 pupils, a splendid reputation and assured growth for the future. It had drawn its clientele mostly from those who would have opted for non-Jewish public schools. It is left with a major problem. When Jonathan Sacks became Chief Rabbi he created Jewish Continuity and the JEDT was then doomed to extinction. It was difficult enough to raise the missing funds for Immanuel College when there was no competing Jewish Continuity/JIA combination. The debt which hangs over the school will have to be funded. My hope is that we have another "Sydney Opera House phenomenon". When this magnificent complex was built in the harbour of Sydney, Australia, its final cost overshot the budget by a phenomenal extent. The Scandinavian architects had skilfully arranged the building plans in such a way that by the time the full horror of the cost became known, the process had become irreversible. Ways and means were found to pay for the Opera House which is today one of the modern wonders of the world, a major tourist attraction and an artistic centre of top class.

Whether anybody would have embarked on creating Immanuel College with the knowledge of its ultimate cost is, to say the least, doubtful. The fact remains that the school exists and plays an invaluable part in the true spirit of Jewish Continuity in the UK.

37

The Worms Report: Securing our Future – An Inquiry into Jewish Education in the United Kingdom

Succcess in the educational field seemed as elusive as ever, particularly since various interested parties were quoting contradictory statistics which resembled party political broadcasts not necessarily based on facts. Stanley Kalms had disappeared from the communal scene. In 1991, the revamped JEDT, under the chairmanship of Michael Phillips, decided to set up a Think Tank to investigate in depth the state of Jewish education in the UK. I was invited to accept the chairmanship and although I had no illusion about the enormity of the task, I could hardly stand aside when this challenge dealt with the very issue I had championed for so many years.

My task was made easier by the quality and devotion of the personalities who joined the committee. They were Rabbi Anthony Bayfield, Allan Fisher, Dr Myer Goldman (who has since tragically passed away), Gabriel Goldstein, Henry Israel and Maurice de Vries. The professional consultants were Dr Stephen Miller, Michael Mail and Syma Weinberg.

The enquiry took 18 months of intensive, virtually unceasing work, involving weekly meetings, travels up and down the country and interviewing 41 professional educators and lay leaders. It transpired that some of our rabbis have great difficulty in uttering the word "pluralism" as though it had perjorative connotations. It is strange that the commission on Jewish education in the USA which includes Alfred Gottschalk, Norman Lamm, Haskel Lookstein, Ismar Schorsch and Isadore Twersky – religious leaders ranging from right to left – does not suffer from a similar debilitating syndrome.

Anglo-Jewish establishments like the Sternberg Centre, the Akiva School, the Spiro Institute are facts of life. They fulfil a need which cannot be satisfied by traditional right-wing bodies. Activists like Sir Sigmund Sternberg and Peter Levy play a positive role in the wider community.

The Worms Report faced these realities in a constructive manner. *Securing our Future – An Inquiry into Jewish Education in the United Kingdom* was published in September 1992. I quote from Chief Rabbi Sacks' foreword:

> As the report makes clear from the beginning, we stand at a critical moment in the history of Anglo-Jewry. We are losing four thousand Jews each year. But at the same time we have a unique opportunity to create a dynamic of Jewish renewal. We have come late – but not too late – to the realisation that Jewish education holds the key to the vitality of our community, intellectually, spiritually and even demographically. Those who know, grow; while those for whom Judaism and Jewish identity are a closed book gradually drift away.
>
> The implications of this report are clear. We must move Jewish education to the highest place on our communal agenda. We must work to recruit to it teachers and lay leaders of excellence. We must communicate the importance of education to the community, especially to parents. Above all we must create a genuinely national structure that will allow us to use our limited resources to the maximum effect.
>
> The single most striking finding to emerge is the sheer fragmentation of Anglo-Jewish education as presently constituted. This means that we have not yet developed effective communal strategies for the recruitment and training of teachers, the construction of curricula, interaction and reinforcement between formal and informal learning contexts, the sharing of models of excellence and best practice, the development of lay leadership and the research and decision-making forums neces-

sary for sound educational planning.

Many dedicated and gifted individuals have laboured long and separately in the cause of Jewish learning. The time has come for us to pool our resources and labour together.

This report is not the end of a process but a beginning. I hope it will lead to a searching communal debate out of which will emerge the shape of a new structure for Anglo-Jewish education.

The *Jewish Chronicle* featured the Worms Report on its front page on 4 September 1992:

CHIEF BACKS MOVES TO SAFEGUARD EDUCATION

Chief Rabbi Dr Jonathan Sacks has pledged to help implement the proposals of the first major inquiry into Anglo-Jewish education.

The proposals include the creation of a national council for Jewish education, combining Orthodox and Progressive groups, and were drawn up by the Jewish Educational Development Trust's Think Tank.

Its report, "Securing our Future" released this week after more than a year's research, coincides with the struggle of many educational institutions to cope with the recession.

Rabbi Sacks said that he would lead moves to put the report's proposals into practice. The "economic crisis is forcing the community to decide its priorities," he said. "Education must come at the top."

Rabbi Anthony Bayfield, the Think Tank's only Progressive member, believed that the proposed Orthodox/Progressive co-operation would not present "an obstacle" to the council's formation. "I can't think that an overwhelmingly United Synagogue group of people would put forward a proposal that they didn't think stood a chance."

It also dedicated its leading article to the Report and summarised its principal recommendations:

NOW, THE HARD PART . . .

Eighteen months of interviews, debates, research and writing culminated this week in the release of what has come to be known as the Worms Report on Jewish Education. The lengthy document is the work of a Think Tank, organised under the aegis of the Jewish Educational Development Trust and chaired by Fred Worms, long a leading advocate for spending more on youth and education in the community.

The group's main recommendation is as straightforward as it is welcome. The report calls for the establishment of a new, community-wide body on Jewish education. Its aim would be to battle against needless competition and duplication among the many existing education initiatives at a time of scarce overall resources, while setting priorities, and raising funds for future projects.

Some aspects of the report may draw open opposition, notably the idea of greater co-operation and co-ordination between Orthodox and Progressive Jews on issues of common concern. But the trend, inevitably if slowly, seems to be running in favour of such joint action.

The more serious threat is that the Think Tank's work, like other initiatives in the past, will be damned by silence, faint praise, or by enough "follow-up discussion" to choke it in verbiage.

Still, the Think Tank is right to stress the need to move from *ad hoc* benevolence to a more organised method of funding. And Mr Worms is right to advocate concrete action on the report by the end of this year. The publication of the report, difficult though it may have been to assemble, was the easy part. What matters most is what comes next.

The principal recommendations (as summarised by the JC) were:

– A National Council for Jewish education should be established as a "representative, umbrella body" for Jewish education. It would encourage collaboration between different organisations and would plan, and raise money for, major projects.

– The recruitment and training of teachers should head the agenda over the next decade.

– Joint degree courses should be established combining Jewish studies with subjects like history and psychology to attract those who might not otherwise consider a career in Jewish education.

– A comprehensive programme of in-service training should be developed to improve the professionalism of Jewish studies teachers.

– A "meaningful career structure" with financial incentives should be established to motivate teachers.

– "Community educators" and "educational fieldworkers" should be appointed to improve teaching in the part-time system. They would act as advisers, teacher-trainers and curriculum-developers to communities.

– Schools and youth groups should co-operate in trying to encourage more teenagers to remain in Jewish education. Some educators should be shared between schools, youth groups and part-time centres rather than being used simply in one area.

– A network of educators should be established to develop curricula in Jewish studies. Two key areas are building links between Jewish studies and the national curriculum; and trying to overcome the difficulties of presenting religious studies to children from non-religious homes.

– An academic unit should be created to research the needs of Jewish education and evaluate the quality of programmes.

– A mobile resource and exhibition centre should be set up to display educational materials to schools and community centres.

– Lay leaders need to be trained for specific roles. Younger men and women need to be recruited into lay leadership and those with "intellectual and interpersonal skills" should be given priority.

38

Jewish Continuity

IN DUE COURSE, Chief Rabbi Sacks expressed the wish that the activities of the Jewish Educational Development Trust should be wound down and that it be replaced by a new body with the title "Jewish Continuity", a term which had been used in the USA some years earlier (see Professor Steven M. Cohen, *American Assimilation or Jewish Revival*, Indiana University Press 1988).

The American Jewish problem may be multiplied 20 fold when compared with our shrunken UK community of some 300,000 souls. With an even faster erosion in numbers, 63 per cent outmarriage and a waning interest in Israel, there are many Jeremiahs who forecast the disappearance of American Jewry (except for the ultra-Orthodox) within three generations.

The Federations, which comprise the principal charitable fund-raising bodies in 300 American towns with a sizeable Jewish population, have woken up from complacent drifting along familiar paths to face the crisis in the 1990s. Jewish education was recognised as the Number One priority. Funds to Israel were drastically reduced to shore up the tottering edifices at home. Mort Mandel, a prominent industrialist, decided to devote his boundless energy to re-structuring the educational scene. Advised by Professor Seymour Fox of the Hebrew University, recognised as one of the foremost educational experts in the world, the services of Alan Hoffmann of the Hebrew University's Melton Centre for Jewish Education in the Diaspora were secured. This powerful triumvirate formed the Council for Initiatives in Jewish Education which is spending many millions a year to re-educate a reluctant community, to shift the emphasis from vicarious Judaism via support of Israel to the creation of a generation of knowledgeable Jews.

Their Commission for Jewish Education published a booklet *A Time to Act*. Members of that body under Mort Mandel's chairmanship included representatives of Orthodox, Conservative and Reform establishments from Yeshiva University to the Hebrew Union College, showing a commendable ecumenical approach.

In the UK Dr Michael Sinclair became the Chairman of Jewish Continuity and Clive Lawton its Chief Executive. Dr Sinclair, a relative unknown, had made a fortune in his business association with American hospitals, had become Orthodox (*Baal Teshuvah*) and was fired with the enthusiasm of the newly converted. Clive Lawton, a former Headteacher of King David School in Liverpool and subsequently an executive with the Merseyside Education Authority, prided himself on his non-conformist style. Complete with long ponytail and open sandals, he tried to combine an anti-establishment appearance with representing a role model for the Jewish youngsters. Some rabbis took an instant dislike to him which did not augur well for the future. He had served on my Professional Advisory Committee for Immanuel College and I knew him pretty well.

When I was consulted about the appointment of Chief Executive I recommended Jonathan Kestenbaum, the Chief of Staff of Chief Rabbi Sacks' office. I had known Jonathan virtually all his life. A modern, Orthodox Jew who had made *aliyah*, he represented the very best of Anglo-Saxon and Jewish culture. Bilingual, learned, determined yet tolerant, he was the prototype of the educated Jew. He worked for Melitz in Jerusalem before being recruited by the Chief Rabbi who told me, in no uncertain terms, that he could not spare him. Indeed, he rendered quite outstanding service to the Chief Rabbinate.

In the meantime the atmosphere had changed completely. Yossi Beilin, Israel's Deputy Foreign Minister, declared categorically that the Diaspora should keep its money, educate its young and ensure its survival. With a GNP of $80 billion, Israel no longer needed handouts from overseas Jews, he said. The decline in the reputation of the Jewish Agency and the World Zionist Organisation were additional nails in the coffin of the "Everything must go to Israel" lobby. The JIA read the signals and decided to join Jewish Continuity by underwriting £12 million over three years.

After one year's operation, Clive Lawton asked me, amongst many others, whether I had any comments, suggestions or criticism. I quote from my letter which I sent to him in January 1995:

> You have asked for my comments on the latest proposals of Jewish Continuity.
>
> You were a member of my "Professional Advisory Committee" which defined the ethos and curricular infrastructure of Immanuel College; you were one of the educationalists consulted by my JEDT Committee which led to the Worms Report on Jewish Education in the UK and you are therefore familiar, at least to some extent, with my approach to this subject. It will not come as a surprise, therefore, when I say that I cannot be included amongst those who applaud either Phase I or the proposed Phase II of Jewish Continuity.
>
> For over a year Simon Rocker, the determined and inquisitive reporter of the *Jewish Chronicle*, has telephoned me at regular intervals to enquire what I think of Jewish Continuity. My answer has always been . . . "The Jury is still out – ask me in a couple of years." Truthfully, I should have given him a different answer.
>
> I found Phase I disappointing. Why? These are the reasons:
> 1. The JEDT was left in the lurch. The decision that a successor organisation be created put the Trustees of the JEDT into an impossible situation. A body which has been condemned to death can hardly compete with the JIA/Jewish Continuity combination and clout when asking for communal funds. Ironically, the Chief Rabbi and the JIA leadership were amongst the principal sponsors of Immanuel College, whose establishment costs have not yet been fully funded and which remain the Sword of Damocles of the JEDT.
> 2. Not everything new is good and not everything that exists is bad. Inviting new proposals from the community resulting in an expenditure of £700,000 into scores of activities, some of a

questionable and marginal nature, is not going to perpetuate the survival of Anglo-Jewry.

Firing shrapnel shots in the hope of hitting something is no substitute for a well-thought-out structural plan. There are no quick fixes and no instant panaceas.

3. Existing organisations that work well but are hampered by lack of funds have been ignored. Take Rosh Pinah Primary School as an example. It can only accept 50 per cent of its applicants. I can tell you of heart-rending stories of families who could not get their children into Rosh Pinah who have reluctantly been compelled to send them to non-Jewish schools.

First priority should surely be given to tried and tested educational establishments that need funds to carry out their work properly. One could, of course, multiply this example several times over. This needs urgent reconsideration.

4. Jewish Continuity should not be seen as a purely Orthodox organisation. The reservations expressed by Felix Posen in public and Clive Marks in private should not be swept under the carpet.

The JEDT had no such problems nor do our colleagues in the US suffer from the "exclusivism" factor. As you are no doubt aware, Mort Mandel is presiding over the Commission on Jewish Education in North America which has representatives at the highest level from all sectors ranging from Yeshiva University to Hebrew Union College.

When perhaps 50 per cent of our people have opted out, we cannot afford to delegitimise Jewish organisations "left of the *halachah*".

Which *halachah*? Stamford Hill or Munk Shul and Hendon Adath, which have already declared that the *Eruv*, when it comes about, is *treife*.

5. We now come to the new "Hands-On Master Plan". I cannot express a definite opinion until I see a budget i.e. how much has been allocated under the various headings.

How much will be set aside for augmenting teachers' salaries, as proposed in the Worms Report? The most experienced Jewish educators in the world, Seymour Fox and Alan Hoffmann, who have given a lifetime into researching the subject, will tell you that this is the crux of the matter.

The teaching profession, as such, is underpaid. This applies even more to Jewish teachers who, in a relatively small market, also lack a career structure. This is why, in the past, we have not attracted the brightest graduates. They preferred to go into medicine, accountancy or law. It so happens now that the professions suffer from a surfeit of candidates and jobs are hard to find.

We have a unique opportunity. We can now get the charismatic double first activists to become teachers, if we pay them properly. Talk to the immediate past Chairman of UJS, who is typical of a number of graduates who have approached me in my capacity as President of Hillel. We are talking in round figures about an extra £10,000 pa.

"How can we possibly afford to pay that to every teacher?" you will ask.

"You cannot," is the answer.

We do not have to reinvent the wheel. I am glad that after much pressure on my part, Professor Seymour Fox has, at long last, been invited to advise us on this problem. He has the answers. They work. I do not wish to anticipate what he is going to say, save for one point . . .

Unless you set aside one million pounds per annum out of the twelve million pounds you have over three years, for funding teachers' increments, you will be wasting your time.

I repeat – there are no quick fixes. This is a slow, laborious, long-term process. There can be no objection to the interim measures of teacher training etc. that have been proposed, both in the Worms Report and the Jewish Continuity document, as long as it is recognised that these are not long-term solutions.

A number of friends have asked me whether I feel triumphant that after twenty-seven years of preaching JIA involvement in financing Jewish education it has at long last materialised. The truth is that I have mixed feelings. Better late than never. On the other hand, we have lost ten student generations in these years, as evidenced by our dramatic demographic decline.

The Chief Rabbi has done a great job in travelling up and down the country, preaching the primary importance of Jewish Education. The message has been heard and understood. Let us not fail in the implementation.

I received a non-commital reply from Clive Lawton which did little to reassure me.

Professor Seymour Fox, with his colleague Annette Hochstein, came to London at the beginning of October 1995 to address representatives of Jewish Continuity as well as other communal leaders. I resisted the pressure exerted upon me both by Professor Fox as well as some London colleagues who wanted me to fly back from Israel to attend this two-day conference. I met Seymour both before and after his visit; his views coincided with mine.

He explained to the London meeting that they did not have a strategic concept, that their multifarious plans were far too ambitious to implement with the limited finance and personnel available, that 80 different grants to 80 organisations could not be properly monitored and that they had to decide whether they were a charity which allocated money or an enabling organisation or a hands-on body which would be active in the field with its own staff.

One thing is crystal clear. The Jewish Continuity organisation must be saved. There will not be a second chance. The Chief Rabbi has staked his reputation on its success. Ironically, the JIA needs it to ensure its own survival as the leading Anglo-Jewish charity.

In March 1996 Professor Leslie Wagner published his report *Change in Continuity* which he was asked to prepare by the Trustees. It is a first-class document which sets out clearly the shortcomings and failures of Jewish Continuity Mark I and makes recommendations very much along the lines of the Worms Report to the JEDT published in September 1992 (ch. 37).

The criticism includes:

... the perceived lack of transparency and accountability in its decision-making has created a lack of confidence among key stake-holders;

... a recurring theme was that Jewish Continuity had to work with organisations and its language had to change. It should not persist in claiming that it knew all the answers;

... that power is too centralised particularly as the same person holds the office of Chairman of the Trustees and Chairman of the Executive Board. In practice, decisions are perceived to be taken by the Chairman and Chief Executive consulting as they feel necessary with a small number of colleagues;

... some critics see the style of decision-making as arbitrary rather than systematic;

... Failure to address these criticisms therefore could seriously weaken Jewish Continuity's ability to raise funds and generate support in the future;

It also explains in some detail that Jewish Continuity is seen largely as an Orthodox organisation and that the Chief Rabbi's continuing prominent association creates significant difficulties. Orthodox religious leaders do not approve of allocations made to non-Orthodox organisations under the aegis of the Chief Rabbi.

The recommendations include the creation of a cross-community Board of Governors, a drastic diminution in the involvement of the Chief Rabbi, who would only be concerned with allocations made to the Orthodox sector and a total reappraisal of the terms of reference of the New Jewish Continuity.

The Wagner Report was overtaken by the announcement in June 1996 that the JIA and Jewish Continuity will merge. I suggested as far back as 1966 that money be raised for Jewish education by the JIA, which is what will now happen.

It is like stepping on the tail of a dinosaur and thirty years later the head twitches. Whilst welcoming this historic development, a caveat must be added. It will only work if the management/allocations committee will operate at arm's length as an independent body. As the *Jewish Chronicle* correctly states, "there will be no third chance".

39

My B'nai B'rith Story

MY PARENTS HAD been members of B'nai B'rith in Frankfurt – the Marcus Horowitz Lodge – which, as I found out to my cost at a later stage, was an exclusive body. Membership was considered a privilege and numbers were restricted. Blackballing was hardly necessary because only those who knew they would be accepted, applied.

B'nai B'rith was founded in 1843 by 12 good men and true who met at Sinsheimers Café in New York to stop the internecine warfare between the different Jewish factions at the time. Although they were all immigrants, Jews soon formed themselves into different *Landsmannschaften* which maintained the tradition of the old country. There was a clear ladder of ascendancy. The Russians considered the Poles beneath them; the Litvaks felt superior to both; the Austrians looked with disdain on any country that lay east of their border, and the German Jews, the Yekkes, talked only to each other.

The founders of B'nai B'rith set sail under the noble emblem of Benevolence, Brotherly Love and Harmony. Yet it took nearly 100 years before a Supreme President of B'nai B'rith did not hail from German Jewish stock. Alfred Monsky's election in 1938 broke the mould. The 1940 Census of American Jews showed that 80 per cent were of East European origin. During the first century of its existence, the Order defied its motto and left the running at top level to those who knew best, namely the Yekkes. They had established a great track record as the leading merchant bankers and owners of great stores but, alas, they also led the pace in assimilation. Phil

Klutznick once showed me a list of founders of some of the pre-1880 B'nai B'rith Lodges in smaller towns in the United States. Very few of the families listed in these documents had remained Jewish.

I was not aware of this exclusivity mentality until I put my foot in it in no uncertain manner when I was installed as President of the First Lodge of England in 1960. In those days some importance was attached to the Presidential Installation Speech and one took great care to prepare oneself thoroughly. I thought it might be appropriate if I were to refer to the great days of B'nai B'rith in Germany, particularly since strenuous efforts were then being made to revive it during the Adenauer period.

I thought I had delivered my task in a reasonably satisfactory fashion until a few days later I received a hand written letter from an old established member of the First Lodge, a solicitor named Samuels who has long since departed to a non-exclusive fraternity. He wrote that he had never been so insulted in his life; it was bad enough that when he had tried as a young man to join the Lodge in Frankfurt he was turned down because he was an *Ostjude* but that some 30 years later he should have to listen to this very same Lodge being referred to in laudatory tones was just too much. He expressed the hope that I would not endeavour to reintroduce the kind of snobbery that prevailed in Germany into the First Lodge of England. I visited him and thanked him for having drawn my attention to a state of affairs of which I had known nothing and assured him that the traditions of the First Lodge would be carried on in the spirit of its founders who had established it in 1910.

B'nai B'rith in the United Kingdom has had its ups and downs often through circumstances beyond its control. There were some very distinguished names amongst my predecessors. The first President was Herbert Bentwich; his successor was Haham Dr M. Gaster. Others over the years included Dr J. Snowman, Augustus Kahn, Paul Goodman, Dr Mortimer Epstein, Dr Israel Feldman, Gordon Liverman, Rabbi Dr Daiches, Rev Perlzweig, Dr George Webber, Theo Birks, Daniel Schonfield, Rabbi Cassel and Hugh Harris. During the First and Second World Wars it became semi-dormant but there were always a few stalwarts such as Julius Schwab who ensured its survival. His sons, Harry and Walter, continued to play prominent roles in the Anglo-Jewish community. Walter passed away in June 1996.

District 15 of Great Britain and Ireland was formed in 1926. By the time I was elected President in 1960 the First Lodge was in a pretty sorry state. My installation took place in front of an audience of some 15 brothers in the basement of Folman's restaurant in Holborn. Waiters kept passing through, toilets were flushing and my first impression was not a favourable one. My Council and I energetically set about raising the standard to try and regain its former glory.

The generally distinguished record of the First Lodge has formed the subject of three books, by Paul Goodman, Walter Schwab, and Dr Alan Webber respectively. They are well worth reading because they show what a remarkable role the Lodge has played in the annals of Anglo-Jewry, particularly in helping to bring about the Balfour Declaration, and as the very first body that provided accommodation for Jewish students, which later led to the creation of the Hillel Foundation. It also spawned the B'nai B'rith Housing Association. During my term of office we introduced the B'nai B'rith Award for outstanding communal service. Its first recipient was Alderman Moss of Manchester (1961). Over the years many distinguished members of Anglo-Jewry received this award and the ceremony became one of the annual highlights in the First Lodge calendar. The names of the early recipients are engraved on the large silver menorah which I presented to the Lodge at the conclusion of my term of office.

Climbing up the B'nai B'rith ladder I eventually became an International Vice President and Co-Chairman of the International Council. This involved travelling to Washington and New York at least two or three times a year, to Australia, South Africa, Canada and Venezuela as well as visiting a variety of European countries where conventions were being held.

B'nai B'rith International reached its zenith under the Presidency of Philip Klutznick from 1953 to 1959. Phil had served in a senior position in the American government under Presidents Franklin Roosevelt, Harry Truman and Jimmy Carter and he became President of the World Jewish Congress. He was also a leading residential developer and built whole townships such as Park Forest, Illinois. He was a brilliant orator, a great peace-maker, a man of seminal ideas who had the ability both intellectually and financially to ensure their implementation. He was one of the founders of Ashdod, he built the Hilton in Jerusalem, and used the proceeds of the Israeli ventures to endow the Hebrew University Professor Moshe Davis' Centre for the University Teaching of Jewish Civilisation.

We became great friends and he took me under his wing. During his term as International President the claim that B'nai B'rith had 500,000 members worldwide was probably true. Ever since, the Order has been on a steady decline. Having formed two outstanding organisations which continue to expand, namely Hillel and the Anti-Defamation League, it has failed to involve the enthusiasm of the younger generation for whom a weekly or monthly Lodge meeting is not particularly attractive. The freedom to assimilate in the United States and the age of television and soundbite entertainment are not conducive to Jewish togetherness which formed the bedrock of B'nai B'rith. There are still exceptions. In this country, the German Lodges, so-called because they consist mainly of refugees from Germany, maintain the continental tradition of weekly or monthly meetings, total dedication and generosity which leaves them well endowed to pursue charitable activities. Alas, their members' average age is well into the seventies.

The great Rabbi Leo Baeck, a survivor of Theresienstadt, came to England after the War. The Leo Baeck Men and Women's Lodges were formed by refugees to commemorate his name. Born in 1873, he grew up in a Germany where Jews felt secure. He was the spiritual leader of German Reform Jewry and when Hitler came to power in 1933, he became the elected head of the *Reichsvertretung der Juden in Deutschland*. He wrote *Das Wesen des Judentums*, a philosophical analysis of the Jewish faith. He was a majestic figure with his white beard, tall stature and gentle demeanour. He left an unforgettable impression on all those who were privileged to know him.

B'nai B'rith's ecumenical approach, uniting all Jews regardless of their religious or political affiliation was demonstrated in 1952, when Rabbi Leo Baeck was the Guest of Honour at a First Lodge

Dinner. The *Jewish Chronicle* featured the event in a leading article.

It was, in its special way, an historic occasion for Anglo-Jewry, for on this platform, provided by this fraternal Order, there were gathered together to pay tribute to this most distinguished rabbi, scholar and philosopher, who is president of the World Union for Progressive Judaism, such diverse figures, among others, as Rabbi Brodie, Chief Rabbi of the Orthodox Jewish communities; the Rev Dr A. Cohen, also a representative of Orthodox Jewry; the Hon Lily Montague, of the Liberal Synagogue; Rabbi C.E. Cassell, of the Reform Synagogue; Viscount Hailsham, a member of the Church of England; Lord Packenham, a member of the Roman Catholic Church and the Rev W.W. Simpson, a well-known Nonconformist. That all these and some scores of other men and women representing all shades of religious opinion could meet together amicably in praise of one man whose name rests on his religious outlook and influence is a measure of the greatness of the guest of honour.

As Dr George Webber put it, in proposing the toast to the Guest of Honour, to see the Chief Rabbi and Rabbi Baeck sitting side by side as brethren of B'nai B'rith typified the tenets of the Order.

It was in October 1966 that I was installed as National President, an Installation which coincided with the first London meeting of the International Council. I remained in office until 1972. The *Jewish Chronicle*, in its own inimitable style, wished me well but pronounced two caveats. The first was that B'nai B'rith, which was doing good work, was a mutual admiration society and always worked to its own satisfaction, and the second was that, whilst Fred Worms was then known as the Chairman of European Maccabi, and as a plain-speaking fellow, they were wondering whether he would fall into the usual trap of becoming pompous, which they thought goes so often with communal office.

I have borne these remarks well in mind. As to the first, anyone who has attended meetings which I chaired could not possibly apply the epithet of "mutual admiration" to us. As far as pomposity is concerned, my mother was waiting for me to grow up and my wife and children continue to treat my puns with the contempt which they deserve!

The Leo Baeck Lodge's 25th Anniversary celebration took place at the Guildhall in the presence of James Callaghan, Quintin Hogg and Sir Bernard Waley-Cohen, the Lord Mayor of London, who had become a director of our company, Tudor Accessories Limited.

Jim Callaghan asked me, "Tell me, Fred, how many times a year do you say these prayers?" He was referring to the elaborate grace after meals, joyfully sung through its extensive blessings by the guests.

"Three times a day," I told him, "but when you say it quietly by yourself it goes rather quicker." I am not sure whether he believed me!

In May 1970 we gave the annual B'nai B'rith Award to Sir Barnet and Lady Janner. The principal speaker at that function at the Royal Garden Hotel in Kensington was Roy Jenkins who, before he put on weight, looked remarkably like me – or maybe I looked remarkably like him. Another guest was a relatively young lady, one Margaret Thatcher, who was Member of Parliament for Finchley.

During my term as National President I travelled up and down the United Kingdom visiting every single Lodge. Amongst the many tasks that a President had to undertake at the time was to participate in the COJO meetings, another one of Nachum Goldmann's creations. In addition to the World Jewish Congress, he created COJO – the Conference of Jewish Organisations – which met periodically and which lasted as long as restitution monies subsidised the travelling costs of its delegates. I was a relatively inexperienced participant but, as usual, felt little inhibition in saying what I thought. After a particularly tedious session I asked "Are we not wasting our time here? Could not the money have been better spent on something more creative?"

Dr Goldmann would have been perfectly entitled to blunt my teeth as they say in the *Haggadah* when the wicked son asked a question which was considered in bad form, but he was too experienced for that. He said, "My young friend, I have got a story for you. A small crowd of Chasidim followed their *Rebbe* on a walk in the countryside when they saw a train rattling by. "Tell me, *Rebbe*," asked one of the students, "what makes the train go? It has no horses." The *Rebbe* said, "It is a bit complicated but I will explain it to you. You see, in the train, sit people like us and they have a discussion and one talks and one talks and in that way things move on."

I was one of the speakers at a B'nai B'rith convention in Toronto in 1982. This was during Begin's prime-ministership. One of his most loyal followers was Eli Ben Elissar. He, Kenneth Bialkin of the Anti-Defamation League and I debated the attitude of the State of Israel *vis-à-vis* the Diaspora. Needless to say Ben Elissar followed the Begin line. Ken sat on the fence and I thought that Begin's negative attitude towards President Reagan when he should have passed the buck for saying "No" to the Arabs, was not perhaps in the best interests of Israel. It was an eye-opener to me that the largely American Jewish audience booed me and cheered Ben Elissar. That taught me another lesson.

It has been the practice of all American Presidential candidates to open their campaign by addressing the International B'nai B'rith Convention and the Senior Representatives of the Order invariably were introduced to them. I thus met all the American Presidents from 1966.

B'nai B'rith led to my involvement in Hillel, in building homes for the elderly and a bridge in Jerusalem. It has given me welcoming friends in every major city in the 40 countries where the Order operates. Representing Jewry at the United Nations, lobbying for Israel, the Music Festival, its youth movement, work in Eastern Europe – these are but the tip of a very large iceberg. Alas, it is melting. Dr Alan Webber in his authoritative *History of B'nai B'rith*, writes that the largest number of members in District 15 was under my Presidency when we had over 6,000 paid-up brothers and sisters.

However, the number of Lodges and members continued to drop and by 1986 the total membership had declined to approximately 1% of the then Jewish population (estimated at 330,000). In 1986 there was a small increase in both lodges and members, but this was short-lived and membership continued to decline. It has now stabilised at just above 2,000 in 45 lodges. A matter of concern was, and still is, that on the whole, younger people were not joining the Order, and the membership was ageing – to some extent mirroring the situation of the population as a whole.

The decline in membership in the US has been equally dramatic. It must be said, however, that a proud parent is entitled to glory in the success of his offsprings. In America, the Anti-Defamation League and Hillel continue to grow, their respective budgets are $33 and $23 million compared with B'nai B'rith's $11 million. In the United Kingdom Hillel and the B'nai B'rith Housing Society have outgrown B'nai B'rith in financial terms. The six-foot children continue to respect and work with the parent although, as is usual when past middle age, he may have shrunk a little.

Stewart and Alan Cohen, Alan Webber and some younger colleagues are trying their utmost to reverse the trend with some new ideas, which may well be anathema to the "old guard". For example, the consultancy operation on private enterprise which they organised on behalf of District 15 in Czechoslovakia and Hungary with the financial support of the British Government, was an imaginative and innovative venture. B'nai B'rith's genius in the past has been its adaptability. Let us hope it is going to succeed again.

40

The B'nai B'rith Hillel Foundation

I MUST DISCLAIM any pretension that what follows represents the authorised version of Hillel's history in the UK. It is not. It is a highly subjective account of my personal involvement. Dr Alan Webber published his well-researched book on Hillel on the occasion of its 40th anniversary. With his permission I have taken full advantage of his valuable work in writing this chapter.

The concern of First Lodge with Jewish students dates back to 1927, when the Lodge organised a symposium on "Students and the Community" and links were established with the Inter-University Jewish Federation (IUJF) which was founded in 1919 and was the national Jewish students' organisation. A year later the President of the Lodge, Arthur Blok, followed up the initiative. Another symposium was held, at the request of IUJF under the chairmanship of Sir Israel Gollancz, on "Where the Anglo-Jewish community fails the Jewish student". In association with the B'nai B'rith First Women's Lodge and IUJF, it was agreed to establish a Jewish Students' Common Room in Woburn House, London. The Common Room was duly inaugurated on Thursday, 5 May 1932, in the presence of Viscount Bearsted, Chief Rabbi Hertz, the Vice-Chancellor of London University and other communal dignitaries.

In 1952 J.C. Gilbert, a prominent member of the First Lodge, proposed the formation of a Hillel organisation in London. This did not meet with universal approval. There was considerable suspicion and some outright opposition both amongst the student corpus and some prominent members of the community.

In the *Jewish Chronicle* of 21 March 1952, under the headline "The B'nai B'rith Scheme for a Hillel Foundation", two articles were published: "For" by Dr George Webber and "Against" by Professor Norman Bentwich. Dr Webber explained the decision that had been taken by B'nai B'rith to set up a Hillel Foundation in Great Britain and the widespread support this had received. Whilst based on the American concept, he made it clear that modifications would be made to meet British conditions. In America each student centre had a full-time director, usually a rabbi, who promoted Jewish studies and group activities – the "Hillel Programme" – which was structured to provide the student with some knowledge of Jewish history, culture and ethics. Other elements included social activities, community service, personal guidance and inter-faith relations. Dr Webber continued:

> No one would suggest that the Hillel Foundation should be established in England upon exactly the same lines. Social conditions differ; university life does not follow the same patterns; and students justly prize their liberty and autonomy. In the main universities the Jewish Societies have flourished for more than thirty years. These Societies have a variety of "Hillel" activities which they conduct without a director.

Norman Bentwich, on the other hand, maintained that the Foundation was not required in England. He argued that it would lead to greater segregation and the resources would be better employed to support the Hebrew University in Jerusalem. Happily, his advice was not taken.

During the early part of 1953 the building at 1 Endsleigh Street, central London, in the desired university area became available. It was purchased for the sum of £10,000 with monies raised by the First Lodge and IUJF.

The House was consecrated on Sunday, 31 October 1954. Chief Rabbi Israel Brodie performed the ceremony in conjunction with Lord Nathan and Victor (now Lord) Mishcon. The BBC was present and it merited time both on radio and television. The *Jewish Chronicle* published a special supplement to mark the occasion. One of the articles stated:

> Hillel House, London, is a centre in which every Jewish student will take pride, but it is not on the physical amenities alone that it will be judged, but rather on the spirit generated and the atmosphere developed. To students away from home, from whatever part of the world, Hillel Houses will give a warm welcome at all times, but especially on Shabbatot and Yomim Tovim. For the first time ULJUS and other groups will have adequate premises and IUJF will have their long and patiently awaited headquarters. Finally, it should be remembered that whenever Hillel Houses are opened in other cities, the London centre will be drawn upon as a guide, so that the happy partnership between students and the Hillel Foundation may develop into that family feeling of comradeship which will have a marked and beneficial effect on the community.

As agreed by the Executive the students had organised their own opening ceremony the previous evening, which was addressed by Rabbi Louis Jacobs, who had recently come to London.

The first Honorary Treasurers were Roger Nathan and Oscar Rabinowicz. They were followed in 1956 and 1957 respectively by Alexander Margulies and Leslie Paisner who were to play an increasingly important part in the growth and development of Hillel. Israel Finestein was the Honorary Secretary and E. Alec Colman, was Honorary Secretary of the "Friends of the Hillel Foundation".

Once the building at Endsleigh Street was opened, students started flowing through, as they did from day one. Henry Shaw, its first director, became the primary point of contact between them and the Foundation. He soon earned their confidence and respect. Henry and his wife, Sybil, week after week, presided over *Shabbat* and Festival meals, and created a warm, homely atmosphere which is still fondly remembered by the early alumni.

The annual Hillel Lecture became an established communal event. Subjects included: "Introduction to Jewish Law", "Jewish Theory and Practice", "The Jew in a non-Jewish Environment", "The Fundamentals of Judaism", "Jewish Philosophy" and "Israel To-day".

Amongst the distinguished lecturers were: Professor Dr Altmann, Professor Leon Roth, Rabbi Dr Louis Jacobs, Professor Raphael Powell, Dr Isaac Levy, Rabbi Jacob Kokotek, Israel Finestein, Professor Norman Bentwich and Dr Chaim Pearl. The lectures were published in 1959 and 2,000 copies were sold.

However, it became clear over the years that whilst nearly everybody was willing and happy to applaud Hillel's activities, adequate financial support from the community was not forthcoming. In fact, by the time Hillel reached its "Bar Mitzvah" in 1966, it was running at a serious deficit which comprised 40 per cent of its expenditure. This was in spite of the fund-raising efforts made by its Honorary Officers, particularly Joe Gilbert. The kosher meals' service which the Foundation provided for the students was showing substantial losses, and the building itself rapidly deteriorated. Yet it was attracting more and more students; it was bursting at the seams and two to three hundred would regularly turn up for Friday night meals in its small refectory.

The lusty Hillel baby which was reared with so much optimism in the 1950s had become a heavy liability. In the old Jewish tradition that one cannot rely on miracles yet confidently anticipates them, Leslie Paisner prevailed upon two members of B'nai B'rith, John Rubens and Barnett Shine, to purchase for Hillel the adjacent building at No 2 Endsleigh Street. This was in the hope that perhaps one day sufficient funds could be found to put up a new and larger Hillel House to answer the growing and welcome demands from the students.

Whilst Hillel was struggling on in its Endsleigh Street home, B'nai B'rith was actively looking for central headquarters, the equivalent of what was known on the Continent as a *Logenheim*. B'nai B'rith assets in Germany, which were seized by the Nazis, were substantial. B'nai B'rith Headquarters in Washington decided that only a global claim would produce the best results. This raised considerable opposition from the many Lodges throughout the world, which included Jews from Germany and other central European countries. Negotiations took place in the early 1950s between leaders of the Leo Baeck Lodges and the late Frank Goldman (Supreme President), and subsequently with Philip Klutznick, in which substantial claims were staked by the Leo Baeck members, who felt that they were in a unique position, since their Lodges contained more refugees from Nazi Germany than any other Lodge in the B'nai B'rith world. Relations with Washington were difficult and, at times, stormy.

In 1964, the Grand President of British B'nai B'rith, Jack Morrison, invited me to take charge of the negotiations which by that time had ground to a halt. At an historic meeting which took place at the home of Jack Morrison's mother in Grosvenor Square, we met Philip Klutznick, who was then the President of the B'nai B'rith International Council, having earlier completed a most distinguished six-year period as Supreme President. It was agreed that, subject to ratification by the Board of Governors and the International Council, a sum of $60,000 would be made available to us provided that the money be used exclusively towards the cost of the erection of a B'nai B'rith building. To say that I was happy would be an exaggeration. I pointed out to Philip Klutznick that we considered $60,000 a relatively unsatisfactory settlement of the long drawn-out dispute and we felt that we were entitled to a larger proportion of the restitution funds. His conciliatory reply was that the restitution monies were expected in two instalments, that at that time it was still somewhat doubtful whether the second half would be received, but that the matter could be reconsidered.

From that moment onwards, the search for a suitable building or site commenced with renewed vigour. Negotiations were entered into with the Federation of Synagogues for the purchase of their site in Finchley Road and, although discussions reached a fairly advanced level in the end, and fortunately as it turned out for the B'nai B'rith Hillel Foundation, agreement could not be reached. Other sites were investigated and buildings were inspected, particularly by Karl Halle, Robert's father. We were most anxious to have a B'nai B'rith House in the north-west London district, where the majority of our members resided, but the enormous cost of property which had skyrocketed since the War made this very difficult.

It was with these two conflicting demands of B'nai B'rith's search for headquarters and the problem of the Hillel Foundation that I was faced when I was elected Grand President of District Grand Lodge in the autumn of 1966, following Jack Morrison who had held this post for some 15 years. I came to the conclusion at the time that the movement could not afford two buildings. If B'nai B'rith was to have its home and strain every effort to raise the necessary funds from amongst its members, and use the restitution monies from the United States, there was no chance for Hillel to expand into the building at 2 Endsleigh Street. I was also concerned about the widening gulf between Hillel and B'nai B'rith. My first task was to bridge the gap, which was made relatively easy because of my personal friendship with the Hillel Honorary Officers, particularly with Joe Gilbert with whom I had been associated through Habonim and other Jewish causes for many years.

I suggested that the only answer would appear to be to combine the requirements of the Lodges with those of Hillel, by putting up a combined B'nai B'rith Hillel House on the site of 1 and 2 Endsleigh Street. Joe Gilbert and his Honorary Officers were delighted. To them, it was the turning point for Hillel, hopefully assuring it of a brighter future through a renewed and deeper commitment of B'nai B'rith. On the other hand, some of the leading B'nai B'rith people had their reservations. The original sponsors and activists of the idea of a *Logenheim* were not at all enthusiastic about moving to the West Central area. Yet there was no doubt that the support of the Leo Baeck Lodges was vital for three reasons.

Firstly, they had promised a contribution of £25,000 towards a central B'nai B'rith building. Secondly, the restitution monies from the United States were inextricably linked with a house which the Leo Baeck Lodges would occupy and, thirdly, the contribution which they would make in terms of manpower in the administration and maintenance of such a building were then considered vital.

I was invited to address their Board and Council and subsequently their members in a general meeting. They gave me a cordial reception. My mother was a past President of the Leo Baeck Women's Lodge, and other members of my family were active in their Lodges. Ultimately, we received almost unanimous support for the project. Having helped to establish B'nai B'rith Hillel House, the Leo Baeck Lodges later acquired their own premises in Fitzjohn's Avenue in north-west London.

The enthusiastic and unqualified support which I had at all times from the members of the First Lodge was a source of great encouragement. They formed the core of the ongoing operations.

I invited the architect Colonel Richard Seifert, who was responsible for so many hotels and skyscrapers in London to act for us. Not only was he prepared to accept but he did so with enthusiasm. We formed a Building Committee, consisting of the following: Fred Worms (Chairman), W. (Bill) Ayliss, Frank Falk, Joe Gilbert, Joseph Kutner, Leslie Paisner, Z. Pick, and Daniel Schonfield, JP with the Chairman of the IUJF representing the students.

Our next task was to consolidate the renewed partnership between B'nai B'rith and the Hillel Foundation, and to establish a new legal entity which would inextricably intertwine the two organisations. Herbert Garfield, Leslie Paisner, Dr George Webber and Israel Finestein, QC, accepted my invitation to create the "B'nai B'rith Foundation", a legal partnership between the B'nai B'rith District 15 and the Hillel Foundation. The B'nai B'rith Foundation became the sole owner of the building, the Hillel Foundation having transferred the freehold sites of 1 and 2 Endsleigh Street to it in consideration of permanent security of tenure both for Hillel and B'nai B'rith.

Whilst the building was being erected, fund raising went ahead. Apart from the relatively small money-raising efforts in which I was involved in connection with the flatlets for elderly people, I had had no previous experience in this esoteric field. On the other hand, my colleague, Joe Gilbert, had become a past master during 30 years as a JPA and Habonim fund-raiser *par excellence*. We decided at an early stage that we would not make a general appeal to the community but that we would concentrate on selected individuals and Charitable Trusts, whose Trustees and Settlors were aware of the vital role which the Hillel Foundation was playing. Primarily, we would address ourselves to members of B'nai B'rith and to Lodges throughout the country. In less than two years, without a fund-raising committee, we raised a large proportion of the total of more than £300,000 which was required. Over 60 per cent had been contributed by B'nai B'rith sources.

In 1968 Joseph Kutner, a leading member of the Leo Baeck Lodge and I travelled to Washington to attend meetings of the Board of

Governors and the International Council. We reminded Philip Klutznick of the conversation which we had had at Grosvenor Square some four years earlier. We pointed out that the second tranche of the restitution money had since been received and, with the support of Supreme President William Wexler and Executive Vice-President Jay Kaufman, the Board of Governors voted us an additional $60,000. At the same time, the Joint Memorial Committee of the Board of Deputies, under the leadership of Alderman Michael Fidler and Barnett (later Lord) Janner, was established to create a permanent memorial to the six million dead of the Holocaust. They proposed to raise £50,000 for the creation of a memorial floor in the B'nai B'rith Hillel House. Alas, they were unable to raise the funds and a nominal amount only was received.

The building was designed to contain 20,000 square feet of floor space on eight different levels. This compared with some 3,000 square feet in the old building. It was to become one of the few edifices in London which has more space under ground than above street level.

Whilst the building operations at 1 and 2 Endsleigh Street were in progress, I went on a much needed skiing holiday in Switzerland. When I came back, Joe Gilbert, the eternal optimist, rang me up and said "Congratulations!"

"Thank you very much – what are we celebrating?" I asked.

"We have just bought a Hillel House in Brighton."

"Splendid," I replied. "What did we use for money?"

"Oh," he said, "we used some of the money on deposit for Endsleigh Street."

I was speechless. In fact, I was furious.

"Joe, you can't do that. That money is earmarked. It has been given by donors for a specific purpose. You cannot redirect it!"

"Oh, we'll sort it out," said Joe.

Much as I admired the man, he and I had somewhat different outlooks. With his enormous charm and ability to raise funds, he would take a risk in the confident hope that something would turn up whereas I, with my extra caution, perhaps caused by my father's cavalier attitude to money, have always acted in a super-conservative fashion.

I rang Pat Matthews, the very active Chairman of the First National Finance Corporation. Pat was a product of the booming 1960s. He had built up his merchant bank into one of the principal property lenders. Unfortunately it suffered severely in the 1974 recession but the company survived under new management. However, at that time an atmosphere of tremendous optimism prevailed.

I asked him, "Will you lend us a substantial amount – a six figure sum – for the acquisition of a freehold house in Brighton to become a new Hillel House?"

"Who are the people behind it?" he replied, and I mentioned Joe Gilbert, Leslie Paisner, Alexander Margulies and myself.

"Good enough, you will have the money."

It was as easy as that in those days. Leslie dealt with the legal documentation, the money was advanced to Brighton Hillel, which was under the energetic leadership of Dr Herzl Sless and his wife Ruth, and was repaid over the years.

We had an outstanding team of Honorary Officers in London who had proved their worth in B'nai B'rith and Hillel for a number of years. There was Lottie Green, who virtually lived with the project and took responsibility for the furnishing of the building, apart from being closely involved with the Catering Committee. Dr Robert Halle, a professional hotelier, was particularly helpful, first as an Honorary Officer and later as Director. Ken Gradon and Ralph Emanuel, both past Presidents of the First Lodge of England, looked after the building and its staff. Harry Schwab became the Honorary Treasurer of the Foundation, Bernard Garbacz, its Auditor, and David Rothenberg the Honorary Treasurer of the Building Fund. Arnold Horwell, as Chairman of the Room Allocation Committee, assisted by Gerald Cromer and the highly experienced Miss E. Mitzman (Mitzi) of the B'nai B'rith staff, needed the patience of Job and the judgement of Solomon to satisfy all interested parties. Hayim Pinner, for many years the Executive Director of B'nai B'rith, was involved in every facet of our activities. His experience and unflappability stood us in good stead.

The new B'nai B'rith Hillel House was formally opened on 10 January 1971 by Avraham Harman, President of the Hebrew University, and dedicated by the-then Chief Rabbi, Dr Immanuel

Jakobovits, assisted by the Haham, Dr S. Gaon, and the Emeritus Chief Rabbi, Sir Israel Brodie. More than 350 dignitaries representing Anglo-Jewish religious leadership, B'nai B'rith membership, student bodies and Hillel sponsors crowded into the auditorium for the occasion. It was a historic event applauded by the *Jewish Chronicle* and the community.

Having achieved their primary objective, the students began to agitate for residential accommodation. The Honorary Officers were not opposed to the aspirations of the students. Who could quarrel with such an admirable aim? Lack of finance was the stumbling block. The Brixton Synagogue suggested that four students could be housed in surplus accommodation adjoining the synagogue and this little Hillette was opened in 1975. In 1980 temporary provision for 16 students was made in two houses in Shepherd's Bush and for 12 people in Golders Green in a building belonging to the Jewish Blind Society. The First Women's Lodge had founded the Stepney B'nai B'rith Clubs and Settlement prior to the Second World War. With the movement of the Jewish population from the East End of London, some space became surplus to their requirements. Hillel agreed to rent this area, and in 1979, opened the Stepney Hillel with places for 20 students. This temporary arrangement has lasted to this very day.

The real breakthrough came in 1982 when I had a telephone call from B'nai B'rith in Washington inviting me to nominate a prominent British Jew who had done most for the community to receive the Gold Medallion for Humanitarianism – a most prestigious B'nai B'rith Award. I proposed Sir Marcus Sieff (later Lord Sieff of Brimpton) and this was readily agreed to. When I called on Marcus to give him the good news he was delighted to accept. I made it a condition that I needed one of his senior co-directors to help me organise the ceremony and he proposed Henry Lewis. Together we ran a function at the Plaza Hotel in New York to which 120 Marks and Spencer suppliers flew over, to be joined by leading American politicians and communal leaders. I also asked Marcus whether he would like a principal speaker from this country and without a moment's hesitation he suggested Sir Hector Laing who was then

Chairman and Chief Executive of United Biscuits and a director of the Bank of England. I met Sir Hector at his Knightsbridge apartment. He was courtesy personified and readily agreed to fly to New York where he made a brilliant speech. Sir Hector is one of those men who does not miss an opportunity. Since he was also the Honorary Treasurer of the Conservative Party, within a short time I had a letter from him inviting me to do my bit for the Conservative victory. I have never wanted to be involved in politics but on this occasion I made a donation to Balliol College, Oxford for research into the Conservative Party's strategies.

The enormous sum of £750,000 was raised. One third was sent to the Weizmann Institute by prior arrangement with Marcus Sieff, one third was retained in America for B'nai B'rith purposes and the other third was earmarked for a residential Hillel in London.

Two adjacent dilapidated houses were purchased in Acton Street, a few minutes walk away from Endsleigh Street near the university area. The houses were sensitively remodelled under the supervision of the architect, Daniel Rosenfelder, to provide 18 student rooms with ancillary facilities. The basement became a large meeting room, for use by residents and non-residents and a kitchen was installed for communal Friday night meals. The hostel was named J.C. Gilbert House at the special request of Marcus Sieff.

Hillel over the years has faced an enormous educational challenge. The average Jewish university student is bright, willing to learn, with an adult outlook yet with a pathetic Jewish education. With the increase in Jewish primary and secondary schools, the situation has been somewhat alleviated but only for a minority.

The profile of the majority is that having attended Hebrew classes until Bar or Bat Mitzvah, they are turned off "religion and all that stuff" by incompetent teachers. Boredom produced apathy, so that our potential scholarship students were virtually illiterate in Jewish matters. They would escape from their Sunday Hebrew classes heaving a sigh of relief, not realising what they were missing during the most formative years of their lives. When they went up to university they were wholly unprepared for the challenges they had to meet. From its early years Hillel ran a highly successful Education

Committee in conjunction with the Inter-University Jewish Federation and later with the Union of Jewish Students.

Unbelievable as it may seem today, the JIA decided to cease supporting Hillel in 1981. It was almost a fatal blow. The *Jewish Chronicle* wrote on 18 September 1981:

> Senior members of B'nai B'rith, furious at this week's news that the Joint Israel Appeal has withdrawn its annual grant of £20,000 to the Hillel Foundation, are now considering redirecting funds they usually give to the JIA to Hillel instead.
>
> News of the JIA's unexpected decision was given by Mr Fred Worms, the Deputy Chairman of Hillel, at its annual meeting. He said, "We have an increased deficit and an overall expenditure of £128,000. Technically, Hillel is insolvent, and as our only source of regular income from the JIA has been phased out, Hillel may now face the threat of closure. We cannot give an income budget," Mr Worms declared, "because we are living from hand to mouth. Hillel is not only serving students but the wider community. It costs, for example, £40,000 a year just to maintain our London building, and if these costs continue to rise we will face the threat of closure."

We set up a Committee of Enquiry under the Chairmanship of the Honorary Treasurer, Bob Glatter, to investigate possible ways of resolving our financial crisis. The principal recommendation was that the building in Endsleigh Street should be sold, half the monies realised should be used to buy another property in a cheaper location and the remainder to form an endowment fund.

This drastic solution produced an animated correspondence in the *Jewish Chronicle*, some of it positive – that there should be compulsory levies on synagogue bills – others repeating the previous idea that the House should be residential only. The extent of the argument indicated how important an element Hillel had become in the community. The *Jewish Chronicle* pronounced that "instead of waiting, as usual, for the post-mortem on such communal matters, London Jewry should act now and involve itself in the future of its students".

The Honorary Officers did not accept the recommendation of the Committee of Enquiry. They decided to hang on and work hard for the creation of an endowment fund, which I had proposed ten years earlier.

Chaim Bermant wrote in the *Jewish Chronicle* on 22 July 1983:

> I may have some of the details wrong, but one incontrovertible fact remains: the Hillel Foundation is broke and unless it can raise about £1 million for an endowment fund in the near future, the Hillel House we have known and loved and which has now been in business for thirty years is to close ...
>
> B'nai B'rith is the one Anglo-Jewish institution which is respected by all sections of the community (except for those who are determined to stay outside it) and if it is not given the financial support necessary to run the Hillel centre, nothing will rise in its place.

On 18 June 1984, the thirtieth anniversary of the opening of the House was celebrated with a dinner at the Plaisterers Hall. The guest of honour was Menahem Savidor, Speaker of the Knesset; the host was Dr Davide Sala. Sir David Wolfson (who had just received his knighthood) was the Dinner Chairman. The speakers included, for the first time, the Chairman of UJS, Matthew Kalman, recognising the enhanced status of the student leaders. The sum of some £200,000 was raised, of which £150,000 was set aside to start the much-needed endowment fund. Thereafter, a prestigious fund-raising dinner or lunch became an annual event.

Israeli politics and financial crisis interfered with the arrangements for the 1984 and 1985 dinners. In both years Yitzhak Navon, the former President of Israel and a close personal friend, had agreed to be the guest of honour. He was unable to attend the first time because he was number two on the Labour Party's election list and, on the second occasion, when the Prime Minister, Shimon Peres, banned all ministers from travelling abroad unless absolutely essential to save foreign currency.

Mr Peres telephoned me and told me that with all due respect for

Hillel, he would not wish to make an exception but he advised that Professor Amnon Rubinstein, who was already abroad on state business, would be prepared to make a detour and fill in for Mr Navon. This was, in fact, what happened.

In subsequent years we started the much-copied "business" lunches with leading figures from the commercial world as speakers including Michael Heseltine, Cecil, now Lord, Parkinson, the Hon (now Sir) Rocco Forte; Godfrey Bradman; Sir Jeffrey (now Lord) Sterling and David Goldstone.

When I became Deputy Chairman of Hillel, I said to Joe Gilbert: "I'll do anything but raise funds." Alas, it has been one of my major preoccupations ever since. It was suggested that my 65th birthday would be an opportunity for some more substantial fund raising. Dr Robert Halle became the principal organiser for a dinner which was held in March 1986.

Tributes were received from many of my personal friends including the then Chief Rabbi, Sir Immanuel Jakobovits; Lord Sieff of Brimpton; the President of the State of Israel, Chaim Herzog; the Israeli Ambassador, Yehuda Avner; the Deputy Prime Minister of Israel, Yitzhak Navon; the by-then Chancellor of the Hebrew University, Avraham Harman; the President of B'nai B'rith International, Gerald Kraft; the Chairman of the Maccabi World Union, Dr Israel Peled and Philip Klutznick. That dinner was a considerable financial success and consolidated the Endowment Fund.

The *Jewish Chronicle* wrote at the time:

In the beginning there was but one Hillel House, a narrow edifice, where one could move up or down, though not sideways, and which was in such a state that one could hardly move at all without demolishing some part of the fabric.

All that, however, was a long time ago, when the world was young, Churchill was Prime Minister ... and Fred Worms was hardly heard of. Today wherever students foregather, no matter how remote their campus, there is a Hillel or a Hillette ... The Hillel Foundation is so central to the life of the community in general, and the students in particular, that one wonders how we ever managed without it.

In the early years there had been attempts to establish a "Friends of Hillel", but this had not met with great success. It was relaunched in October 1972 and in the late seventies the chairmanship of the "Friends" was assumed by Roger Cowen. By 1979 the number had grown to some 500 and continued to increase. Lionel Shebson followed Roger Cowen as Chairman in 1985, and in 1988 was succeeded by his wife, Vivien. They have provided a solid base for Hillel in terms of financial and moral support.

A committee under the leadership of Marion Cohen organised a series of lectures, reviving the tradition of earlier years. The first lecture was delivered in 1988 by Jeremy Isaacs, Director of the Royal Opera House, Covent Garden. Subsequent speakers included Sir Edward Heath, Professor Michael Baum, Professor of Surgery at the Royal Marsden Hospital, and Chief Rabbi Dr Jonathan Sacks.

The publication of *Hillel News*, a quarterly newsletter, was resumed on a regular basis in 1987, and since 1989 has been under the editorship of Dr Alan Webber. The *Hillel Diary* continues to be published and provides a valuable source of revenue under the energetic Fay Fagelston. Charles Corman together with Jonathan Lewis and Peter Sheldon, have been consistent stalwarts in producing advertising support.

On 29 June 1993 a dinner was held at the Langham Hilton Hotel to celebrate the 40th anniversary of the establishment of the Hillel Foundation and to mark my retirement as Chairman, a post I had held since Joe Gilbert passed away in 1982. I was reluctant, like Mark Twain's character, once again to listen to my greatly pre-dated obituaries but my colleagues persuaded me with the argument that it would help to fill the venue. "Ah well," I said, "anything for the Endowment Fund." A most distinguished company, including many leaders of the Anglo-Jewish community and the Israeli Ambassador attended. Stanley and Joy Cohen were the generous hosts.

The President of the BBHF, Judge Finestein, who chaired the function said:

I want to draw your attention to a remarkable abuse of the English language contained in the invitation to this distinguished event. One Fred S. Worms is described therein as the "retiring Chairman" of the Hillel Foundation. I know English is a rich language, but there are limits and there is no one less retiring than Fred Worms.

I do not know whether you are clapping what I have said, or clapping Fred Worms; all I can tell you is that he is self-willed, sometimes brusque, egocentric and not easy; we love him for it and we respect him because he is frank and says what he means, and means what he says. He knows what needs to be done, and he does it, and he gets other people to share his convictions. He is a great persuader.

Mr Gladstone, a hundred years ago, always got things right in the end. He was Prime Minister four times. One of his critics said of him: "The old man always has the ace of trumps up his sleeve. I don't blame him for that. What I do blame him for is that he keeps saying it was the Almighty who put it there." Well, Fred Worms has nothing up his sleeve. Everything is on the outside; you know where you stand with him.

Then, we had some generous hyperbole ...

Furthermore, I want to tell you this, ladies and gentlemen; he is a writer of distinction. I use my words with care. Those of you who have read his articles, who have read the searching interviews that he had with famous men, will know what I am referring to. I have sometimes said to Fred, "Write and write and write again" and I hope that he will do that with the limited spare time that we allow him to have.

I have a nagging fear that the Judge may change his mind after reading this book.

Bob Glatter, Hillel's Honorary Treasurer, followed:

I have been told that I have probably worked longer with Fred than anybody else. Before any of you challenge this statement, let me tell you that I first met Fred in 1954, almost 40 years ago. He was already a bustling successful industrialist, and I was a difficult obnoxious teenager. Over the years Fred has mellowed, as each year has gone by, and we are not here to talk about me this evening ...

In all those years I think I can truly say that Fred and I have never had a cross word, except when I went to him a month or so ago and I told him that we had in mind to call Hillel House after him to pay tribute to him, and he almost showed me the door, because Fred prefers giving to receiving.

Then I spoke:

It is with a modicum of emotion that I stand here today and listen to all these praises which have got completely out of hand, because this is supposed to be the 40th anniversary of Hillel, not my Bar Mitzvah.

It's rather agreeable to read one's own obituary, as I did in the *Jewish Chronicle* last Friday. You don't want to believe everything that you read in the *Jewish Chronicle*. The editor, Ned Temko, who is present tonight, is a friend with whom I play tennis. He is in fact a very fine tennis player. The famous feuilletonist and writer, Chaim Bermant, has also been known to us for quite a few years. His article said that I have been Hillel's Chairman for 25 years. That is not so. I was Deputy Chairman, and became Chairman only after Joe Gilbert passed away. It was clearly understood that as long as Joe was alive I was not prepared to step into his shoes.

There is a beautiful sentence which occurs four times in the Old Testament, invariably at the end of a paragraph ... "and the country was quiet for 40 years".

Extraordinary! Why was this worth recording?

It shows that wars throughout our history in the land of Israel were a permanent feature until 70 AD, and when there was one whole generation which lived peacefully, it was worth recording. The 40 years must not be taken too literally; it has a kind of generic symbolism of a generation's timespan.

The Hillel Foundation, likewise, has not had an easy 40 years. When you read Dr Webber's history, you may be astonished to find that when Hillel was founded in 1953 there was enormous opposition.

Who was against it? That leading activist, Zionist, university professor, Norman Bentwich, who became a great friend felt that the introduction of a Jewish body into the university ethos could only have negative ghetto-like influences.

It was more or less the same opposition as we had in the early years against Jewish schools. Norman Bentwich lived long enough to rue his words. However, the bigger opposition came from IUJF. The students believed it was an establishment plot to diminish their independence. How ironic that when Hillel House was rebuilt in 1969 and Henry Shaw had to move into temporary premises in Gray's Inn Road, the students sat *shivah*. They said – "how can we possibly manage without a Hillel for a couple of years?" – a recognition of the fact that Hillel had become part and parcel of their lives.

We had financial difficulties in the 1970s and 1980s, but with the help of God and the help of some of the people who are here, and in particular our sponsors and our patrons, we have not only survived but we have prospered. We have had a phenomenal growth. In 1953 IUJF had about 1,400 members. UJS today has 6,500 members. There is intense activity in about 40 campuses and we have no less than 20 Hillels up and down the country.

One of the reasons why Hillel has been successful is that we have this continuous rejuvenation. It is the only body in the Anglo-Jewish community where you have an annual injection of new blood. A student leadership generation lasts exactly one year. You have hardly got used to the chap and you begin to remember his name when he retires. Every year the wheel gets reinvented, new demands are being made, complacency is out and it is a most fantastic experience to work on this Executive.

In *Goodbye Mr Chips* the old headmaster looks back on thousands of pupils during his term of office. So do I and it has its uses. When I have a puncture in Jerusalem I just wait until one of my ex-Hillel boys comes along and helps me out.

I would like to take this opportunity of objecting – and you might think this is not the right platform – to what President Ezer Weizmann said a fortnight ago. Once again he has been shooting from the lip. He has said that the *Galut* is finished; all the eggs must be put into the Israeli basket. He has probably been reading the latest demographic reports from the USA and this country.

My friends, the only answer to make sure that the Diaspora is not finished and is going to survive, undoubtedly lies in Jewish education. But if the President of the State of Israel says "don't bother" then a lot of people will say "who are we to go against the advice of the President of the State of Israel?" He has not done Israel a favour either, because there is no way in which nine million Jews will go to Israel next week. Koestler made the same remarks 40 years ago, and it was an equal *non sequitur*. He said "assimilate or emigrate". It did not work.

Today, Israel needs a viable, educated Diaspora. I have been preaching almost as a lone voice for the last 30 years that Jewish education must receive priority number one, that is over and above everything else. Slowly – slowly, the message is being heard and understood that unless we change our ways and we re-slice the communal cake for the benefit of Jewish education, Ezer Weizmann will be right and we shall phase ourselves out of existence.

Avraham Burg, whom I had known for many years and who shares my views on Jewish education as a key for Jewish survival, came from Israel for the occasion and was our Guest Speaker. Then Chairman of the Knesset Education Committee he has since become Chairman of the Jewish Agency:

I ask myself why, from all the people Fred knows, here in this room, here in Great Britian, in Israel, all over the world, he asked me to come tonight. And after listening to him I think Fred asked me to come because my being here makes him look less controversial. We have a kind of relationship which started more than a decade ago. I think we both share a similar vision of the future. Thank you for enabling Yael and myself to be with you tonight, on such an important evening not only for you, but also for the future of this community.

When we speak about Jewish education we actually open a dialogue on the relationship between us and our past. Every individual in our modern world is born with a key. And the name of the key is education. There is nobody around this room who will deny the importance of education as the key to the future, for social mobility, for personal success, for prosperity, for status, for achievement, for excellence, for many things ...

There are some people, for example, the Jews, who get a second key. The name of that key is Jewish education and this is the key which is supposed to open the door to our past. It is not necessarily the key which opens the door to the future.

Now, there are some who say one key is enough, general education is enough. We have heard this debate since the Enlightenment. I call these people secular fundamentalists. And they evaporate, disappear and disconnect themselves from the destiny of the Jewish people.

There are others who choose the second key only. Jewish education the traditional way of life – that is all they need, and they become Jewish fundamentalists. These are people who deny any connection between Jewish existence and modernity.

There are those people, not enough alas, who say we want to live our lives with the two keys simultaneously. We would like to open both doors, we would like to be generally educated and be part of the modern world, rooted in Judaism, but well-informed, knowing our past and sharing our common memories. This challenge of operating with two keys is the challenge of Jewish Education in our generation.

Following this dinner our Endowment Fund reached the £1 million mark.

In retrospect, there were two major developments during my 25 years with Hillel which had a deep, lasting and positive effect on our relationship with the students.

Henry Shaw set a pattern of a benign, paternalistic approach which was followed by subsequent Hillel Directors, including the energetic Rabbi Cyril Harris now Chief Rabbi of South Africa. Over the years, it became clear that however charismatic the personality of the Director, the students preferred to paddle their own canoe. For some years UJS has been led by a team of full-time student leaders, elected annually, who take a year off their studies to dedicate themselves to the running of the organisation. This has been an unqualified success. Every year we felt that we had such terrific human material that surely the following year there was bound to be a diminution in quality. Yet, year by year, the high standard was maintained, if not exceeded. It was not an easy task to convince the provincial Hillel leadership to follow our example and abdicate responsibility to the younger generation. When there was a crisis at Birmingham Hillel and its dormitories were emptying, we suggested they try our formula. They did and there have been waiting lists in Birmingham ever since.

The expansion of Hillel in the provinces has been another success story. Under the sustained and patient leadership of Jeffrey Green, a Deputy Chairman of Hillel, the network has been expanded until there are today no less than 20 units in the UK. They are independently run by provincial committees but many have relied on London Hillel for financial assistance and educational guidance, not only in their formative years but whenever major problems have arisen. The Charles Wolfson Trust, through Lord (David) Wolfson and his co-trustees, were particularly helpful in the provision of Hillel Houses in a number of provincial towns where they have placed the Trust's freeholds at our disposal for an annual peppercorn. I believe we are actually in arrears with paying them five peppercorns per annum. Roger Wingate, through the Harold Hyam Wingate Charitable Trust, has given us a house at his old Alma Mater, Reading University, and he has continued with annual financial support and encouragement.

The Association of Jewish Sixth-formers (AJ6) is a thriving offspring of Hillel. Established for the specific purpose of preparing sixth-formers for university life, it has created its own ethos for their particular age group through outstanding leadership. Their full-time

Field Workers included Rabbi Pinchas Rosenstein, Leonie Lewis, David Ross, Sara Sless, Nikki Goldman, Wendy Sugarman, Jeremy Lawrence, Jason Arram, Debbie Sinclair, Zeddie Lawrence and Olivia Marks.

Of all the organisations I have been associated with Hillel was the one with which I was most closely identified. For 25 years it was a hands-on daily operation. During the whole of my time at Hillel I cannot recall ever having serious differences with my colleagues. Perhaps the answer lies in the fact that they all became personal friends.

Bob Glatter and Martin Korn, successive Treasurers, both partners of Blick Rothenberg, together with Dr Alan Webber who quietly worked for his Ph.D. whilst beavering away for B'nai B'rith and Hillel, Jeffrey Green, Dr Robert Halle, and Gerry Baron-Cohen formed the nucleus of the team. They were joined by Brenda Katten from whom I extracted a promise that as soon as she was free of her WIZO responsibilities, she would allow her name to go forward for senior office. She became my successor as Hillel's Chairman. Henry Shaw and Rabbi Cyril Harris were followed by Michael Copeland, Robert Halle, Margot Levine, Sue Benjamin and Gerry Lucas. For many years Mervyn Cohen has been the tried and trusted accountant who must, by now, be familiar with the name of every existing and potential donor in the Anglo-Jewish community.

There were many others who were involved over the years in making Hillel House the success it has become but there is one lady, who above all, deserves recognition. She never held an official post but year after year Ellen Dorfmann virtually dedicated her life to Hillel catering, perhaps the most controversial and difficult of all the activities that go on at Hillel House.

During the years of my chairmanship Judge Israel Finestein was Hillel's President. I relied a great deal on his wise counsel, unflappability and phenomenal historical memory. When I followed him in the post of President, he received the unique distinction of being elevated to Honorary Life President prior to his election as President of the Board of Deputies of British Jews.

We were also very fortunate that men of exceptional achievement became Hillel's Honorary Vice Presidents. Sir Isaiah Berlin, the historian Sir Martin Gilbert, the Hon David Sieff who carries on a valuable family tradition of involvement, Sir Harry Solomon, the level-headed industrialist and Lord Weidenfeld who is *sui generis* and who has become a one-man party for European co-operation, were all helpful in one way or another over the years. Their continued association with Hillel has given us gravitas in the communal hierarchy.

There was only one weakness in the structure. Too much of the ongoing annual fund raising remained on my shoulders. I kept reminding Brenda Katten that one of her priorities should be to form a fund raising committee, preferably chaired by a businessman with some financial clout, to allow me to reduce my involvement over a period. "I have a brilliant idea," she said one day. "We'll have a lunch to celebrate your 75th birthday."

"It is not going to work," I replied. "My name will become counter-productive. The public is fed up fêting me every five years. Think of a better platform to base your appeal on."

We reached a compromise. With some slight historical manipulation a double birthday event was to take place. The Inter-University Jewish Federation, the forerunner of the Union of Jewish Students, was resurrected because it had been formed some 75 years previously. The lunch took place in October 1995 in the impressive Old Hall, Lincoln's Inn with Malcolm Rifkind, the Secretary of State for Foreign Affairs, as the guest speaker.

To my surprise and delight the function was oversubscribed, many would-be participants could not be accommodated and Hillel's reputation and finances were consolidated.

41

Housing the Elderly and the Central Council

WHEN I BECAME President of B'nai B'rith First Lodge of England I looked round for a special project to mark the period of my office. My father-in-law, Mick Rosenberg, found the solution. He drew my attention to the housing problems which so many of his contemporaries faced at that time. Our community was set on a steady decline in numbers which, alas, continues to this very day. From a post-War high of 480,000, the Anglo-Jewish community now counts less than 300,000 souls. This haemorrhage has had severe social consequences. The traditional pyramid of a large working base supporting the relatively small apex of the over-60s is gradually being reversed. People live longer. The average lifespan of an Englishman at the turn of the century was 55 years. Today the average age of the tenants of the various B'nai B'rith Housing Society sheltered flatlets is 88. The trouble was, and continues to be, that only a small minority of the elderly can face their retirement in the secure knowledge that their existing home and income will be adequate for the remainder of their lives.

Sir Keith Joseph, as he then was, said in Parliament on 3 March 1961:

I now turn to the old people who are beginning to feel, "I do not want to go and live in a home. I like my own little house or flat; however, I am beginning to feel that I cannot go on living by myself in safety." Perhaps the modern way of achieving immortality – the equivalent of the endowment of chapels in the

Middle Ages – is to launch and run a housing association for the elderly.

I could not resist such an eschatological reward. After forming a housing association we looked around for a suitable property in the north-west London area. These were the swinging sixties with an unprecedented building boom. As soon as sites came on to the market, professional developers with virtually unlimited banking finance snapped them up. Housing associations were severely handi-capped under those circumstances. Before they could buy they needed the approval of the funders, that is the Housing Corporation and the Local Authority which, like all bureaucracies, were not very quick in making up their collective minds. Furthermore, the cost of the site naturally had to be incorporated in the overall project cost which in itself was subject to a Government yardstick. Often this prevented us from going ahead because sites were just too expensive under these criteria.

I took the unprecedented step of writing to every institution of a quasi public nature, including schools, in north-west London asking them whether by any chance they were contemplating the disposal of their property and, if so, whether they would rather sell to a charity than to a commercial enterprise. Surprisingly, this worked and we were offered the site of a school which was closing down. The local authority, Harrow, was sympathetic and we arranged a leaseback scheme with them. Gordon Court was built during the early 1960s and opened in 1966. Thirty-four flatlets with 38 tenants cost £98,000. The project was called after the late Gordon Liverman JP, a Grand President of B'nai B'rith. His widow laid the foundation stone. Chief Rabbi Brodie and Sir Keith Joseph attended the opening ceremony. My early committee members included Daniel Schonfield, of the famous rabbinic family, Ralph Emanuel, Kenneth Gradon, Walter Schwab, David Stern and Alan Cohen.

Alan, an Alderman at the time, was particularly useful in opening doors for us. He has been sitting next to me in the Norrice Lea Synagogue, Hampstead Garden Suburb for some 30 years. Because of this proximity, communal developments were conceived right there. I am sure the Almighty will forgive us because we never discussed any private business but only subjects which in Talmudic language were in the name of Heaven, in other words, for the benefit of the public. Della's and my friendship with the Cohen family spans five generations. Alan's grandfather, together with Ellis Birk's father, were the founders of the Hampstead Garden Suburb synagogue in 1935. I knew them both as well as I know Alan's grandchildren. Della and Alan, together with Philip Morris who was the Youth Leader, were amongst the co-founders of the HGS Synagogue Youth Club when they were teenagers. Alan became the National President of B'nai B'rith in 1994, following my challenge to him some years ago that he and his brother, Stewart who is now International Vice-President of B'nai B'rith, should get involved.

From these small beginnings grew a Housing Association with £15 million worth of properties. One may well ask where the money came from. The answer is either from the Housing Corporation or the Local Authority. The formula, prior to the passing of the Housing Act 1988, was a perfectly simple one. When a site was acquired and the approved building had been erected, the rent officer would come along and fix rentals for each flatlet. These rentals bore no relationship to commercial realities. We never discovered on what criteria the rent officer based his absurdly low calculations. The rents and service charges were totally inadequate to service a normal mortgage. An astonishing calculation would then be made. If the finance provided by the Housing Corporation was £1 million but the rental surplus based on artificially low figures would only service a mortgage of £100,000, then the shortfall of £900,000 would be written off immediately. The balance of £100,000 would be paid off over a 60 year period. Furthermore, if, at the end of each year, approved expenditure exceeded income, the revenue deficit would be made up by a Housing Association grant. The basis underlying this policy was a sound one. The Government had recognised that a body of qualified volunteers would give far better value in providing housing than a central bureaucracy.

All this changed dramatically after 1988. Government allocations to the Housing Corporation were cut year by year; only 3 per cent of the total was earmarked for housing the elderly; emphasis henceforth, was to be laid on providing home help in existing premises, however unsuitable they might be. Pre-1988 tenants are still protected on the old basis, but others who moved in after the crucial date have to pay a rental and service charge which is quickly accelerating to open market value. The result is that two identical flatlets occupied by two ladies of the same age attract completely different rentals. Under this particular formula blessed are the poor! Tenants who have no savings have the whole of their rental and service charges paid by housing grant. Those whose total assets exceed £16,000 are the new poor. They have to pay the full new rent and service charge, in many instances greater than their pensions.

In 1974 Daniel Court was opened on the former Hendon aerodrome site. When it was decided to convert the old airfield into a residential neighbourhood, the local authority invited housing associations to apply for a land allocation. Of the 28 applicants two were chosen and we were one of them. We built 30 flatlets at a cost of £280,000. The building commemorates the name of Daniel Schonfield whose involvement in the launching of the housing society in the early 1960s was of such seminal importance.

Harmony Close, off Princes Park Avenue in Golders Green, was opened in 1979. It was and remains our biggest project at a cost of £2.4 million. Some 69 flatlets accommodate 90 tenants. The unique feature of this project was the incorporation of a hostel for single young people. It had taken us some years to put the site together. The unprecedented scale of the scheme was made possible by the ecumenical co-operation of the adjacent Carmelite monastery which in fact is a convent. The Mother Superior was most supportive and we were happy to pay tribute to her during the opening ceremony which was performed by Lord Fisher, then President of the Board of Deputies of British Jews.

1985 saw the opening of Young Court, Willesden. Louis and Helen Young had been great benefactors of B'nai B'rith and left the B'nai B'rith Housing Trust a substantial legacy. Sixty-two flats in Willesden Lane, with accommodation for some 90 tenants, cost £2.6 million. That building was opened by Sir George Young (no relation) who was Under-Secretary of State for the Environment. Here again the site accumulation had been a very difficult one which had taken a number of years. Enormous patience and perseverance was required to convince the individual freeholders and trustees of the North West London Jewish Day School Trust to do business with us. The late Rabbi Maurice Landy proved particularly helpful in these negotiations and in the land exchanges with the London Borough of Brent.

In 1987 we crossed the River Thames for the first time by building South Lodge in the grounds of the Streatham South London Synagogue. Twenty single and six double flatlets cost £1,340,000.

The Golders Green Beth Hamedrash, the ultra-Orthodox community also known as the Munk Shul, approached me through my old friend, Frank Posen, a nephew of Rudolf Kahn who was my classmate in Frankfurt and who later worked for me in Tudor. They wanted to have their own housing unit for an Orthodox clientele but at that time the formation of new small housing associations was strictly discouraged. We took them under our umbrella and put up a very attractive unit in the heartland of Golders Green at a cost of £1.55 million for 20 flats. Maurice Wohl made a contribution towards this and his name is commemorated in the building.

Throughout these years Chief Rabbi Jakobovits and John Marshall, the local MP, were of enormous help and attended all our festive occasions.

1989 saw us south of the Thames for the second time. We fulfilled a demand from those elderly ladies and gentlemen who wanted to retire to the seaside. We acquired an old hotel in Cliftonville and converted it to provide 15 flatlets for 19 tenants at a cost of £1 million. We called it Montefiore Court, since this part of Kent and in particular Ramsgate has been closely associated with Sir Moses Montefiore, the legendary leader of Anglo-Jewry through most of the nineteenth century.

Meta Worms Court, an additional complex at Princes Park Avenue, was opened in 1993 at a cost of £911,000 providing 16 flatlets for 20 tenants. The committee honoured my mother, who was a founder member and President of the Leo Baeck Women's Lodge, a leading activist in the *Kindertransport* from the dangerous German end, and also the founder Chairman of the Leo Baeck

Children's Care Committee, now known as the Meta Worms Children's Committee, which has sent hundreds of deserving children on holiday for many years.

Since the very viability of the smaller housing associations up and down the country became increasingly fraught, we took the initiative under the umbrella of the Central Council for Jewish Social Services to form the National Network of Jewish Housing Associations, of which I became the Founder Chairman. Some 26 housing associations now meet on a regular basis, consult with each other and have become a formidable lobbying force.

A word here should be said about the Central Council. The concept of forming an umbrella organisation for Jewish Welfare Services and ultimately for most Jewish charities goes back to the early 1970s when Roland Franklin, Ellis Birk, David Lewis, Stuart Young and I met at the offices of Keyser Ullman to see to what extent we could follow the example of the American Jewish Federations. Over the years the Central Council was chaired by Roland Franklin, George Pinto, Stuart Young, Sidney Bloch, and Victor Benjamin. Lord Young assumed the Chair in 1993. Throughout this period Melvyn Carlowe has been the outstanding Chief Executive of the Jewish Welfare Board, Jewish Care and the Central Council and has provided a solid link of continuity.

David Young is a remarkable man. Twenty-five years ago he said to me, "I run my life in five to seven year cycles." When he joined the Government he repeated this and, true to his word, after having served in the Cabinet under Mrs Thatcher ("other people bring me problems, David brings me answers") he became Executive Chairman of Cable & Wireless where, alas, his own timetable of leaving in 1997 was anticipated by his fellow directors in November 1995.

When he surveyed the diminishing Anglo-Jewish community with its multitude of charitable organisations – in London alone there are no less than 89 Jewish charities – he felt the time had come for a drastic reorganisation. He wanted to make the Central Council into a potent force which would play a prominent part in streamlining our voluntary work. His initial enthusiasm was not maintained and he resigned the Chairmanship at the beginning of 1996. The need for a strong Central Council remains as urgent as ever. His successor, the experienced Philip Sober, realises that he faces a major challenge.

At the 30th anniversary party of the B'nai B'rith Housing Society held in September 1995, I announced that we would set another good communal example by merging with the JBG Housing Society in the course of 1996 and that I would resign as Chairman in favour of my younger colleague, Eric Shapiro.

This chapter cannot be concluded without recording the names of the remarkable team that has managed the affairs of the B'nai B'rith Housing Association for some 30 years.

First those who have been with us for a long time: Ken Gradon, Erna Kahn, Roy Filer, Heini Wohl, Vivian Caplan, Eric Beecham, Leslie Jacobs and Martin Korn. They were joined later by Michael Keidan, Tony Gold, Michael Moss, Michael Blake and Dvora Safier, Anne Schwab, Edith Bentley, Jean Beecham, Freddie and Sheila Brodtman, Nan Gilbert, Manuel and Majorie Ferris, Delia Cedar, Frank Posen, Marienne Ullman, and Walter Sulzbacher,

The following played an invaluable part in our team in past years: Alan Cohen, Daniel Schonfield, J. Cowen, R. Brodtman, Alan Silverman, David Stern, Ralph Emanuel, Walter Bentley, Walter Schwab, Richard Crown, Robert Halle, Leslie Gilbert, Monty Cohen, David Mirsky, Lewis Goodman and Maurice Lissack.

Since the very beginning the professional administration was in the hands of Danny Dannhauser and Harry Schwab. Danny is the Talmudist of housing legislation. He reads the fine print and analyses it as other people would study Rashi or the intricacies of the latest Finance Bill. Harry, the conscientious ex-Marks and Spencer executive, made sure that our records were always immaculate. These two stalwarts were later joined by Danny's son, Michael.

David Stern, Daniel Rosenfelder and Alex Flinder were the architects of most of our projects, Armand Safier was our reliable Quantity Surveyor and Stuart Trogal and David Kut our Structural and Service Engineers.

There cannot be many organisations that have enjoyed such loyal, consistent service from so many devoted and gifted volunteers. Let us hope that Sir Keith Joseph, of blessed memory, will use his influence on high that his benevolent forecast will be fulfilled.

42

The British-Israel Chamber of Commerce

THE ISRAEL ECONOMY has always been a subject of fascination for me. Through my bank directorships I had a fair insight into some of its principal industries. What I found most astonishing was that within my own business' lifespan, the economy multiplied over fivefold from $15 billion to $80 billion, an achievement unequalled anywhere else in the world.

Israel Sieff, the first Lord Sieff of Brimpton, had the idea that Anglo-Israel trade should be promoted by two reciprocating Chambers of Commerce. The British-Israel Chamber of Commerce would sit in London, and its counterpart in Tel Aviv. Over the years the B-ICC has made its contribution in achieving two-way trade which now exceeds £2 billion.

In 1972 its President, Marcus, the second Lord Sieff, invited me to become Honorary Treasurer. Lewis Goodman was then the Chairman. When Lewis and I came to the end of our term of office in 1979 we had over 900 members. I was elected a Vice-President and continue to take an active interest in the Chamber's affairs. Amongst the other leading players over the years were Monty Sumray, Martin Mendoza, Bernard Garbacz, Bob Glatter, Colin Lehmann and Ken Marks, to name but a few, and latterly Henry Knobil. When the Chamber found itself in a state of decline in 1994 a Council of Elders was called. We sat together and decided to offer the Chairmanship to Henry. I was deputed to go and see him. Fortunately he accepted and he has been successful in revitalising the Chamber, assisted by its Chief Executive, Denise Arden.

Some of the above names are featured in other chapters. It demonstrates once again that Jewish communal service, which reduces one's leisure time, is carried out by a relatively small nucleus of committed people.

In this connection I would like to mention two charismatic personalities passionately concerned with the promotion of Anglo-Israel Trade.

They became confidants, wise counsellors and listeners par excellence. Yehudah (Gubi) Avner (formerly Haffner of Manchester Bnai Akivah fame) was an outstanding Ambassador representing Israel at the Court of St James. Of equal importance was his active interest and positive influence within the Anglo-Jewish community from 1983 to 1988. We are distant relatives via his wife, Mimi, a cousin of Gene Kevehazi. Gubi Avner, after his retirement from his last ambassadorial post in Australia, was appointed as personal advisor on Diaspora Affairs to Prime Minister Peres, a post which he first held under Menachem Begin. It was a clear demonstration of his integrity and impartiality which clearly transcends party politics.

The present popular and unflappable Ambassador Moshe Raviv has continued this tradition during his second term of duty in London, which coincides with an unprecedented trade relationship between Britain and Israel to which he has contributed so much.

43

European Jewish Publication Society

ON 30 JANUARY 1995 the following press release was sent out:-

The establishment of the European Jewish Publication Society was announced in London.

The Society's primary aim is to promote and assist by ways of grants and subsidies, the publication of manuscripts on Jewish subjects of literary, educational or historical interest, that might otherwise not be publishable commercially.

The Society is interested also in encouraging publishers to promote the work of young authors and scholars and will support the marketing and distribution of their publications.

The Chairman of the Society, Mr Fred Worms, states that while there has recently been a welcome revival of cultural activities in the Anglo-Jewish community, the publication of books of Jewish interest remains very precarious.

On 17 February 1995 the *Jewish Chronicle* commented in a leading article:

VALUING EXCELLENCE

Anglo-Jewry has many talents. But surely one of the more dubious is our long-time genius for focusing on what ails us, and for running ourselves down. This is all the more reason to welcome a number of recent initiatives to promote and invest in areas of often-overlooked excellence in the community.

Two such moves, in barely as many weeks, have sought to invigorate Jewish literary, artistic and cultural endeavour in Britain. The launch in London of a European Jewish Publication Society, reported in the JC at the start of the month, will provide sorely needed funds for the publication of Jewish literary, educational and historical works that otherwise might be shelved as uneconomical . . .

Why did I get involved in another venture at a time when I was anxious to rid myself of some of my communal responsibilities? It is not that I cannot say "No" – I say "No" all the time, but this particular challenge was only taken up after consulting my favourite guru, Sir Isaiah Berlin.

One day Peter and Martine Halban called on me. They were old friends and neighbours at Yemin Moshe, Jerusalem. Peter, who has a distinguished record as a publisher, said he was no longer able to subsidise books of Jewish interest, books which needed publishing but for which there was a limited market. He gave as an example Dr Harry Levy's manuscript on Belsen. Reverend Levy was the senior chaplain to HM Forces and was amongst the very first to enter that frightful concentration camp. After many years of hesitation, he put his experience on paper if only to provide another eye-witness weapon against those who would deny the Holocaust. In due course, *Witness to Evil* became the first book to be published under the auspices of the EJPS.

After sounding out some of my friends I found that it was the same group of generous philanthropists who would join with me in providing the necessary finance to launch the Society. They were Peter Levy, David Lewis, Sidney Corob, Felix Posen, the Rothschild Foundation, Martin Paisner and Israel Weinstock. We created an independent editorial board with Professor Aubrey Newman, Judge Israel Finestein, William Frankel and Martin Paisner and Dr Sidney Brichto as co-ordinator. Sir Isaiah Berlin agreed to become our President.

It has been fashionable for many years to accuse the Anglo-Jewish community of being totally philistine, to be Jewishly illiterate and of eschewing the purchase of books on Jewish topics. Like all generalisations, there are exceptions. We are testing the water and perhaps we shall be successful in reversing the trend.

There was some difficulty in getting charitable status. The Charity Commissioners wondered why the people of the Book needed more books that were not commercially viable. At a meeting at Paisner's office I asked one of the Commissioners how many Jews he thought there were in England.

"I guess between one and a half and two million," he replied.

"Would it surprise you if I were to tell you that we are down to 300,000 and losing 4,000 souls every year?"

He looked at me over his glasses.

"You have made your point. You must stop the erosion."

In the short time since its formation the EJPS has assisted in the publication of four books which would not have seen the light of day without its help.

PART 5

Pen Portraits

44

Mutti who later became Oma:
1894–1988

MY MOTHER WAS one of six children. Mutti and her five siblings had a happy childhood in Hoesbach, where they got on very well with their non-Jewish neighbours. Her oldest brother was Adolf, a cattle-dealer who lived in Aschaffenburg; next came Julius, then Herman and Benno and finally Claire. Herman married into the restaurant business in Strasbourg, the Klein-Bollags, who had been there for generations. They were very Orthodox and Herman who, like the rest of my uncles, had been rather easy-going until that stage, adapted himself very quickly.

After my mother's escape from Germany, her mother, Clock Oma joined Herman since she could not get a visa for England. They survived the War under trying circumstances in the south of France and later, after my grandmother had joined us in England, the Herman Lowenthals emigrated to Israel where, initially, they had a very tough time. The Jewish Agency settled them in a moshav – Tifrach – in the Negev. This became a very Orthodox establishment and the first thing the men built was a *mikvah*. Later on, Herman and his family moved to Bnai Brak, the ultra-Orthodox town in Israel. There his children began to multiply and I have worked out that within four generations there will be at least 1,200 emanating from the loins of Esther, Herman's loyal wife.

In the early 1990s my aunt Claire Kevehazi, who now lives in the Maccabiah Village in Israel, got into correspondence with a German genealogist, a Dr Ingrid Heeg-Engelhart, who had made it her life's task to trace the antecedents of the Jews of Aschaffenburg and surrounding villages. Dr Heeg-Engelhart wrote to me after I became involved in the correspondence to tell me that my great-great-great grandfather, who lived in the eighteenth century, was the man who built the Jewish school in Goldbach, a hamlet near Aschaffenburg.

My mother, as a particularly gifted child, was sent to the best school in the area, namely the Englisches Fräulein Institut in Aschaffenburg. She had to attend on Saturday mornings which involved walking an hour each way since the family was Orthodox and travelling on *Shabbat* was forbidden. This stood her in good stead because right up to the age of 83 she walked regularly from Beaufort Park, her apartment near Henly's corner, to Norrice Lea Synagogue and to our house in The Bishops Avenue. After high school she was sent to an upmarket hotel in Bad Nauheim, where she received proper professional household training which included cooking, baking, table-laying, laundry care and entertaining to an extent that would have enabled her to run a hotel later on.

She married my father and lived a life of good middle-class luxury for nine years in Frankfurt. She brought a considerable dowry but had to adapt her lifestyle after her divorce in 1930. After the difficult years in Frankfurt, running the family business courageously under Hitler and playing a leading part in the *Kindertransport*, she arrived in England at the end of 1938. My mother had a trying time as a "domestic" working for other people before we moved into Ashford Court in Cricklewood and became regular attenders of the Walm Lane Synagogue where Rabbi Louis Rabinowitz was in charge. In due course he would become Chief Rabbi of South Africa, and later settled in Israel where he was particularly friendly with the Hoffmanns, the South African family into which my daughter, Nadia, married.

The War years showed Mutti's true qualities. Under very difficult circumstances she made a real home for my sister, my cousin Laurie Lowenthal, Ilse Ledermann, a young friend who also hailed from Frankfurt, a Dutch couple who were paying boarders and for me. In spite of severe rationing she had an open house, entertained fellow refugee tenants who lived in the same block and offered a hospitable refuge to my uncles Julius and Benno, whose marriages were under strain. She even organised the wedding dinner at Ashford Court, when Ilse married Justin Kahn, an American serviceman of German Jewish origin who was stationed in England. In due course I moved into a one-room flat in the same block which I shared with Laurie.

After the War we moved from Ashford Court to Beaufort Park, near Henly's Corner. This was a newly developed residential estate where we managed to get one of the largest flats. We lived under a benign matriarchy. Mutti was content but she pined for her mother and as soon as possible after the cessation of hostilities, Barney Janner who had become a good friend, flew to France and personally collected my grandmother. I will never forget the picture of our small crowd waiting at Croydon airport for Barney and Clock Oma to land. One photograph shows my mother, tears streaming down her face, holding the 79-year-old lady by the arm with Uncles Julius and Benno smiling broadly.

Clock Oma lived another 10 years during which she suffered a great deal, but perhaps not as much as my mother did, who took care of her night and day and virtually sacrificed her health. The constant demands of the old lady were not inconsiderable. Unfortunately she died a year before Claire and Zolly Kevehazi were able to leave Hungary in 1956. They, too, settled in an apartment at Beaufort Park until they emigrated to Israel.

One of my and my sister's great ambitions was to compensate our mother as far as we could for the enormous sacrifices which she had made for the family over so many years, and I believe we had some success in this. Mutti ran a cultured, civilised, elegant household. She gave regular parties and her annual Chanukah dinners were legendary. People vied with each other for invitations and it became the highlight of their year. She was always immaculately dressed in the latest fashions, made by her designer daughter, Vera.

As President of the Leo Baeck Women's Lodge, she took her responsibilities very seriously. Never lacking in self-confidence, she would stand up and speak, often without notes, relying on her memory after careful dry runs which Cecily Lowenthal, my cousin Laurie's wife, had rehearsed with her. She became the founder of a Committee which sent deprived children on holidays to Switzerland. After her death it became known as the Meta Worms Children's Care Committee and it continues to be active to this very day.

The high school in Aschaffenburg in which Mutti was educated was run by Catholic Nuns. She was therefore familiar with the finer points of Christianity and showed respect and understanding to all her *au pair* girls, most of whom hailed from Switzerland. These young ladies were very lucky because they received a quasi professional household training and were paid for it. My mother was firm and fair. If a girl made a mistake she had no hesitation in pointing it out and where appropriate made her perform the same task again. I have often said to Della that if anyone were to talk to *au pair* girls in this fashion nowadays they would pack their bags and walk out. Never with my mother. They adored her and kept in touch with her. They brought their husbands, and sometimes even their children for her inspection. Her magnetism was such that for a period after Della and I were married, we lived at 26 Beaufort Park, my sister Vera and her husband Ken Gradon lived at No 25 and my mother at No 27. In 1953 we built our house in The Bishops Avenue and in 1958 Vera and Ken moved to Meadway Gate.

Unlike my father who spent money easily, my mother was very careful. I arranged for permanent car hire to stand by but I still caught her, even on windy days, waiting at a bus stop. We started employing full-time gardener/chauffeurs mainly so that my mother would have ready transport available which she then used to her heart's content because she did not want to "waste the poor fellows' time in doing nothing".

She enjoyed travelling and visited family and friends in various parts of the United States where she stayed with her niece Helga Greenbaum (née Lowenthal) and her husband Kurt, and Leon and Ruth Gildesgame in select Mount Kisco. Every year she vacationed either in Italy or Switzerland to take the waters and when she felt like travelling with a companion, we invited her old Frankfurt friend Lucy Spier to go with her. She travelled "in state" on the *Queen Mary* and had herself photographed with Clark Gable, but most of all she enjoyed her circle of friends. Nearly all of them were her "brothers and sisters" of the Leo Baeck Lodge. Amongst them were families Lehmann, Mattes, Moss, Strauss, Halle, Lissauer, Erle and Livingstone.

One of her great pleasures was to go to the opera. We took her regularly to Covent Garden, Glyndebourne and to concerts at the Festival and Albert Halls. She visited Israel with us practically every year, the last time in a wheelchair when she was no longer mobile.

Her 70th birthday was celebrated in our home with a big party. In 1974 she celebrated her 80th birthday at the Gradon's house at Meadway Gate, and then 20 members of the family spent a week in Majorca. The party included my New York cousin Helga and her husband Kurt, our three children, the Kevehazis, Herta Lowenthal and of course Vera. Those were halcyon days as the family sat on the balmy hotel verandah amongst luxuriant growth of exotic flowers taking great pleasure in my mother's enormous enjoyment of seeing her nearest and dearest around her.

In 1979, on the occasion of her 85th birthday, we gave a party at Hillel House. There were some 150 guests. We sang songs, produced sketches of her past and Caroline, our youngest daughter, made the keynote speech. My mother replied movingly, beautifully, without notes. The Bnai Akivah choir performed with the participation of the Garbacz boys and Rev Freilich led grace after the meal. Chief Rabbi Jakobovits and his wife Amelie were amongst the many prominent guests.

Oma, as she was called by now, continued enjoying life until her late eighties. Her 90th birthday was celebrated at cousin Laurie's health club in Hendon under the slogan of the 150th anniversary party which included the completion of 60 years of Laurie's life. Her last few years were spent at one of the Leo Baeck retirement homes, the Clara Nehab house, where she was very well looked after. My sister and I visited her every single day unless we were abroad. She passed away in 1988 and is buried at Bushey cemetery. The inscription on her tombstone reads: "Her children rise to sing her praise" – a quotation from a Friday night prayer-song. We still talk about her all the time, in particular about her great Friday lunches, when the family assembled and whoever was in town was expected to attend. Enormous quantities of various cakes were on offer which my mother had baked together with her *au pair* at 5.30 that morning. Her legendary plum yeast cakes and her *streuselkuchen* have been unequalled to this day and all of us went to our respective homes loaded with enough cakes to see us through the weekend. Yet to look at her hands, her slim fingers, the long, beautifully manicured nails, one would have thought that she never did any housework.

We have commemorated her name in a variety of ways. Not only are there a number of Meta Worms endowments, but there is the Meta Worms Garden – a beautiful quiet lawn with large palm trees in the Maccabiah village in Ramat Gan, there is the Meta Worms Residential Block at Princes Park Avenue, London NW11 and there is a Meta Worms Room at the Clara Nehab house. Most importantly, her name is engraved in our hearts for as long as we live.

Since her passing, the family in London has lacked a cohesive catalyst. We are all busy and it is difficult to meet occasionally, never mind once a week. The irresistible attraction of her imperial command is no longer there. Of course, we meet on *Semachot* but some of the cousins and second cousins, nephews and nieces have become distant relatives. For some years now I have been sending out a quarterly newsletter to the wider family. It has become popular but it is a poor substitute for the Friday *Kaffee Klatsch*.

45

Pierre and Maniusia Gildesgame

PIERRE WAS BORN in Poland in 1903, spent the First World War years in Palestine, then literally walked back to Poland via Vienna together with his older brother Leon, to rejoin their family who were wealthy, cultured and multi-lingual. Pierre studied in Liège, Belgium, and married Maniusia when they were both in their early twenties. They enjoyed one of the great model marriages, alas not blessed with children. Pierre and Maniusia joined Leon in England in 1929. The brothers became successful industrialists, built up a close relationship with Simon Marks and Israel Sieff and became a leading supplier of underwear to Marks and Spencer.

Pierre was a brilliant motivator, raised enormous sums of money for his various causes and, with his remarkable gift for making friends, the Gildesgame hospitality and dinner parties became proverbial. Throughout the 1960s and 1970s Della and I travelled with the Gildesgames through several European countries, many times to Israel, often to Switzerland where they walked and we skied during our winter holidays. When Pierre finally managed to sell his business he looked forward to semi-retirement with enormous enthusiasm.

Whilst he was at the zenith of his career he created a charitable trust, appointed me as a trustee and also made me an executor of Maniusia's and his estate on the assumption that as a younger man I would survive them both. As co-trustees he nominated an accountant, and a lawyer who was an eminent and aloof personality from the City of London. Pierre had made one of his rare errors of judgement in choosing them. Working with these men on the charitable trust side for a number of years, I realised that they had no idea and never would have where Pierre's real interests in life lay. They could not understand his enormous enthusiasm for Jewish causes. True he had been made a Commander of the British Empire for services rendered to the UK Olympic Committee but Pierre's heart and soul as "Mr Maccabi" lay in the promotion of Jewish sport and culture. I said to Pierre, "I shudder to think what is going to happen when you are no longer here. I shall be out-voted by these two gentlemen and it will be very difficult for me to follow your intentions which you have made clear to me on so many occasions."

"What do you suggest?" he asked.

I said, "Let's have a couple of chaps whom we know and whom we can trust."

"Who?"

"Well, I would have thought the choice is pretty obvious. Martin Paisner and Bob Glatter."

Pierre and I had been friendly for many years with the late Leslie Paisner, an eminent lawyer, an activist in the Jewish Community and a man who ultimately retired from his enormously successful legal career in tragic circumstances, brought about by serious illness and his unwitting involvement in a very bitter libel case. During this period Leslie and his wife Suzanne came to Israel and the last Seder of his life, and the saddest of our lives, was spent in our Herzliah apartment where Leslie was crying and Joe Gilbert, who had just lost his wife, was also in tears.

In earlier, happier days, the triumvirate of Joe Gilbert, Alexander Margulies and Leslie Paisner was famous for getting things done. They acted where others debated. They founded Carmel College and nurtured the fledgling Hillel Foundation. Leslie was Honorary Solicitor to many Jewish organisations including Maccabi. We had some difficulty in getting charitable status since sport is not a recognised activity under English charity law. Leslie made an appointment with HM Chief Inspector of Taxes and took Pierre Gildesgame and me to assist him with technical background. The Chief Inspector was well briefed.

"My sources tell me that Judas Maccabeus was a mighty warrior, a saviour of the Jewish people but not, I would have thought, the epitome of charitable activity and, if I may say so, the same goes for Bar Kochba, as one of your clubs is called."

We explained that our ultimate objective was Jewish education, that sport was a means to an end and since both education and religion were charitable objectives we should qualify. We had a stimulating debate. This could only happen in England, I thought. We achieved our objective.

Leslie's sons, Harold and Martin, have built up the family firm to a size of which their father would have been proud. They enjoy a high reputation and it is said, only half in joke, that if Martin is not a trustee or an executor of a charitable trust in the Anglo-Jewish community, it has got to be a fairly small one.

Bob Glatter, like Eric Beecham, was one of my friends and colleagues on whose life I had a certain influence. Bob worked with Harry Finck, the accountant with whom for a number of years I had a loose working association as Simon Worms and Finck. He had a very small practice without a great future. I introduced Finck and Glatter to Blick Rothenberg & Noble where Helmut Rothenberg was in charge. In due course, Bob became one of the senior partners. He followed me into Maccabi, into Hillel, into the Chamber of Commerce and in all three organisations he reached high office. He is now President of Maccabi England, Vice Chairman and former Treasurer of the British-Israel Chamber of Commerce and Vice President of the B'nai B'rith Hillel Foundation. We are very close, in constant communication and a day rarely passes when we do not talk to each other. On my recommendation he was made a director of the Bank Leumi (UK) Ltd following my retirement.

In 1981 Maniusia had to go into hospital for a minor operation. Della visited her in the evening and Pierre was also there. Since the St John and Elizabeth Hospital was only within ten minutes' walking distance from Abbey Lodge, Regent's Park, where Pierre and Maniusia lived, Pierre decided to walk home. A hit-and-run motorist drove into him on a zebra crossing, carried him along on the bumper, shook him off and disappeared. Pierre was dead.

That same evening we were telephoned by Alec Fishberg, a friend and one of the tenants at Abbey Lodge who had heard of Pierre's tragic death from the Head Porter. I immediately got in touch with

Dr Naftalin, their great friend and doctor. It was Joe Naftalin's and my dreadful task to go and see Maniusia the following morning and break the news to her. It was probably one of the worst moments of my life. It is always difficult to tell a spouse of such a tragedy but in this case it had a special poignancy. I have known no other couple who lived so completely for each other which is simply not possible when your love and precious time has to be shared with children. In this particular instance, each one was a receptacle of the spouse's outflow of affection, admiration and total dedication cemented by living together for almost 60 years. The driver was subsequently caught and got away with a nine months' prison sentence.

Maniusia survived another 12 years. Bob Glatter, Martin Paisner and I, together with our wives and her nephew Lionel Bloch and his wife, Sue, looked after her. She was remarkably brave and slowly recovered her *joie de vivre* although the shadow of her missing Pierre was always looming over her. Maniusia passed away peacefully in 1993.

Apart from being Mr Maccabi, Pierre was also a great lover of art and had accumulated a fine collection of post-Impressionist paintings. Together with Doris Morrison and Alexander Margulies he started a committee known as the British Friends of the Art Museums of Israel with which Della has been associated for over 25 years. In his Will Pierre left his collection and a substantial amount of money to the Israel museums. Whilst the Gildesgames never wanted any buildings named after them in their lifetimes, Pierre made it clear that he would have no objection to their name being used after their demise.

Today we have the Pierre Gildesgame Sports Museum in the Maccabiah Village. The Tel Aviv Museum now has a Gildesgame Gallery and the Israel Museum in Jerusalem has the Mifgash Gildesgame, a quiet retreat where people can sit peacefully and rest in the sublime atmosphere of the Jerusalem Hills. The Efrata School in the Baka district of Jerusalem enjoys the attractive facilities of the Gildesgame sports grounds. There is a Gildesgame Community Centre, a project of British Emunah, in Netivot in the Negev. In England there is Gildesgame House at MAL and in Earl Shilton,

Leicestershire, where Pierre had his factories, a park in their names has been endowed. Two of the London Maccabi Clubs have Gildesgame Endowment Funds to support their work.

I learned more from Pierre than from any other man. To me, he became the substitute paternal figure which I had missed since my childhood.

46

Rabbi Dr Kopul Rosen

ONE OF THE MOST charismatic men that I met in a lifetime of coming across Presidents, Prime Ministers, academics and religious leaders was Rabbi Dr Kopul Rosen. Tall, distinguished, with a black Herzlian beard, he carried himself with a natural dignity and the erect bearing of the sportsman that he was. He founded Carmel College, the Jewish public boarding school at Wallingford in Berkshire, in the midst of a green belt area. The River Thames meandered peacefully by the bottom of his private garden. His house was filled with modern art. He was a powerful orator, an original thinker and an educationalist *par excellence* with seminal ideas. He was also, rather like his three distinguished sons, the *bête noire* of the religious establishment, yet he was a man of unshakeable faith in the Almighty. When he was in his late forties he suffered a bad fall on the slipway of the boathouse. Thereafter, he developed cancer. I wish to quote from just one of his letters written to me shortly before he died:

> The unfortunate thing about this is that somehow people believe that a new idea in education is a form of religious heresy. If you say one has to go on plodding away at *Lech Lecha*, it is assumed that you are "froom" [Orthodox], but if you say that it is more important to know the contents of the Bible than to translate a limited number of words, you are immediately suspected of some form of incipient heresy.
>
> Where there is no courage and no vision, one sticks to the old familiar routine even though circumstances of life and conditions have changed.

The highest medical opinion says that I have a small chance, and they underline the word "small". My reply has been that this year's Derby winner was an outsider and although I may not be the best of runners, my jockey is marvellous and performs miracles. I have never known such peace and inner tranquillity as I have now ... "

His wife, Bella, and son Jeremy, carried on at the school for a time. Jeremy became a rabbi and businessman; Michael (Micky) founded Yakar, outstanding educational establishments in London and Jerusalem which he defines as "an attempt to be like a twentieth-century *Shtiebel*. That is to say that both strive to be a place of spiritual quest where a person can hear an echo of the divine yet at the same time it is not prepared to compromise the intellect. The learning at Yakar is characterised by question and not by answer, by struggle and not by platitudinous piety." David, the youngest, who is an uncanny image of his father, fulfils a number of important roles in Jerusalem as rabbi (he performed the wedding ceremony for Caroline and Nitzan), as an expert in Inter-Faith relationships and adviser to the B'nai B'rith Anti-Defamation League. Angela, the only daughter, is a distinguished lawyer working for the Government in Jerusalem.

Kopul is commemorated by Yakar which is an acronym of his Hebrew name.

47

*Professor Sir Ernst Chain**

ERNST BORIS CHAIN was born in Berlin in 1906 of a German mother and a Russian father who had built up a successful chemical factory. Ernst came to England in 1933. He was a typical product of the German university. Sure of himself, somewhat arrogant and impatient, he was full of contempt for what he considered the backward laboratory equipment and approach of the English. He was lucky enough to be offered a job at University College Hospital Medical School.

The Liberal Jewish Synagogue gave him a stipend of £250 to tide him over the first year but so great was Chain's disdain of the archaic facilities that the inevitable break came after only a few months. With the help of Professor J.B.S. Haldane he received an introduction to the School of Biochemistry at Cambridge, but again, after a short time, left to join the William Dunn School of Pathology at Oxford, which at that particular time was chaired by an ambitious young Australian, Howard Florey.

Professor Charles Harington wrote to Florey:

> I feel that if his race and foreign origin will not be unwelcome in your department, you will import an acceptable and very able colleague in taking him. Incidentally, I have found that his remarkable genius as a musician has made him acceptable in certain social circles here – a point which I think is not without some importance.

* Extracts of some of the letters were published in Ronald W. Clark's biography of Ernst Chain.

He got the job at £200 a year and thus began the legendary relationship with Florey which, fraught with suspicion, jealousy and friction, ultimately led to the commercial exploitation of penicillin and the joint award of the Nobel Prize.

The early years in England were unhappy ones. As a refugee from barbarous Germany, depressed by the thought that he had left his family behind, he was unable to mix freely with his English colleagues; his contempt for their trivial pursuits and his lack of sporting prowess made him an isolated figure. Music was his great escape. For a time there was a possibility that he would become a concert pianist. Thus whilst Florey and his colleagues were on the tennis court, Ernst was sitting at the grand piano. He feared that he would never be accepted as an equal.

Consolation came with the announcement of the Nobel Prize. Congratulations were received from one Anne Beloff who was working at Harvard and who, three years later, became his wife. "Dear Ernst, I have become sufficiently Americanized to consider the use of the surname an unnecessary formality. I hope you don't object."

By now it had become clear that Chain's frustrations were not conducive to giving his best under the direction of others, and he was looking for an outlet where he could be his own man. The solution came, surprisingly, not from England or the USA but from Italy. A certain Professor Marotta was not only a brilliant chemist but also a member of the Italian Establishment, with considerable influence in political circles. He was determined that Italy should be put on the map as far as scientific development in the biochemical field was concerned, and it was he who secured the services of Ernst Chain as Director of the Instituto Superiore di Sanita in Rome. There Chain built up a superb team. Almost unlimited funding opened up many possibilities in the development of a whole new range of penicillins with specialised curative characteristics.

Chain's reputation and that of his Institute grew by the month. He lectured all over the world, including Iron Curtain countries, and was involved in controversy over whether the know-how of penicillin production should be made available to the Russians and the Czechs. Although politically he had moved steadily to the right, he felt that as far as medicine was concerned political boundaries were intolerable.

Despite all his phenomenal success, his worldwide reputation, his consultancy work with some of the world's leading medicinal firms, he yearned to return to England. He was particularly concerned that his three children should receive an English education. The difficulty was finally overcome when, through Sir Isaac Wolfson, £200,000 was provided towards the cost of the highly sophisticated equipment that at that time was not available in England. That grant was later increased to £300,000 of which £25,000 was earmarked for a private apartment to be built for the Chains on the roof of Imperial College. This penthouse became one of the most desirable residences in London.

Chain continued to receive honours from universities and governments of many countries yet years after his return he felt singularly neglected by his adopted country. In 1969 he wrote to his colleague, Bernard Katz:

It has always seemed to me absurd and incongruous that I am the recipient of high decorations by foreign governments (see *Who's Who*) which I have to display at official national and international functions, whereas the government of my own country has not taken the slightest notice of my existence. If I were to pass on tomorrow my obituary would make curious reading and my biographer would have a hard task to explain these facts away ...

Taking all these facts into consideration, I have absolutely no doubt that if my case, with all the considerations outlined in this letter, is ... represented to the Prime Minister by the President of the Royal Society, possibly with the support, which I am sure would be fully forthcoming, of the present secretary of the MRC (a large unit of which – the Metabolic Reactions Research Unit – is housed in my Department under my direction) and the president of the Royal College of Physicians (of which I am an Honorary Fellow) the whole matter which forms the subject of this letter can be settled in minutes. The outcome of such a step can only be positive and, I know, will be welcomed by many people in this country and abroad . . .

Four days later he received a letter offering him a Knighthood in the Queen's Birthday Honours.

Whilst travelling all over the world in connection with his lectures, consultancies and scientific pursuits, Chain spent an increasing amount of time on his Jewish interests. His father had been a member of B'nai B'rith in Germany and Ernst joined the First Lodge of B'nai B'rith where he became a most popular member, performing at their functions at the piano (in later years accompanied by his son, Benny). Surprisingly, he veered gradually towards the fundamentalist religious Creed. He wrote:

While we have witnessed astonishing technological progress over the last 4,000 years, human relations have remained essentially unchanged since the time the Torah was written, and have to be regulated by very much the same laws. For this reason the fundamental teachings of Judaism, as expressed in the Old Testament, and developed by the great sages of the Middle Ages, one unitarian Almighty, benevolent, all-pervading, eternal divine force, of which the spirit of man was created an image, is for me still the most rational way of accepting man's position and fate in this world and the Universe . . . is entirely reconcilable with modern scientific concepts. It gives us, above all, an absolute measure of good and evil, an absolute scale of values without which no orderly human society can exist, and which no philosophical system and certainly no scientific method can give us . . .

He believed that Jews had a special responsibility which would be negated by assimilation. In a speech in 1965 he declared:

In the Diaspora a large part of the effort must be directed towards keeping the Jewish identity and preventing assimilation. Assimilation is a loss of orderliness, and therefore a step towards an increase of entropy i.e. chaos. It is most important to realise this and to understand that we benefit most of the community among which we are living by preserving our identity, and not by losing it through an equalizing assimilation process.

Della and I had become close personal friends of the Chains. At a dinner party at Esher House he spontaneously came out with the statement "when a supercharged cylinder travelling through space is punctured, the cylinder will disappear but space will not be enriched."

The Chains' relatively modest house in Wimbledon was the only one that I had ever seen where two grand pianos stood side by side. Had Ernst lived longer he would have made an ever-growing impact on the Anglo-Jewish community and he would have rejoiced in the professional success of his and Anne's children.

48

Lord Nathan

MY FIRST LAWYER was Herbert Garfield. He, too, came from Germany. He was a partner at Herbert Oppenheimer Nathan & Vandyk, a venerable old City firm in which Lord Nathan was the senior partner. Harry Nathan had followed the late Selig Brodetsky into the Presidency of the Maccabi World Union. He was a man of tremendous charm but also fully aware of his own importance. The first impression he generally gave was one of pomposity, but as one got to know him better this gave way to an appreciation of his sense of humour and integrity. He held more presidencies and chairman-ships of voluntary organisations than any other man I have ever known. Yet surprisingly he seemed to be well-informed and involved in practically every one of them, whether it was the Royal Society of Arts, one of the City Guilds or the Maccabi World Union. He was also the first Honorary President of Hillel.

We had become friends during the period when I was Chairman of the European Maccabi Executive. Lord Nathan would invite me for breakfast once a month which would either be taken in his apartment off Berkeley Square or at Browns Hotel. He would most skilfully and delicately pick my brains, seek the latest information on Maccabi and communal news and from time to time we would discuss general business matters.

In 1953, shortly after the coronation of Queen Elizabeth, Pierre Gildesgame – who had to go abroad, invited Lord Nathan and me to act as hosts for Sam Bronfman, who was President and Chief Executive of Seagrams, one of the world's leading drinks corpora-tions. The idea was to prevail upon Mr Bronfman to provide the major portion of the finance for the Canadian Maccabiah team. Mr and Mrs Bronfman were entertained by us at the Empress Club and for the first hour or so Lord Nathan recited in considerable detail the remarkable achievements of his firm, their international involvement, their experience in multi-national organisations and their contact with various governments. I found it quite hard to steer the subject back to the main purpose of our meeting. Lord Nathan went on to give a detailed description of the Coronation Ceremony which he had witnessed inside Westminster Abbey. Mr Bronfman listened with great courtesy and in semi-whisper finally said: "Thank you, Lord Nathan, for this wonderful description, but I would like you to know that my wife and I were also in the Abbey."

He did make a substantial contribution to the Canadian Maccabiah team.

The First Maccabiah in the new State of Israel was held in 1950. The country was still living under a strict regime of austerity and rationing. The only decent hotel in the country at the time was the Sharon Hotel run by the Levi family and at the conclusion of the Games, which were a real fillip for the local population, a small dinner party was arranged at the Sharon at which Prime Minister Ben-Gurion was present. He had acccepted the invitation on the strict understanding that there would be no speeches. He said he was very tired and wanted to relax.

When the relatively simple but excellent meal was over Lord Nathan got up and said: "Mr Prime Minister, Ladies and Gentlemen, I know the Prime Minister said that he didn't want any speeches but I cannot allow this opportunity to pass without saying a few words on this auspicious occasion ... " He then went on to make some appropriate remarks which he concluded with, "When I was in China I was astonished by the total absence of after-dinner speeches. I asked my host why that was, and he said with a twinkle in his eye, 'In China we shoot after-dinner speakers.' I hope Mr Prime Minister, you will forgive me for making these few remarks. I look forward to your reply."

Ben-Gurion responded instantly, "Lord Nathan, Ladies and Gentlemen, I agree with the Chinese ... " and he walked out!

During the Opening of the Congress which followed the Games,

Abba Eban, who was to stand as a candidate in the forthcoming elections, greeted the delegates fluently in five languages. Lord Nathan, who was in the Chair, responded: "Thank you, dear Aubrey, that was splendid. If you don't get elected you can always open a Berlitz School."

Some years later, on the occasion of the European Maccabi Games in Copenhagen, Lord and Lady Nathan entertained Della and me at a fashionable restaurant in the Tivoli. He was a wonderful host and took enormous trouble to make sure that everything went well. The waiter service in those days was notoriously slow, and he made a special point of going over to the restaurant earlier in the day to put the fear of God into the manager. The meal went like clockwork. It was most enjoyable. We concluded with a *bombe-surprise*. It was a concoction about two-foot high which consisted of a variety of frozen gateaux, fruit and whipped cream. I had never seen such an outsize dessert. Lord Nathan, who suffered chronically from overweight, divided it into four equal portions. Lady Nathan and Della made no impact on theirs. I diminished mine by about 10 per cent; he finished his completely and when coffee was served he carefully took a sweetener out of a silver box. "Too much sugar is not good for you," he said with a wink!

After his death Oppenheimers had a rapid succession of senior partners. They squabbled. Then the unbelievable happened. The revered old firm fell apart and sank without trace. Some partners joined Denton Hall Burgin & Warrens, others went to Nabarros. Ronnie Fox started his own practice – Fox Williams. If there is such a thing as turning over in one's grave, then surely old man Oppenheimer, that strict disciplinarian, Lord Nathan and Herbert Garfield will have done just that in disbelief that a pillar of the City's legal establishment should have been allowed to be wiped off the map and to be forgotten so soon.

49

Sir Bernard Waley-Cohen

As MY COMPANY, Tudor, progressed I thought the time had come to look for an outside director with a national reputation to strengthen our Board and I invited Lord Nathan to join us. "I am very flattered, my boy," he said, "but I have decided that apart from Gestetners I will not take on any directorships. I am too busy in too many directions. However, what about my son-in-law, Bernard Waley-Cohen?" Sir Bernard was well known in the City of London as a senior Alderman and magistrate, and in due course Lord Mayor of London. His term of office as Lord Mayor was remarkable for his extensive travels. He was one of the best PR men the City ever had. He was also a prominent member of Lloyd's, the famous London insurance market as well as a Vice President of the United Synagogue and Treasurer of the Jewish Board of Guardians. And so it was that Sir Bernard became a member of the board of Tudor Accessories Limited.

I became a member of Lloyd's and Laurie Lowenthal, my cousin, became a member of Lloyd's and the MCC – Middlesex Cricket Club. Bernard had offered membership of the MCC to me as well but I turned it down because I really felt that my limited interest in cricket did not justify taking away a much-coveted place from the very long waiting list.

Sir Bernard was a larger-than-life character. Like his father before him, he looked upon traffic lights as handicaps for other people which could be totally ignored by him. Many a time when I was sitting with him in his open-topped Bentley, driving from one place to another, he would jump the amber lights or possibly even ignore the red ones, sometimes to be met with a wagging finger from a smiling policeman. "Now, now, Sir Bernard!"

He had an impish sense of humour. "Joyce, bring the kitchen brandy," he once shouted from his dining room in St James when I asked to have a little Grand Marnier together with his fine old Courvoisier. At Board Meetings he would close his eyes and appear to be fast asleep. Yet he missed very little. Precisely one hour after his arrival the alarm on his wristwatch would ring. "Sorry chaps. I've got to be off to my next meeting."

In spite of his physical disability from childhood polio, he was a good horseman and was Master of his local hunt in Somerset where he farmed. Joyce, Lord Nathan's daughter, is a formidable woman in her own right equally at home on a horse or hosting a great dinner party. Bernard's twin sister was married to the late Oliver Sebag-Montefiore who also became a friend.

The collapse of Lloyd's came as a tremendous shock to him, as it did to so many City establishment figures. His particular world of doing business with the utmost good faith had pre-deceased him.

50

Meir Gertner

MEIR GERTNER WAS the nearest contact to an *Illui* (genius in Talmud study) that I have had in my life. I am not enough of a *Mavin* or expert to judge whether his or Rav Steinsaltz's knowledge of the Talmud was greater. What I do recall clearly is that whatever incidental reference was made in the course of a wide ranging conversation, Meir would pluck a Talmudic source from his mind, give the Hebrew cross reference in true Yeshivah tradition and explain its relevance.

He was a born educator and my teacher for four consecutive years from 1972 until his sudden death in 1976. We met every Friday morning for two to three hours in my office for an unstructured *shiur*. The constant factor was that we spoke in Modern Hebrew only. It is perfectly feasible to learn Torah and study Talmud in the original Hebrew without being able to converse freely in the contemporary language. That seems to be the fate of many Yeshivah *bachurim* in the Diaspora and I, too, found myself entrapped in this particular warp. Whilst enjoying the weekly portion of the Torah in the vernacular, I was tongue-tied when it came to talking with an Israeli, apart from the bare salutations and health enquiries. I knew the words but was not able to string them together. The fact that subsequently I was able to participate at board meetings of the Union Bank in Tel Aviv conducted in Hebrew or in executive meetings of the various charitable bodies to which I belonged is entirely due to Meir.

I quote from his biography which I wrote and which appeared in *Meir Gertner, An Anthology* edited by Dr Albert H. Friedlander and Fred S. Worms.

Meir was born in Rosalia, Transylvania in 1905. Transylvania formed that north-western part of Romania which changed nationality with regular monotony. It was the historic shuttle-cock between Hungary and Romania. Throughout its chequered history it retained a strong affinity with Hungary and its established Yeshivoth. The Hassidic influence was predominant.

By the time he was fourteen he had been studying at various Yeshivoth for eleven years. The language of study and communications was Yiddish. The reading of secular material was frowned upon. At best it was considered a waste of time, at worst – blasphemous.

He recalled that one day he carried a journal which did not look like a talmudical publication. The eagle eye of the Rosh Yeshivah soon discovered this irregularity. The following conversation ensued. (Alas, the poignancy of the plaintive questioning in Yiddish is lost in the translation): "What are you hiding, boychik?" Meir silently handed him the paper. The Rosh Yeshivah read slowly from the heading: "*Darkenu, Yotze La'or Mitaam Misrath Agudath Yisrael*" (*Our Path* published by the Agudath Israel). Needless to say that the Agudah then, as now, was an ultra-Orthodox Jewish organisation; "Nu boychik, tell me – is this *Loishen Koidesh*?" He considered the use of the Holy Tongue (*Lashon Hakodesh*) to have been profaned by its secular use, albeit in an Agudah publication. The youth with his large black *kippah*, long sidelocks, shaven head and pale face, felt exceedingly uncomfortable. If the *Rebbe* only knew how deeply he was involved in secular studies, that he read poetry and history, and that he longed passionately to break out from his Yeshivah confinement.

After his Bar Mitzvah he left *cheder* in Rosalio and entered the Yeshivah of Wisho, which was presided over by Reb Menachem Mendel Hager, a son of the famous Vizhnitzer *Rebbe*. By then, his tremendous intellectual curiosity had been aroused. He began to earn money by giving Talmud lessons. His earnings were spent entirely on private studies in secular subjects.

At the age of 20 he left Romania for Hamburg. There could have been no greater contrast between the Yiddish Shtetl, with its bearded inhabitants in their Kaftans, fur hats and shoulder length sidelocks, and the elegant Hanseatic town of northern Germany. Immediately after his arrival he cut off his *peyoth* [sidelocks], grew the magnificent mane of hair which he was fortunate enough to retain for the rest of his life, and changed into an elegant double-breasted suit complete with matching waistcoat. From East European Yeshivah *bocher* to north German Young Gentleman – the metamorphosis took great courage but "please God in Heaven" he prayed "don't let my mother find out!"

To the young yeshivah graduate who had come straight from the protective walls of the ghetto into this pulsating restless atmosphere, this must have caused considerable problems of adjustment. He spent some of his time in further Talmudic studies under Dr Carlebach, but he became increasingly involved in German literature. Goethe, Schiller, Heine, Rainer Maria Rilke, Herman Hesse, Max Brod and many others, opened a new vista to him and gave his outlook an entirely new dimension.

In 1938 Meir left for Israel. Much has been written about Palestine in the 1940s, the gradual involvement of the Yishuv in the Second World War, the traumatic realisation of the Holocaust, the War of Independence and the establishment of the State in 1948. Meir was in Jerusalem throughout that period. He was employed as a teacher by the Keren Hayesod; he joined the Haganah and fought in the Battle of Jerusalem which led to the tragic division of the city. Meir was in charge of a small platoon, consisting mostly of new immigrants who had received hardly any weapon training.

In the many hours of discussion which I had with him over the years, when he used to recall experiences from different phases of his life, he made remarkably few references to his 10 years in Palestine under the Mandate. His sister told me that he mixed mostly with intellectuals of German Jewish origin, read widely in German and Hebrew and spent much of his time translating novels in the two languages. It was at that period that he translated Max Brod's *Der Meister* into Hebrew.

The truth is that Meir's outlook on life had undergone a radical change. The certainty of his childhood in the infallibility of his traditional upbringing had given way to serious doubts. The horror of the Holocaust had shattered his most strongly held beliefs. Both God and the Germans had let him down. He kept away from synagogues and struggled within himself to find a new philosophy which would reconcile his love of Jewish tradition with the realities of the day as he saw them. He missed his brother Levi. Levi had left Rosalio in 1929 and studied history and philosophy at Berlin University. He emigrated to Palestine in 1936 and carried on studying at the Hebrew University. He was sent to England by the Jewish Agency to improve Jewish education and arrived three days before the outbreak of War. Levi became one of the outstanding educators of our generation, running the Zionist Day Schools, seminars and many other educational activities right until the day of his death in 1976, the very year in which Meir passed away.

Meir came to England for a sabbatical year and was soon engrossed in what became the great fraternal didactic partnership – Levi and Meir Gertner – whose dominance in the field of Zionist education in the Anglo-Jewish community became proverbial. Every time Meir and his wife, Thea, wanted to return to Israel, new academic temptations were laid in their path. He taught at Carmel College, obtained his Ph.D. in Oxford, taught at the London School of Oriental and African Studies and at the Oxford Centre for Postgraduate Hebrew Studies, lectured for ten years at the Leo Baeck College but, most importantly, participated regularly at the seminars organised by his brother, Levi.

Meir taught in depth. He would open the book that was to be studied, say a chapter in the Bible, but he would rarely get beyond the first sentence. His tremendous range of knowledge, his phenomenal memory, would cause him to examine each word individually. He would quote the views of dozens of commentators. He would analyse the origin of the word and find Hebrew, Greek or Latin synonyms. He would explain the transition of the meaning of the words as used in the Bible and as applied to Modern Hebrew. He would hold his audience spellbound.

In another age Meir would have been lauded as one of the *Gedolim* – the great ones – whose name would have attracted an international following. His gentle nature, his aristocratic manners, his courtesy, his depth of knowledge of the Tenach, his charisma in teaching, his combination of Central European Yeshivah background with his professorship at Western universities, made him a figure the like of which we shall not see again in our lifetime.

5 1

The Goeritz and Pollak families

AMONGST MY ROLE models during my bachelor years was the distinguished Goeritz family. Erich and Senta Goeritz hailed from Chemnitz in Germany. He was that rare combination of painter, art connoisseur and successful businessman. She was an outstanding beauty with flaming red hair, one of Max Liebermann's favourite models. Part of their valuable art collection went to the Tel Aviv Museum, the rest was inherited by their two sons, Thomas and Andrew. I was a frequent guest at their Park Lane home.

Later Thomas became my special friend. He had an elegant apartment off Sloane Street which, by my frugal standards during the late 1940s, was the height of luxury. A regular visitor was Victor Mishcon, his friend and lawyer. (Victor's and my communal paths have since crossed on many occasions. He was active in Hillel before me and has been a constant supporter. He received his peerage from Harold Wilson and distinguished himself in public and communal affairs, as Chairman of the now defunct Greater London Council, as personal adviser to members of the Royal Family or as discreet intermediary between the Israel Government and the King of Jordan. Not bad for a Brixton rabbi's son! He is a neighbour in Herzliah, and as a recent octagenarian works as hard as ever under the good care of his wife, Joan.)

Thomas Goeritz had a fine sense of humour. When we and a party of friends came out of a cinema he produced a pair of ladies knickers from his pocket (a sample from his lingerie factory) and asked innocently, "Any of you girls lost this?" It was surprising what a Pavlovian reaction this got.

He married Rachel, a rabbi's daughter from Finland. If ever there was an example of sons marrying their mother, this was it. She looked the very image of Senta's youthful photographs. They moved to a splendid apartment, full of impressionist paintings, in Regent's Park. They were blissfully happy, had a daughter Michelle, but when she was four Thomas died following a minor operation. It was a very great tragedy.

Some years later Rachel married Israel Pollak who was many years her senior. Their wedding at the Marble Arch Synagogue was attended by 15 personal friends including Marcus and Lily Sieff, Della and me. Israel was a brilliant renaissance man. Born into a textile family in Romania, he supervised clothing factories in Russia of all places, built up a big business in Latin America and was enticed by Pinchas Sapir to move to Israel. There in Kiryat Gat he founded Polgat, an amalgam of Pollak and the locality, which became a powerful textile combine and leading Marks and Spencer supplier.

Apart from Isaiah Berlin, there was no other man with whom I enjoyed conversation more. He was a consummate painter. When we celebrated our 170th anniversary party (Della 60, I 70 and married for 40 years), the children held a family celebration in Jerusalem to which Rachel and Israel were invited. They brought us one of his paintings, something I had always coveted. It hangs in a place of honour in our Jerusalem home.

The Pollaks became part of the establishment. They endowed many charities, were active on Boards of Governors of universities and museums and were intimates with every leading politician. Whilst no longer a synagogue-goer, Israel had respect for religion, an encyclopaedic knowledge of the Talmud and in our many discussions was always able to quote from the Sources.

Their penthouse in Tel Aviv and their villa in Caesarea became a mecca for "High Society". He gave Rachel and Michelle, who adored him, many happy years before he passed away after his 80th birthday.

52

Davide and Irene Sala

THERE IS ONE family, above all, whom the Anglo-Jewish community is sorely missing. I refer to the late and lamented Dr Davide and Irene Sala. They belonged to that small and distinguished band of Baghdadi Jews who have achieved international fame. Many of them are inter-married. The first time I heard the name Sala was at the Suvretta Hotel in St Moritz where his cousins, the Zilkhas, held court year after year in the winter season.

The Salas were forced to escape to Persia from Iraq. They moved to Italy but there they were under threat of kidnap, and so came to England. Anxious to join the Anglo-Jewish community and, knowing my name through friends in Milan, they called on me a week after their arrival.

Having made a fortune in the specialised business of supplying oil rigs, the Salas were determined to give most of it away in their lifetimes. In their quiet way they donated millions to many institutions in England and in Israel and their hospitality in their Park Lane home was renowned.

Davide, an active Zionist, became the catalyst in the involvement of the Sephardi community which, prior to his arrival, stood aloof from the mainstream of Anglo-Jewry. He took a passionate interest in our students, loved Hillel, provided scholarships and set a unique example of combining cheque-book charity with deep personal involvement. In middle age Irene acquired a Ph.D. in archaeology and became one of the driving forces in a number of international expeditions.

When she was killed in a tragic plane accident in Latin America in

1991 the flame that had lit Davide's path was extinguished. The Salas had a tenuous relationship with religious practice. Following Irene's death Davide asked me to organise a "Memorial Celebration" at Grosvenor House where every guest received a pink rose – Irene's favourite flower. No one then imagined that a similar function would be held for him within the year. He died in 1992 of what can only be described as a broken heart.

Della and I had known the Salas from the time of their arrival in England and we became intimate friends, spent holidays together and co-operated in a number of communal fields. What a pity that they did not see our close relationship expressed in a tangible form at the Israel Museum. The Sala Ethnographic Wing and the Cochin Synagogue are physically interconnected.

I treasure a silver letter opener which I use every weekday to open my post; it is inscribed: "To Fred, on your 65th birthday, Davide and Irene."

If ever one can say that a family has become irreplaceable, it applies to the Salas.

53

Henry Moore

I THINK OF this great man with nostalgia, not only because of his genius which took such a long time to flower into public recognition, but also because of his great courtesy, his bluff Yorkshire no-nonsense approach to life in general and artistic humbug in particular and his intolerance of the intolerant. We were first introduced to each other by his Geneva publisher.

On a private visit to Hoglands, Henry Moore's home in Hertfordshire, I was able to render him a small service which, in retrospect, is even more idiosyncratic than it appeared at the time. He had just had a new studio built with some sophisticated lighting arrangement which refused to work. I, the most impractical of men, who will not change a fuse at home, managed to get it going. His gratitude was overwhelming and I treasure the book into which he drew a convoluted personal dedication.

His lounge was full of *objets trouvés*, African sculptures and a large Derain. I recall him telling me that all the Pop Art he had seen was junk. He followed a rigid regime. Alarm at 7 a.m., up at 7.40 a.m. (oh, for another ten minutes in bed!), dealing with the post and reading every letter at 8.45, then work until 1 p.m. Afterwards lunch and a rest with *The Times* until 3.30 p.m. Back to work and occasionally dictating letters, which he hated. He walked with a limp from a badly set broken bone following an accident.

His Swiss Army knife was with him all the time. Moore and his wife Irina, born in Kiev and brought up in Moscow, were fruit experts. They had an orchard with apples, plums and pears keeping "2.5" gardeners busy. He said for inspiration he could only live in

England although he very much enjoyed his annual visit to Italy. As we wandered through his estate from one studio to another, he confessed that he was depressed. He was unhappy because at a time when he had all the worldly goods and recognition, he had become estranged from his daughter. I believe this was patched up later on when she produced a son but she never saw eye to eye with the executors and trustees of the Henry Moore Foundation.

Roger Berthoud, who has written his outstanding biography, records two aspects of Jewish interest:

> Moore made his only trip to Israel (in 1966) where his work was shown under British Council auspices at the Israel Museum in Jerusalem, and at the Tel Aviv Museum. Henry's visit, his furthest eastwards, clinched his feeling of having a special relationship with the spiritual home of many of his keenest collectors. His four-day stay included lunch with Jerusalem's durable mayor Teddy Kollek, a memorable session with school-children in the educational wing of the Israel Museum and from Tel Aviv with that museum's director, Dr Haim Gamzu, a trip through the Negev desert to the Dead Sea.

Later on, both the Israel Museum and the Tel Aviv Museum acquired important large Moores which are prominently displayed in the Sculpture Garden in Jerusalem and the large piazza in front of the Tel Aviv Museum respectively, where they sparkle in the sun, an extraordinarily successful juxtaposition of northern European art under a cloudless Middle-Eastern sky. It gives me a sense of satis-faction that the veteran *Jewish Chronicle* was amongst the early stalwarts who appreciated Moore's extraordinary talents at a time when he was subjected to the most vicious attacks by part of the art establishment.

The *Morning Post*'s critic led the charge in 1929:

> ... the exhibition must raise furious thoughts in the minds of those responsible for the teaching at the Royal College of Art ... A master in a national art school should be a man of taste with a keen sense of form. Yet, in the Suckling Child, though the

head of the baby was admirably modelled, the mutilated breast was "revolting." Other statues were "lumpy masses bound by clumsy contours ... the best of the drawings are quite ordinary; nothing shall be said of the worst."

The *Jewish Chronicle*, under the headline of "A Genius of the First Order" wrote (alas, the name of the critic is not known):

Good sculptors are so extremely rare, especially in England, that when one appears we find it hard to resist hailing him with all the superlatives that should be reserved for genius ... It is impossible to foresee where the development of this extraordinarily vital art will stop ... that it should be produced by so young a man, and in England, in the present century, is almost incredible. Three of the greatest names in present-day sculpture are Jewish names – Epstein, Zadkine and Lipchitz. No admirer of these should neglect the opportunity of seeing an exhibition which constitutes the most serious challenge they have yet received.

Nowadays Henry Moore is recognised as probably the outstanding sculptor of the twentieth century. The "Order of Merit" was a fitting tribute to a great man whose contribution to art will probably be timeless.

54

Lord Mancroft

STORMONT MANCROFT, KBE, MBE, TD, considered himself a Jew; not much of a practising one, yet his feeling for his religion went beyond the traditional respect of a son for his father's background. His mother was Christian.

I first met Stormont Mancroft in May 1969 when, as Chairman of Cunard, he accepted a menorah which I presented to him as President of B'nai B'rith on the occasion of the opening of a synagogue on the *Queen Elizabeth II*.

Well over six feet tall, erect, with a distinguished appearance, he was charm and courtesy personified. A wry wit, he made himself a reputation as London's best after-dinner speaker. He was a fine musician, had an impressive career as a soldier, barrister, banker, journalist, orator and Lord-in-Waiting to the Queen. His geniality over the years was sadly tempered by the drug problems of his son and heir.

The scores of lunches which we shared after Bank Leumi board meetings over a period of 12 years were a source of pure delight and the highlight of my colleagues' and my working week. When it came to somewhat technical balance sheet discussions and the Chairman would go round the table to seek our views, Stormont would frown, pucker his elegant forehead and say "on the whole I agree with Fred".

When the Arabs threatened the Norwich Union Insurance Company because it had a Jewish Director on the Board the affair made him a national figure. His reputation was further enhanced by his dignified resignation during that sordid episode. He never became a "tycoon" because he lacked the necessary ruthlessness and it was this "failing" which endeared him even more to some of his friends.

He thought my continuous quest for exercise was ridiculous. "The only exercise I take," he said, "is when I walk up the stairs of the hospitals visiting my jogging friends."

He told me that he left instructions in his Will that he did not want a religious memorial service. "I would quite like one in synagogue but my Christian wife would object to it. So it's best if nothing is done. I expect they will ignore my wish." He was right. They did.

His memorial service was held at St Margaret's, Westminster. Rabbi Julia Neuberger was one of the participating clergy. She intoned: "I will now recite the Kaddish in Aramaic, the language Jesus spoke, and then I will read it in English."

The congregation knelt, some sat with their heads bowed. The order of the day was reasonably ecumenical. Prayers came from the Psalms, Ecclesiastes and Proverbs. Yet Jesus was subtly introduced by invoking his blessing for the Royal Regiment of Artillery which sounded the last post and reveille in memory of their departed Colonel.

Lord Rawlinson, who gave the *Hesped*, pointed out that Lord Mancroft had requested on his deathbed that there should be no memorial service but surely, the speaker inferred, such excessive modesty could not have been allowed as the last word.

After the conclusion of the service I suggested to Julia that this was probably the first time that she had said Kaddish to a kneeling congregation. "Nobody was more surprised than I," she replied.

55

Lord Weidenfeld of Chelsea

GEORGE WEIDENFELD, together with his then new wife, Annabelle Whitestone – a tall, blonde lady who had loved and cared for Arthur Rubinstein to the end of his days, were also amongst Lord Rothschild's guests both for the opening of the Supreme Court in Jerusalem and for the family reunion in Frankfurt.

Annabelle converted to Judaism and after marrying George at Chelsea Register Office had another religious ceremony at Yemin Moshe, whilst the Supreme Court celebrations were going on.

George has had a not dissimilar background to my own. He came from Vienna in 1939 as a penniless refugee and by charm, application and cultivating the right circle, became an adviser to Chaim Weizmann, a leading publisher, and an intimate of Harold Wilson who gave him his knighthood and his peerage.

In his autobiography *Remembering My Good Friends* he lists two thousand names including half the English aristocracy. I reminded him of our friend, Wim van Leer, a wealthy industrialist who settled in Israel and wrote in his autobiography that he had slept with two thousand women. When I tackled Wim on this improbable claim he replied: "Fred, this is the only understatement in the book!"

Nachum Goldmann referred to George's lifestyle as "Jews, women and song". There have been variations e.g. "Jews, women and books or opera" but no one can under-estimate the gravitas side of Lord Weidenfeld's career. A protagonist of German reunification, he used his international network of powerful politicians at seminars and conferences for his persuasive lobbying. He is at his best when taking up the cudgels for Israel in the House of Lords. He did this when the State was not the flavour of the month and it took real courage to explain patiently, convincingly and powerfully why the Arabists at the Foreign Office did not have all the answers. As a Vice-President of Hillel he spoke frequently and chaired our luncheon parties. He has offered his home in Chelsea regularly for the Jerusalem Foundation, Ben-Gurion University, of which he became Chairman of the Board of Governors in June 1996, and a variety of good causes in which he plays a leading part. He remains Anglo-Jewry's most popular bon viveur.

56

The Zilkhas

AMONGST OUR NEIGHBOURS in Yemin Moshe were Abdulla and Zemira Zilkha. Abdulla came from an eminent Iraqi banking family and carried on the family tradition in France and Switzerland. He was from that select band of Baghdadi Jews who, like the Sassoons, have had a considerable influence in international finance.

The Zilkhas in their time maintained four grand homes. Their principal residence was in Paris, with holiday homes in the south of France, St Moritz and Jerusalem. In later years they moved from Paris to Zurich and only kept up their St Moritz establishment. When their main home was in Paris they retained the services of one of France's top chefs. He complained, however, that he could never prove his worth to us because of our insistence on *kashrut*.

Before they bought their St Moritz home they spent part of the winter at the Suvretta Hotel in St Moritz where they would entertain us royally and where they would go cross-country skiing every day. After moving into their Zurich home Abdulla played a round of golf by himself before breakfast every morning.

Zemira Zilkha comes from the old established Mani family which includes many other distinguished Israelis such as Ruth Cheshin of the Jerusalem Foundation and her sister Dalia, the wife of Eli Hurvitz of Teva Pharmaceuticals.

In September 1985 Abdulla and Zemira celebrated their 50th wedding anniversary to which they invited a charmed circle of their friends, amongst whom very fortunately Della and I were included. We celebrated for a week with dinners and luncheon events at the King David, Hilton and American Colony hotels in Jerusalem with

342

special parties at the Weizmann Institute and at the citrus farm of their relative Binjamin Machness near Rishon Le Zion.

We keep in close touch with the Zilkhas and see them from time to time in their villa next to the Dolder where Zemira continues to copy the world's great paintings in inspired tapestry form.

57

Tennis and Ned Temko

TENNIS HAS ALWAYS been an important part of my life. Unless I play at least twice a week I feel out of sorts. In the 1960s I joined the Hampstead Garden Suburb Lawn Tennis Club, a euphemism and a hyperbole combined. It was true that it was in Hampstead Garden Suburb but there was no lawn and the standard of tennis was questionable. It had certain attractions particularly the friendly and comradely atmosphere on the courts. Members like Alfred Kleiman always had a joke and the quantity of the banter far exceeded the quality of the tennis.

One day, the captain – Phillip Kennedy – rang me up. "Fred, you are playing at Wimbledon tomorrow." "Is this one of your better jokes?" I asked. "No, I am serious." He went on to explain that every year a few weeks before the Wimbledon Championship, the All England Club invites tennis clubs affiliated to the LTA to send two members to participate in the coaching of the ball boys. And so it was that Alec Marmot and I met in the hallowed Wimbledon Club premises where a former Naval Commander who had been in charge of the ball boys for over 20 years greeted us.

"My suggestion is," he said, "that you start off with a good Wimbledon tea." Alec did but I declined since I cannot play on a full stomach. That was my first mistake. He kept us on the court non-stop for four and a half hours. He told us that he was not interested in our standard of tennis, "just do what I tell you. The score is deuce."

The ball boys were taught how to be unobtrusive, to have the balls always ready at the end when the player needed them – a particularly difficult feat when it comes to a tie break. One does not realise how much practice and skill there is in the polished performances of the ball boys and girls at Wimbledon. Later, over Pimms and smoked salmon sandwiches, the Commander told us, "I have seen plenty of tennis players – that doesn't turn me on at all, but to see the ball boys in perfect action, that is something to write home about."

During the last few years since we moved to Highpoint where we have our own courts, I make up my own foursomes including Peter Marks, Geoffrey Selby, Malcolm Gold, Warren Grossmith and Jeffrey Stellman amongst others. One of our regulars is Ned Temko, the editor of the *Jewish Chronicle*. Ned is a natural athlete, a beautiful mover with a very quick eye, and an even quicker temper. A few bad shots in succession and the racket flies against the net. At least that is how it was, but now he is much more controlled. He is a class player whose only serious challenger in our circle is Lee Berman, the ex-Accadia Hotel tennis professional. Ned also skied for his university but I have not yet had the pleasure of sharing the slopes with him.

I can imagine the *Jewish Chronicle* Selection Committee setting down on paper the pros and cons for choosing a new editor. Presumably plus points would be an intimate knowledge of the Anglo-Jewish community and previous experience in the Jewish publication field. Ned's principal professional experience was with that well-known Jewish journal, the *Christian Science Monitor*, and he descended on Anglo-Jewry like a parachutist landing on unknown, but hopefully friendly territory. His appointment was an act of enormous courage on the part of all concerned, some of whom may have had initial misgivings.

Ned came to the *Jewish Chronicle* at a difficult time and as a diffident young man. He would slip into Jewish functions rather like Peter Lorre crept surreptitiously into Rick's Nightclub in the film *Casablanca*, hoping that he would not be seen. He has worked hard by travelling up and down the country as a member of a "Jewish Chronicle Brains Trust" and has become an acknowledged insider of the community whose leading articles are much respected. He has turned the *Jewish Chronicle* into a contemporary publication whose growing size is evidence of communal and advertisers' support and confidence. He says the best is yet to come.

Valete!

IN WRITING AN autobiography one is continuously compelled to
make choices. What one publishes is only the tip of the iceberg and
of necessity much material has to be left out. I have passed over the
many interesting overseas trips that Della and I have made during
the last 45 years and which have formed the subject of travel reports
to the family and friends. Perhaps they will be included in another
book.

I have not referred to the interviews which I have conducted with
some of the leading "thinkers", many in Jerusalem, during the last
15 years at the behest of *Le'Ela*, the Chief Rabbi's journal, lumin-
aries such as Rav Adin Steinsaltz, Professor Yeshayahu Leibowitz,
Dr Michael Rosenak, Rabbi Dr David Hartman, Dr Meir Tamari
and Professor Bernard Reisman of Brandeis University and activists
like Teddy Kollek and Natan Sharansky who have discussed their
lebensanschauung frankly with me.

I have also enjoyed the friendship over many years of the man
who is *sui generis*, the great philosopher, raconteur and musical
expert – Sir Isaiah Berlin, whose modesty is such that he is continuously amazed why so many people should take such enormous
interest in him. We have exchanged some interesting letters and they
too will, with God's help, see the light of day in the not too distant
future.

One is greatly troubled by World Jewry's divisiveness and lack of
confidence, a post-Rabin assassination phenomenon. The defenders
of the faith, the very people who were going to provide the con-
tinuum of our ethos are now suspect. Orthodox rabbis are divided

346

into those who place land over life against others who still stress the primacy of life and the Torah's injunction of justice to the neighbour and stranger.

With all our children and grandchildren in Israel, we have more than an academic or sentimental interest in the peace-process. Our hopes and prayers are that our people will soon rediscover its compassionate soul and enter the second half-century of the State of Israel and the next millennium in peace and harmony with itself and its neighbours.

Glossary

Agudah	an ultra-Orthodox organisation
aliyah	emigrating to Israel
aron	ark containing the Torah Scrolls
Baal Teshuvah	born-again Jew – one who returns to religious practice
bachur/bachurim	student(s)
balei battim	lit. house owners. Respected citizens
Bar Kochba	Jewish hero who died 135 AD fighting the Romans
bein hashmashot	lit. between the sun and the moon. Dusk
bevakashah	please
bimah	central pedestal from which the Torah Scroll is read
birkat hamazon	grace after meals
bocher	lit. boy. Usually applied to Yeshivah students
Bnai Akivah	religious Zionist youth movement
Brith Milah	circumcision
CBF	Central British Fund
Chagim	The three Jewish Foot festivals: Passover, Pentecost, Tabernacles
Chanukah	Festival of Lights
chanukiah	menorah = eight-armed candlestick
Charedim	ultra-Orthodox
Chasid/Chasidim	ultra-Orthodox Jew(s), follower(s) of Chasidism
chaver/chaverim	friend(s)
chazakah	traditional unchangeability
chazan	cantor
chazanut	cantoral art
cheder/chadarim	Hebrew class(es)

cherem	excommunication
choma/chomot	wall(s) (lit) of the Old City of Jerusalem
Chumash	five books of Moses (Torah)
Chuppah	wedding canopy
Clock Oma	Family nickname for great-grandmother. In German Urgrossmutter means great-grandmother and Uhr means clock
Daf Gemore	a page of the Talmud
dati	religious
davening	praying
Dayan	Rabbinical Judge
Derech Hayashar	lit. the straight way. The middle way
Dybbuk	possessed soul
Echah	Lamentations
Ehyeh Asher Ehyeh	I am what I am. (God's definition of himself, Exodus 3:14)
Ein Kemach ein Torah	without material assistance there can be no learning
Emunah	lit. Faith. Also Women's religious Zionist Organisation
Erev	evening
Eruv	a symbolic boundary line (e.g. a wire) which will enable Orthodox Jews to carry and push prams on the Sabbath
Eretz Israel	the land of Israel
Frum	Orthodox
Gabbai	warden
Galut	Diaspora/exile
Gedolim	famous Rabbis of the past
Gemeinde	(German) Community
Habonim	left-wing Zionist youth movement
hachsharah	preparatory training (for *aliyah*)
Hadassah	another name for Esther. Also women's Zionist Organisation
Haftorah	reading from the prophets every Saturday and Jewish holidays
Haggadah	Passover story
Haganah	Pre-independence Jewish illegal defence force
Haham	Chief Rabbi of Sephardi Jews in Britain
halachah	interpretation of Jewish law

349

Hashem	The Name (of the Lord)
Haskalah	Enlightenment (nineteenth century)
Hesped	Funeral oration
Hodu Lashem	A phrase which can mean "Thank the Lord" or "India is the Lord's"
Illui	Genius in Talmud study
IRG	Israelitische Religions Gesellschaft (the Breuer Community)
Kaddish	mourner's prayer
kashrut	Hebrew noun for Kosher in dietary laws
kavana	devotion in prayer
kehunah	priesthood in biblical times
kfar	village
kippah/kippot	skull-cap(s)
kiddush	blessing over wine
Klal Israel	the whole of the Jewish people (in a unifying sense)
Kohelet	Ecclesiastes
Kollelim	pl. of Kollel = religious study centre for adults
Kol Nidre	the evening prayer prior to the Yom Kippur fast
Kotel	the Western Wall
Landsmannschaften	(German, used world-wide) groups originating from a particular country
Lashon Hakodesh	lit. the Holy Tongue. Hebrew
layning	reading from the Torah in a prescribed cantillation
Lebensanschauung	philosophy of life
Lech Lecha	paragraph in Genesis in which God commands Abraham to leave his birthplace and go to Canaan
Lehrhaus	house of study
Limudei kodesh	Torah and Talmud study
Loishen koidesh	Yiddish for Holy Tongue
Maccabiah/Maccabiot	World Jewish Games (pl.)
madregot	steps
Madrichim/Madrichot	pl. masc./fem. for Youth leaders
Magen David Adom	Israel's equivalent of the Red Cross
Maftir	the person called up last to the Torah before he chants the Haftorah
Mavin	expert
Mea She'arim	ultra-Orthodox quarter in Jerusalem
meclal leprat	from the general to the particular – Talmudic rule of logic

Melitz	one of the leading educational institutes in Jerusalem
mesechta	a section of the Talmud
Meshuhrarim	freed/black Jewish slaves
mikvah/mikvaot	ritual bath(s)
minchah	afternoon prayer
Minhag	custom
moshavim	agricultural settlements
Moshe Rabenu	Moses our teacher
Ner Tamid	everlasting light
nusach	traditional tunes
Olim	Immigrant to Israel (lit. going up)
Ostjude	A Jew from Eastern Europe
pasuk	sentence
Pesach	Passover
petek	personal note
peyoth	long side-locks
Poale Zion	Labour Zionist organisation
Purim	Feast of Lots to commemorate the deliverance from Haman
Rambam	Maimonides (acronymn for Rabbi Moses ben Maimon – famous exegete 1135–1204)
Rebbe	Rabbi
Rosh Hashanah	Jewish New Year
Rosh Yeshivah	Head of Religious study centre
Seder	ceremonial dinner held on first and second nights of Passover
sefarim	prayer books
Shabbat/Shabbatot	Sabbath(s)
Shalvah	calm
Shamas	Beadle
Shavuoth	Pentecost
Shechina	God's aura
Sheket bevakashah	Quiet please
shiur/shiurim	study group(s)
shivah	seven days of mourning
Shoah	the Holocaust
shul	synagogue
Shtetl	lit. little town. Ghetto
Shtiebel	a small informal Orthodox place of prayer

Simchah/Semachot	festive occasion(s)
sinat chinam	causeless hatred
Sukkah/Sukkot	temporary dwelling booths on the feast of Tabernacles
Tehillim	Psalms
Tenach	The writings of the Old Testament including five books of Moses, the Prophets and various ancillary scrolls
tillim	missiles
Tisho B'Av	9th of the month of Av – a day of fasting and lamentations
Torah	the Pentateuch
Torah im Derech Eretz	study of both Torah and secular education
Tramping	hitch-hiking
treife	not kosher
Tzofim	Scouts
Yahadut	identification with knowledge of Jewish heritage
Yekkes	German Jews (derived from the word "jacket" which as formalists they always wore. Ironically, today, the long black jackets are worn by the ultra-Orthodox whose antecedents are from Eastern Europe)
Yerushalayim	Jerusalem
Yeshivah/Yeshivoth	Religious study centre(s)
Yisha'yahu	Isaiah
Yishuv	Jewish population of Palestine and later Israel
Yom Hashoah	Holocaust Remembrance Day
Yom Tov	Jewish holiday
Zugelaufeners	(Yiddish) New arrivals

Index

Grange, Kenneth, 116
Granot, David, 150
Green, Jeffrey, 286–7
Green, Lottie, 274
Greenbaum, Helga, 306–7
Greenbaum, Kurt, 306–7
Greenwood, Jeffrey, 150
Greig, Peter, 106
Grossmith, Warren, 345
Guggenheim, Benny, 50, 51, 69
Guggenheim, Evi, 69
Guggenheim, Lydia, 51, 69
Gutfreund, Hanoch, 179
Guth, Wilfred, 144

Hager, Rabbi Menachem Mendel, 327
Hailsham, Quintin, Baron (previously Viscount), 262–3
Halban, Martine, 299
Halban, Peter, 299
Haldane, J.B.S., 316
Halevy, Jonathan, 195
Halle, Karl, 270
Halle, Robert, 270, 274, 279, 287, 295
Hallegua, Queenie, 175, 177–8
Hallegua, Sammy, 175, 177–8
Hanak, Arthur, 224
Hanfstaengel, Puzzi, 24, 25
Hargreaves, Alison, 52
Harington, Charles, 316
Harman, Avraham, 274, 279
Harris, Cyril, Chief Rabbi (of South Africa), 286–7
Harris, Hugh, 259
Hartman, Rabbi David, 160, 346
Harverd, Arthur, 56–7, 141
Harverd, Bernice née Woolfson, 56–7

Harverd, Daniel, 57
Harverd, Dorit, 57
Harverd, Leora, 57
Heath, Sir Edward, 280
Heeg-Engelhart, Ingrid, 303–4
Hennesey, Sir Patrick, 108
Hertz, Joseph, Chief Rabbi, 32, 266
Herzl, Theodor, 139, 232
Herzog, Aura, 139
Herzog, Chaim, 95, 279
Heseltine, Michael, 279
Hesselbach, Walter, 83–4
Heth, Meir, 149
Heth, Nachum, 149
Heuberger, Georg, 86–7
Heuberger, Rachel, 87
Hirsch, Rabbi Samson Raphael, 11, 12, 23, 94, 239
Hitler, Adolf, 14–6, 24, 37–8, 47, 79–80, 174, 228, 261, 304
Hochhauser, Lilian, 159
Hochhauser, Victor, 159, 193
Hochstein, Annette, 256
Hoffmann, Alan, 59–60, 69–70, 74, 157, 166, 251, 254
Hoffmann, Ayelet, 60, 85, 89, 161–3, 166, 203
Hoffmann, Matan, 60, 87, 166
Hoffmann, Nadia née Worms, 52, 54–5, 59–60, 63, 69–70, 74, 85, 89, 114, 155, 157, 166, 191, 203–4, 227, 304
Hoffmann, Noam, 60, 70, 155, 203–4
Hoffmann, Tal, 60, 86
Hogg, Quintin, see Hailsham
Horovitz, Marcus, 12
Horwell, Arnold, 274
Hurwitz, Dalia, 342